New World Order

Just Say No!

by

Eric F. Magnuson

Fimbul Winter Books

New World Order

Just Say No!

ISBN-13: 978-1500396169

ISBN-10: 1500396168

Copyright 2012, 2022

Eric F. Magnuson

All Rights Reserved

New World Order

Just Say No!

Globalist Tyranny vs.

Libertarian Nationalist Revolution

A multitude of free sovereign nations competing in a free world market has natural workability superior to any form of world government and can be less easily subverted to collectivism.

Table of Contents

Seek and Destroy	9
World Libertarian Revolution	
Introduction	155
Part I Liberation of Society	
Evolutionary Principles	166
Liberty and Natural Order	174
Lending and Spending	179
Economics and Power	186
History and Propaganda	196
Evolution and Devolution	203
Charity and Welfare	211
Society and Apathy	216
Government and Collectivism	223
Opponents and Strategies	238
Solutions and Implementation	246
Revolution	272
Part II Liberation of the World	
New Look at Western Civilization	278
World Power through Misdirection	282
The New World Order	287
Superior Options for the Future	291
Declaration of World Independence	295
Liberty Works Best Everywhere	298
Part III The United States	
Proposed Additions to US Constitution	313
Invasion of the United States	316
Part IV The Future	
State of the World 2034	317
Part V Quotations	
Quotations for World Liberty	327
Quotations for Good Living	234
Part VI World Libertarian Order	
About the WLO	336
History of the WLO	342
WLO Membership	346
The United Nations	347
Free Market Economists	351
Internet Forums	352
Subverted Media Alternative	356
About the Author	359
Fimbul Winter Books	360

To

Samuel Adams and the Signers
of the Declaration of Independence

Ludwig von Mises and the other
great Free Market Economists

that their

Highest Aspirations be Manifested

Alternative to IMF Banks

One thing can give us worldwide liberty, prosperity, and peace, quickly eliminating the imagined need for Globalism, Socialism, and Communism. That is to get counties everywhere to pull out of the IMF, and nationalize their central banks. General education is the first step. Once the truth is well known, implementation will follow. The material below explains the entire business with succinctness and clarity:

Most of the big problems on Earth are caused by International Monetary Fund (IMF) bankers who, via privately owned member central banks, like the US Federal Reserve, manipulate currencies, and with the help of subverted politicians, engineer wars and economic upheaval so they can lend money to governments for military mobilization and otherwise unnecessary social programs. Globalism, the New World Order, is simply the one world government that will allow the IMF banks to have total finance monopoly.

Countries do not need to borrow from IMF banks, but can have their own central bank, and control their own currency. Populations are kept from the knowledge of this by cooperating mainstream media, and by subverted politicians who keep IMF control in place by voting for it in legislatures. All that is necessary to have enduring liberty, prosperity, and peace on Earth is to get counties to leave the IMF, set up their own central banks, and tie the amount and value of currency to receipted hours of work, or a mixed store of scarce and durable commodity, the value of which is determined in free world markets.

In the U.S. these changes will eliminate the unnecessary federal income tax, which pays only the interest on the unnecessary national debt. All fiscal expenditures are paid for by excise taxes at state, county, and municipal levels. See the U.S. national debt at the link below.

War and terrorism are a complex study, but the purpose of most war today is to generate 'refugees' aided by the EU and UN to invade countries to destroy indigenous race and culture, so that people lacking identity will except globalization. Terrorism is supported by deep state funding, open borders, and police stand-downs, to make daily life seem so dangerous that we will gladly surrender guns and liberty just to feel safe. Good people need to become proactive about building a better future. We will be rid of these problems only when the Globalists and their invading hordes are just a dreary memory.

* * *

We have just received two comments from France:

"It *is* succinct. All we need with this, are the addresses of those who readers must petition to produce these wonderful changes. It's really a wonder that such massive public fraud could have on for so long in plain view." ~ Brett Manteaux

"We must urge people not to vote for any politician who will not take a direct stand against further involvement with the IMF." ~ Emile Bonvuar

Introduction: Seek and Destroy

This section contains our more recent essays on the threat of globalization. Most of them have also been added to the older books.

Globalist bankers, media bosses, and politicians are equivalent in their effect upon society to rats carrying bubonic plague. Widespread knowledge of this, fused with the principle of leaderless resistance, will, with imagination and diligence, spell their inevitable demise.

War and terrorism are a difficult study. Just when you think you understand an event, new information surfaces showing that it was actually a false flag, usually involving Globalist traitors in your own government working with foreign operatives.

Besides Globalist banker lending, facilitated by cooperating politicians and media, the ongoing wars in the East are waged to generate "refugees" to invade and destroy indigenous race and culture everywhere, so that people lacking identity will accept globalization, and with it, corporate monopoly. The purpose of small scale terrorism is to make the everyday environment so perilous that we will gladly surrender liberty just to feel safe. We will be rid of every major problem in modern life when the Globalists, and if their invading outlanders, no longer exist.

Contents:

The short sections on evolution are included to resolve the unwarranted conflict between science and religion. We have bigger fish to fry. What this means will be clear after reading the material.

In "State of the World 2034" the reader experiences how it will feel to be living after the essential changes have been made. It's the "Ten Steps" reformatted to be after the fact.

Eric F. Magnuson

Update
March 21, 2022
11:05 A.M.

What Evolution Is

Evolution is the process by which living organisms adapt to their environment through change. This is necessary for survival, because the environment itself is always changing. If this happens so quickly that creatures can't keep up, they perish. Rapid environmental change usually has to do with temperature or water levels.

Genes are the cellular component within living organisms responsible for the characteristics of the organism. Genes themselves are continually changing. This process is called mutation and occurs randomly, but is sometimes triggered by environmental stimuli (e.g. increased solar activity).

When a creature's mutating genes result in a characteristic which favors adaptation to the environment, then the creature will live longer and reproduce more. The favorable genes are passed along to the offspring. If the opposite occurs, and the genes are not favorable to survival, then the creatures will die younger and reproduce fewer offspring, so the unfavorable genes are not passed on. This process is called natural selection, or survival of the fittest.

Science isn't science without proof. There are six proofs for evolution:

1. Universal Genetic Code

2. Continuity of Fossil Record

3. Interspecies Genetic Commonalities

4. Prenatal Growth Recaps Phylogeny

5. Postnatal Imprinting Recaps Phylogeny

6. Bacterial Resistance to Antibiotics

Note:

For detail on five of these proofs see Richard Peacock's site "Evolution: Frequently Asked Questions"

What Evolution is Not

Ever since Charles Darwin first explained the evolutionary process, there has been an unnecessary unwarranted feud raging between the religious and scientific communities. There is no real bone of contention here, and never has been, for three reasons:

1. Evolution is not a theory to be debated, but a proven scientific fact.

2. The fact that most observable phenomena are not mentioned in ancient scriptures, does not render them nonexistent.

3. Evolution does not negate the process off intelligent design. It is simply the means by which intelligent design is implemented. Universal intelligence is simply the potential for manifest existence residing in unmanifest existence (e.g. the light bulb before Edison). Natural selection unlocks this potential in the same manner as does an inventor. Both universal intelligence and technology are infinite, so there is a great deal to look forward to. See more about this ahead.

For the Libertarian connection to evolution, here are two root definitions from "Evolutionary Psychology."

1. Evolutionary destiny is the imperative for the unimpeded, ever more varied and complex expression of universal intelligence through evolving organisms.

2. Liberty is the inalienable birthright of every living organism in the universe to manifest justly as a participant in evolutionary destiny. This manifestation, to be both Libertarian and just, must not unnecessarily interfere with the evolutionary expression of any other living organism.

Countdown to Globalization

When the main threats to individual liberty center around the impending loss of national sovereignty and the destruction of indigenous races and culture, then nationalism, by any means necessary, including war, becomes the first principle.

Sleepwalkers of the World, wake up! Forget your limp-wristed religious fantasies, alcohol intoxication, drug dreams, idiot ballgames, and virtual-reality heroism. Stand up on your feet like real men and women, think about the future, and show some proper adult seriousness for once in your pathetic lives. The eleventh hour is past. World Libertarianism is now the only alternative to globalist oppression. All the nonsense you think matters is of no importance, and never has been. If you feel insulted by all this, then you are one who needs to read further. If not, you are probably smiling at this moment, as we are.

Fully educated people know that a multiplicity of free sovereign nations competing in a free world market has a natural workability superior to any form of world government, and can be less easily subverted to collectivism. World problems will not be solved through ignorance. Join us grownups in the Twenty First Century. Read further, so that when the smoke clears you will be worthy to smile along with us, as one who has participated in the throwing down of globalist tyranny. Embark upon the Greatest of All Quests: Liberty Triumphant and Eternal!

Freethinker

Knowledge and Belief

Preliminary Principles:

1. An actuality is a pure state of existence apart from the perception of it by any living organism.

2. A reality is the accurate perception of an actuality by any healthy living organism. This will be qualified to some extent by previous experience and by the perceptual apparatus of the organism.

3. A fact is the conceptual representative of a reality.

4. Facts are the building blocks of correct thinking.

5. Logic is the process of correct thinking, the natural method used to arrange the building blocks provided by facts.

6. Knowledge is the correct natural correlation of facts by means of logic, the finished structure.

7. Truth is the broad and meaningful apprehension of knowledge.

8. Wisdom is the loving and just reaction to truth.

9. A belief, in the pure sense, is an attempt to extrapolate beyond what is known.

10. The amount and strength of an individual's beliefs is inversely proportional to the amount of his knowledge.

11. Philosophy is used to create a feeling of personal integrity and wholeness by attempting to extrapolate beyond available facts. Correct reactions are based upon facts, not upon philosophy.

12. Most philosophy is merely the "explanation" that people lacking facts offer to justify their own particular emotional reaction to their environment. The only worthwhile philosophy is a comprehensive overview of all available factual data fused by love, heroic idealism, good moral character, and courage. This involves an eclectic approach to the attainment of wisdom, not a slavish adherence to "isms" of any kind, including the fashionable zeitgeist of well entrenched science.

Viable Spirituality

In this context, spirituality is differentiated from religion, because it represents something much larger. It includes all of a person's values as these are reflected by actual conduct over the course of a lifetime, rather than by the mere parroting of religious doctrine, often with partial adherence. A person's spirituality comprises everything in life. This may include religious activity or no religion at all.

A truly viable spirituality must have perfect integrity between three basic components:

~ an intellectual premise consistent with all known science and which grows along with science

~ a moral premise reflecting absolute Libertarian reciprocity. This means no unjust encroachment against any creature or the environment to the detriment of any living thing. This also means absolutely no tolerance of such encroachment from others.

~ a source, not of dogmatic belief, but of archetypal inspiration, grounded in one's own ancestral mythology.

Absolute separation of church and state is impossible because what the people are spiritually determines the type of government they will create or condone. Wherever we find the institutionalized lassitude of cowardly religion, we also find Socialism or some other unworkable form of collectivist government. We can't expect an inferior prevailing spirituality to result in a superior way of running society.

Evolutionary Spirituality

This is spirituality based upon evolutionary principles. It will evolve as society grows in understanding. It will transform the world by inspiring people, first to cast off the chains which bind them individually, then to democratically throw down unjust governments everywhere. This is inevitable, but will happen only very slowly through ongoing education about what works and what does not.

Those who claim that human salvation can only be attained through obeisance to some popular savior or another are lying, although they usually believe they are not. The confusion and divisiveness these spiritual monopolists create with their bigoted power-hungry scheming is the one of the most destructive forces on Earth.

Salvation comes though living in accordance with truth and though the practice of righteous Libertarian principles. Simple human decency is what will save the world, not mindless belief in tepid, limp-wristed mythologies.

Popular religions more or less advocate a morality based upon non encroachment against others. This is a good start, but he reason these religions have not saved the world is because they mix this moral truth with mythological falsehood and insist upon absolute literal belief. People see through much of the falsehood and then wrongly reject much of the moral truth along with the falsehood.

Personal Obstacles to World Liberty

There are many falsehoods that seem to give fulfillment in the short term, but which deliver absolutely nothing in the long term. They are only fantasy, and a complete waste of time. Dealing with reality is far more exciting, and produces constructive change, because attention isn't diverted away from things that really matter. The main problem areas are:

1. False Beliefs
One need not embrace ancient fairy tales as literal truth in order to live a moral life. This is not to say that good principles cannot be illustrated with traditional stories and allegories. We simply need to sort out what is real.

2. Non-Libertarian Economics and Politics
Collectivist systems simply do not work. All fully educated people know this. False systems include Communism, Socialism, Democratic Socialism, Social Democracy, Democracy not constituted upon Libertarian principles, Fascism, Populism, Theocracy, etc.

3. Controlled Media
Most easy-to-get information is controlled by those in service to globalist bankers and their subverted government lackeys, re-elected decade after decade by an ignorant apathetic majority. One must seek further for hard knowledge upon which to make important decisions.

4. Drug Induced Euphoria
If you don't like environmental circumstances, change them with action, not merely your experience of them by ingesting

chemicals. Alcohol is used to suppress the cerebral cortex in order to liberate the reptilian complex. It gives timid people false courage in business and romance. One need only affect a reconciliation between Jekyll and Hyde in this regard. Psychedelic drugs seem interesting because they give the user a strange mental life. Since all human societies are based almost entirely upon lies, reading books and learning truth will give a far stranger mental life without bad side effects.

5. Spectator Sports
Ball games are just arbitrary simian competitiveness, a wishy-washy substitute for those afraid to get involved in things that actually matter.

6. Virtual Reality
Millions today resemble those poor souls who freebase cocaine, sitting all day addicted to their own brain chemicals, playing video games which give false feelings of heroism in seeming to defat enemies that do not exist. Wake up! There are real enemies to defat.

7. Excess Entertainment
Novels, movies, and music are great, especially when they inspire heroic Libertarian ideals and action. The amount need only be in balance with the other demands of real life.

8. Unproductive Friendships
This involves not wasting time with fools who suffer from any of the above delusions. Friendship should be casual and light hearted, centered around the mutual love of causes, professions, or hobbies. Meddlesome busy-bodies who encourage validation of life strategies through consensus should be avoided. It is always best to keep one's own council in order to develop inner resources. If you need advice, seek what the greatest minds in history have said, not some doped-up joker you knew in high school. Remember what George Washington said,
"Have no intimacy with worthless men."

Libertarian Basics

The Basic Libertarian Premise: It is wrong to unjustly encroach upon any creature or the environment to the detriment of any living thing. Most people agree with this premise. The disagreement is over what constitutes encroachment.

The innate love of liberty and the concession of this to others is what we may call the Basic Libertarian Impulse. Depending upon the degree of spiritual development, the individual either manifests this or does not. We know that it is unjust to unnecessarily kill, assault, coerce, rob, defraud, slander, or otherwise encroach upon any living creature. Calling these acts by other names and programming an ignorant majority to agree that they are necessary or permissible does not change their nature. To do evil is to trespass unnecessarily upon the liberty of any living organism. Historically this principle has been called the Golden Rule.

In human affairs we accept the premise that is desirable for people to reach their natural level of prosperity and development through their own volition while living in peace and harmony with each other. A human being is an creature which comes into this world with no rights owed him and no obligation incumbent upon him, except the natural right to absolute individual liberty, and since he is not alone on the planet, the logical obligation of reciprocity in this towards others. He need only concede to others the same liberty that he demands for himself, because this is absolutely all that is necessary for continuing harmony on Earth. The one human responsibility then is simply to never make unjust encroachment. The only legitimate function of government is to enforce this natural obligation of humanity. Any person or government attempting to impose any burden other than this upon the individual is guilty of criminal coercion and should be regarded as a mortal enemy even if the oppression is sanctioned democratically.

Liberty is the natural right of every living organism to manifest justly as an unimpeded participant in evolutionary destiny. This manifestation, to be just, must not unnecessarily interfere with the evolutionary expression of any other living organism.

Every problem in every society on Earth can be traced back to a point where someone in government decides to sacrifice individual liberty for some other goal. Like any breech of natural law this produces a distortion. One compromise seems to justify another and soon the cause and effect relationships become obscured by time and complexity. The achievement of harmony on Earth simply involves eliminating the complex of false dependencies that have arisen because of these past mistakes.

Individual liberty is the innate right to be free of unjust encroachment from others. It doesn't matter if the others outnumber us, are organized, and use euphemistic terminology. There are two types of unjust encroachment against individual liberty, illegal and legal. From a Libertarian standpoint both are equally as criminal. Un-Libertarian elements will allege that legal crimes are not unjust because they are determined to be necessary by a majority opinion and that this should supersede any objective measure of workability and rightness. There is no reason for decent people to compromise about this. People who don't want to be free are cowards. People who keep others from being free are criminals. The majority of people on Earth have always been and still are both.

People who have little regard for individual liberty will think that anyone who questions their morality or basic understanding in this regard is being terribly unreasonable. For those, however, who have a heroic vision for future societies, liberty is not a question to be begged, but a moral absolute. It is not negotiable or compromisable. Its value is not merely theoretical or just a "matter of opinion". The Libertarian position is the only viewpoint which is not unreasonable. The people who now oppose individual liberty eventually will be vanquished. Natural order will prevail. The first line of attack is education.

Libertarianism is not power hungry politics, but the structuring of human affairs in accordance with natural law. Anarcho-Capitalism is not chaos, but the one and only system of economics which implements natural order.

The individual has the natural right to live in a free society, failing this, to live in liberty within any society in which he may find himself, regardless of the "consequences" to anyone else. Absolute individual liberty is the one and only thing worth fighting for. The truly Libertarian position is superior to all others, intellectually and morally. There are few however, who really understand or practice Libertarian ideals. No existing government and very few people will knowingly allow complete liberty to anyone if it seems to suit their purpose to do otherwise. If the individual wants liberty, he has to reach out and take it at any cost, must guard it jealously, and to keep it must be willing to fight even unto death.

No matter what else man accomplishes, if he does not immediately deal with the problem of increasing population, nothing else he does will matter. Couples who have more than two children make direct encroachment against all other creatures on this planet. The ideal population level on Earth was passed hundreds of years ago, if by the word "ideal" we mean a level consistent with concepts like individual self-actualization and opulent joy in living, rather than mere subsistence in anguished mediocrity. Evolutionary destiny is served through qualitation, not quantification. Maximum joyful manifestation for small numbers is superior to minimum meager manifestation for vast suffering multitudes. We are not imbued with life merely to endure it.

Trying to make the world Libertarian through writing is like holding a message in a bottle while standing upon a high precipice overlooking the vast expanse of limitless ocean. You are at the brink of heroic destiny, but casting your message into the sea of fate. The message is a knowledge of natural principles, which if generally acted upon by mankind, will ensure worldwide prosperity and peace, the unimpeded evolutionary expression of all living things. You wonder if the message will ever be read by anyone. Your only certainty is that little perceptible change will result in your own lifetime, because there are few who would comprehend the message even if everyone did read it. You wonder if the message will be preserved long enough to make any difference at all or whether the life you have spent has simply been wasted. Then you wonder if anything matters at all. Then you contemplate the other things that you might have done with your life and you realize that there is nothing, nor could there ever be anything, more excellent than this: the Greatest of All Quests.

Essential Facts for World Liberty

"Let me issue and control a nation's money and I care not who writes the laws." ~ Mayer Amsche Rothschild ~

"If the American people ever allow private banks to control the issue of their currency, first by inflation, then by deflation, the banks...will deprive the people of all property until their children wake up homeless on the continent their fathers conquered.... The issuing power should be taken from the banks and restored to the people, to whom it properly belongs." ~ Thomas Jefferson ~

"We are on the verge of a global transformation. All we need is the right major crisis and the nations will accept the New World Order." ~ David Rockefeller ~

Weed Out Falsehood

We are tired of crackpots who claim that predatory globalist bankers are aliens from outer space or another dimension. It seems more likely that those who say these things are working to engineer popular mistrust of the resistance. Additionally, since it is primarily events of the past two centuries which affect us now, the endless attempts to trace all this back to ancient Egypt or reconcile it with ancient prophesies, only complicates and distracts from the real issue at hand, the upcoming triumph of tyranny on Earth.

What follows is not "conspiracy theory" but well documented fact. It is not easy to see against the complex background of world affairs. Because of independent media, public awareness of these matters has been increasing in past months. It's a good idea to print out or get hardcopy when appropriate, because very resourceful people are trying hard to stop Internet access to information about these matters.

The New World Order

The predatory globalists are international bankers, not extraterrestrials, but they love only gold, and in their sick insatiable greed, rob all of humanity of the natural right to liberty, earned prosperity, and peace. They do this by manipulating currencies through privately owned central banks like the Federal Reserve Bank of the United States, and with the help of subverted politicians, engineer wars and economic upheaval so that they can lend money to governments for military mobilization and otherwise unnecessary social programs. This is what is meant by "Welfare-Warfare Economies." There is a large detailed body of historical fact about how they have done this for the past two hundred years.

Internationally these people are guilty of crimes against humanity on a scale greater than anyone in all of human history. In their individual countries they are, at very least, guilty of treason. They are allowed to continue in this only because of public ignorance. We can bring these enemies of all human potential to justice with legal precedents like those enacted at Nuremberg, but before an international tribunal can be convened and indictments issued, there must be increased public demand. Liberty-loving people need to learn about these matters and pass it on to others. This in turn must lead to activism: resolutions and petitions by business and civic groups to international organizations, senators, and congressmen.

At this time in history, there is no greater responsibility, and no higher calling. Taking refuge in endless popular modes of escapist delusion will not ensure the future of life and liberty on this planet. Even if adults no longer care about their own futures, they should get involved at least for the sake of the children. In the voting booth, there is merely the illusion of a choice between two NWO puppets. The only real choice is between World Libertarianism and ongoing "two-party" elections geared to globalist tyranny.

The US National debt is nearly twenty trillion dollars, every penny created by fiat counterfeiting. Nobody earned this money. Other nations will follow the US example when it works. All America needs to do is nationalize the Federal Reserve, repudiate the national debt, and demand reparations from the creditors for the amount already swindled from the American people.

The Enemies of Liberty

Prosperity and peace will follow naturally from worldwide liberty. The enemies of this process are those whose efforts, or lack thereof, put them in opposition to the triumph of Libertarian policies that will bring the closest thing to utopia possible on Earth.

Usually the *intent* of these individuals is much narrower, with little thought given to the bigger picture. The most common goals are the personal attainment of wealth, power, fame, prestige, recognition, acceptance, or stability.

Most are not seeking the deliberate ruination of humanity. Unfortunately the truly powerful people who actually control the world *are* seeking precisely that, and thus far have been extremely successful. World history since 1913 is entirely a product of their machinations.

In this volume we are going to look and a great many categories of people who stand in the way of total excellence in human manifestation. Often a person will be in more than one category, and within these, more than one subcategory as follows, those who are:

Paid For
People given perks or campaign contributions for implementing policy or failing to stress certain areas of truth in their rhetoric. Most of this is legal, but because of the complexity of events, remains *hidden in plain view*.

Status Quo Beneficiaries
These are exploitative elements, along for the ride. Most are worldly syndical people, and this usually involves a high paying position that would otherwise not exist in an honestly run society. Sometimes it involves huge volume manufacture and distribution of product that would otherwise be utilized on a much smaller scale in an honestly run society.

Ideologue
These are the indoctrinated idealists, ignorant intellectually, with an unlimited capacity to rationalize any and all means to the attainment of their ideals. They always defend these as "short-term necessary evils" no matter how destructive or unjust. They don't have a clue as to the real consequences for humanity of the concealed agenda of those who utilize them.

Moral Capability

In humans, he cerebral cortex is the seat of higher moral deliberation. The ability to conceptualize morally is a genetically determined brain skill just like mathematical or mechanical ability. Someone born with effectively no ability to empathize with other living creatures, is what we call a moral moron, or *constitutional psychopath*. They are four percent of the population, one in twenty-five people, and are found in every walk of life.

As with any dichotomy, there is a proportional number of people at the upper end of the moral continuum. Those who are average in the moral sense cluster around the center point

Today, the word *sociopath* is often used as a substitute term for psychopath, but actually denotes two sub-categories:

Psychopath – One vs. Humanity

Dissocial Reaction – One + Family vs. Humanity

This is because the word *psychopath*, in popular use, has come to evoke the image of a violent, wild-eyed individual, with hair-trigger rage reactions. Most of them, however, lead quiet lives of shallow superficial respectability, because they learn early in life that keeping out of trouble is more enjoyable than getting into trouble. Their goals are usually the same as anybody else, but often the means to attainment are very different.

There are many good examples of this among individuals who grow tired of their spouse in a situation where money is involved. The spouse may miss their daily insulin injection, fall down the front staircase, or suffer from a car with leaky brake fluid.

Psychopathy can interact with other behavioral disorders. Criminals are almost always, at very least, constitutional psychopaths. The worst are rapists, snuff and child porn video makes, kidnappers, pedophiles, and those who torture and kill for pleasure. These people are irredeemably evil, and cannot be rehabilitated. The moral integrity and safety of human societies depends upon eliminating them.

Group Psychopathy
There are many factors which determine human behavior, but if one group of people is forty IQ points lower than another group, then it will also be forty moral IQ points lower. If this leads to the taking for granted and general acceptance of certain types of evil behavior, then a tendency for this will be passed along genetically in that group, leading to what is often referred to as a *race of psychopaths*.

Twits will refer to the mature understanding of these matters as *racism*, but tepid knee jerk reactions, after all, is what makes them twits.

IMF Bankers

Most of the big problems on Earth are caused by International Monetary Fund bankers who, via member central banks, manipulate currencies, and with the help of subverted politicians, engineer wars and economic upheaval so they can lend money to governments for military mobilization and otherwise unnecessary social programs.

Globalism, New World Order, is simply the one world government that will allow the IMF banks to have total finance monopoly, e.g. forty percent mortgages, sixty percent refinance.

Countries do not need to borrow from IMF banks, but can have their own central bank and control their own currency. Populations are kept from the knowledge of this by cooperating subverted mainstream media, and by the subverted politicians who keep IMF control in place by voting for it in legislatures.

All that is necessary to have enduring liberty, prosperity, and peace on Earth is to have all counties leave the IMF, set up their own central banks, and tie the amount and value of currency to receipted hours of labor, or a mixed store of scarce and durable commodity.

People of all political parties worldwide must declare that they will not endorse any candidate who doesn't have a detailed plan in hand to get their country out of the IMF, and to nationalize their central bank.

The goal of the Nationalist Revolution novels is to help inspire total worldwide resistance at every level to globalization.

It would be wonderful if we could end world tyranny democratically, but that isn't going to happen. Many will die, but if we don't fight, we will soon have the "cashless society" with national I.D. debit cards, then silicone chip body implants. This will be followed by behavior modification implants, and finally, when they figure out how to do it, a physical matrix for everyone but themselves.

Evil exists. A globalist banker or media boss is a human with the soul of a black widow spider. They cannot be reasoned with, only stopped. We can and will defeat them, but only through heroic action, not with secretly held opinions. The only good globalist is a nonexistent globalist. Free indigenous peoples and cultures will never be safe until they are just an unpleasant memory.

Welfare-Warfare Economy

This is not an anecdotal term. It is the IMF way-of-things at this time, and will remain so until we demand something better either in the voting booth or at gunpoint. Ball games and virtual reality heroism will not accomplish this.

Welfare
A humane society will provide sustenance for those with a history of productivity who have incurred legitimate disability. With healthy economies there will jobs for everyone on Earth who are able and *willing* to work.

Because of ongoing bad economies, there has arisen a permanent underclass of people who feel "entitled" to endless sustenance by government. They oppose anyone who works for a healthy economy. Those who engage in violent demonstrations are the modern counterpart to the Bolshevists who murdered sixty-six million people in Europe.

Warfare
War and terrorism today are a very difficult study. Just when you think you understand an event, new information surfaces showing that it was actually a false flag, usually involving Globalist traitors in your own government working with foreign operatives.

The purpose of endless wars is to generate "refugees," aided by the EU and UN, to invade countries and destroy indigenous race and culture everywhere, so that people lacking identity will except one world government.

Terrorism is supported by deep state funding, open borders, and police stand-downs. The purpose is to make our daily lives seem so dangerous that we will gladly surrender our guns and liberty just to feel "safe." History has shown that the worst enemy people have turns out to be their own government when it gains too much power. Citizen ownership of guns simply represents a balance of power.

Good people need to become proactive about building a better future. We will be rid of these problems only when the Globalists, their subservient minions, and invading outland hoards have been permanently vanquished.

Military-Industrial Complex

This term also, is not anecdotal. All countries must have defensive weapons in place. In a Libertarian Nationalist world, however, the daily function will be only to maintain readiness, not to sustain endless military engagement for the profit of avaricious bankers.

Military Profiteers
Usually these are Globalist agenda-driven elements working for the longer term profits that would come from global finance monopoly,
"Soldiers of Fortune" in the truest sense.

Industrial Profiteers
These are the industrialists who manufacture the machinery of war. In a Libertarian world, they will simply need to retool for farming and space colonization. The good ones will be more than delighted to be able to do this.

> In the councils of government, we must guard against the acquisition of unwarranted influence, whether sought or unsought, by the military-industrial complex. The potential for the disastrous rise of misplaced power exists and will persist. ~ Dwight D. Eisenhower 1061

Subverted Politicians

Globalist bankers keep politicians loyal with campaign contributions and easy access to big loans. They create prestigious organizations to teach and implement their agenda. Among these are the United Nations, European Union, Trilateral Commission, Council on Foreign Relations, National Education Association, National Council of Churches.

Politicians, high military officials, prominent industrialists, and media moguls are invited to join these organizations. All this, combined with entrenched subverted government, *deep state*, is correctly called the E*stablishmen*t.

Subverted Media

IFM bankers have created and subsidized popular media outlets which present or stress information or disinformation which supports their objectives. This usually involves trying to make the public believe that pro Globalist sentiments are already held by a majority of people, and that one will be badly out-of-step if they do not embrace these ideas themselves.

Operation Mockingbird
In the early 1950s, Globalist elements in the Central Intelligence Agency compiled a list of phrases which they felt would elicit knee-jerk responses in the general population. They approached IMF-friendly elements in the mainstream media and persuaded them to cooperate in engineering popular consent for one world government.

It was suggested by the CIA that their phrases be used glibly in a very matter-of-fact way as part of normal daily reportage. The most important of these is *conspiracy theory*.

The CIA knew that lazy apathetic thinkers (almost everybody) would jump on a phrase like this, as an easy-out for rationalizing their own ignorance. e.g. If they don't know about something complex or hidden, it *must* be only theoretical, and the person propounding it must, of course, be *paranoid*, another term on the CIA list. Now the twits can get back to the ballgame.

Subverted Educators

Charlotte Thomson Iserbyt, former Senior Policy Advisor for the U.S. Department of Education, disclosed government policies hidden from the public in her famous book,
The Deliberate Dumbing Down of America.
It was on the New York Times Bestseller List for weeks in the 1980s, but has anything changed?

Today, schools mix truth with outright lies. If anyone questions anything, they are labelled *haters*. Good examples include:

Competition is Cruel
We are all *so* special.
It's insensitive and unfair that anyone ever be graded for the actual level of their performance in anything. Where is our sensitivity?

Gender Fluidity
There are many more than two genders.
Scientific research clearly showing that sexual aberration is a function of genetic mutation, hormone imbalance, or a mistaken learning process, is really just the bigoted intolerance of what are simply normal human differences.

Some schools today have small children socialize intimately with transgender men.
Drag Queen Story Hour. Parents, wake up!

Monoculture is Best
Race is merely a social construct.
Breed up quick, so we can all be the same.

The tedious gray slavery of global monoculture is far more hip and open minded.

The Globalists insure that all these culturally destructive ideas are taught, by giving endowments to schools and colleges, with campaign donations and other payoffs to cooperating legislators.

Globalist accomplices within the education system are usually ideologue twits, many of whom are also entitlement parasites, drug addicts, sex perverts, or invading outlanders. Some are more than one of these. People can only teach with passion from the standpoint of what they are.

Subverted Citizens

Compromised Adults
This is Jean and Joe Six-Pack, couch potato air-heads. They like their ballgames and beer, but never read. They watch only fake news. They never think beyond the end of their own noses, or more than three weeks ahead. A viable future for children, life on Earth one hundred years from today, the evolutionary destiny of mankind, are concepts totally alien to them. Those who do care about these things are seen as trouble-makers.

Misdirected Youth
These are the children ruined intellectually and psycho-sexually by the subverted education system and media. They grow up to be brain dead self-haters.

Reparations Parasites

This usually involves those seeking indemnity for events that happened long ago. Two good examples of this are claimants connected with slavery in the United States, and with what is termed the "holocaust" in WWII Germany.

Falsified History

Sometimes popularly accepted history contains mistakes or exaggerations about events, numbers, motives, or responsibility. At other times outright lies are propounded deliberately.

America
There is an ongoing myth that everybody who were not slaves profited from slavery. In actuality, everybody but the plantation owners, were hurt by slavery, because it eliminated fair completion for the commodities produced, and for jobs in the labor market.

Only two percent of the Caucasian population were slave owners, and this was before the huge influx from Europe after 1850. Today, however, some are asserting that Caucasians, as a group, owe reparations to all descendants of slaves, as a group.

Tell this to Caucasians who lost family fighting to end slavery in the Civil War.

Germany
The six million "holocaust" death-toll number was suggested by a magistrate from Vermont who sat at Nuremberg. The IMF-friendly media jumped on this number, and have never let go. There are a few problems, however:

The World Almanac uses official census data.
For 1940, it reports a world Jewish population of 15,319,359.
For 1949, 15,713,638.

Under the terms of the Geneva Convention, the Red Cross inspected all the concentration camps once every two weeks. Their official estimate of the total number who died in all the camps is 271,301. This includes non-Jews.

American forensic doctors examined hundreds of bodies and found only typhus and starvation as the causes of death, not even one death from poison gas.

When the Russians liberated the camps in Poland, including Auschwitz, they did not allow the press into the camps for five years. When they finally removed the restriction, journalists got to photograph all those gas chambers that nobody remembers seeing who visited the camps during the war years.

IMF bankers, of course, continue to lend money to Germany for the ongoing reparations to Israel based on the six million estimate. Anyone who speaks up is shouted down as a *Holocaust denier.*

Self-Disabling Parasites

These are people who are perfectly able to work, but who use subterfuge to keep from doing so. There are several categories. Some may be in more than one:

Breeders
These are welfare mothers who have eight children while being completely subsidized by government. These are men who brag on the city bus about fathering seventeen illegitimate children. Condoning either is like poising the public water supply.

Wastrels
These are people who find every way possible to keep from working. They include borrowers, gamblers, gigolos, moochers.

Mental Cases
With the exception of aberration having physical origin, the clinical catalogue of dysfunctional behavior is really just a list of the different types of bad moral character.

A good example is the neurotic who develops a *phobia for work* as a reaction to some unrelated incident in youth. Morally ambivalent psychiatrists are often complicit in sustaining this, because they know that loving parents want the young person to take whatever amount of time is necessary to *work through* the problem. There are endless sessions, but very few cures.

Drug Addicts
The moral maturity of a person at the time they begin using a psychotropic drug remains fixed, until they stop using the drug. This includes anti-depressants and tranquilizers prescribed by doctors who receive a manufacturer commission for every prescription.

Today many users start on drugs at an early age. Good business people don't want an adult worker with the maturely of an eight-year-old. Additionally, drug use often interferes with motivation, attention span, and coordination.

Sex Perverts
Colleges today host an endless freak show of transgender monstrosities. There is usually euphemistic terminology for this, like the very computeresque *non binary*. Those who sport these labels believe that they are intellectual pioneers in a brave new world of greater tolerance and expanded consciousness.

Invaders

Legal
These are immigrants whose influx into any country ultimately destroys the race and culture of the indigenous population. Their immigration is legal, but would not be, if the country were not subverted to the purposes of Globalism. In the interest of racial preservation, this problem must be addressed immediately worldwide by any means available.

Illegal Individuals
Many of the gatecrashers who violate borders come back no matter how many times they are deported. There are instances of some who have returned over fifty times. If they knew that they would be executed immediately upon return, most would probably not return.

Illegal Hordes
At this writing (5/26/2019), there is an ongoing invasion across the southern border of the United States. It would be perfectly appropriate to use loudspeakers to warn the invaders, and then at intervals with fighter planes, strafe with machine fire, those who ignore the warning. If a sovereign nation is to remain free, it must enforce its borders.

Who's Who

In 1933, Friedreich Nietzsche propounded the ideal of the Ubermensch, or Superman. This does not involve supernaturalism or anything unattainable, but as a concept has been misunderstood, joked down, and twisted by cowards and lowlifes ever since.

The superman (men and women) are simply people who do not have to victimize or encroach upon others to survive in a free society. They transcend the myths and false moralities of everyday experience, and work in some area of magnificent obsession to make the world a better place. They are here among us, not to be stoned, cool and jazzy, but to save the day.

The subhuman is the opposite of this, people who have no capacity except to encroach upon others in a free society. This is primarily a function of low I.Q. Their intrinsic inferiority puts them in opposition to social policies that will lead to liberty, prosperity, and peace. They are essentially enemies of evolutionary destiny. If evolved humanity is to survive, then the subhuman must be eliminated. The easiest, most humane, and best way is through mass sterilization.

In terms of the narrative at hand, the superman is the Libertarian Nationalist warrior who will oppose Globalism even unto death. The subhuman is any of the people listed herein as enemies of liberty. When they are gone, good people will rest briefly, then the Golden Age of Humanity will begin.

Strategies

Apathetic Non Resistance
This is not a viable option. In the long term, globalization would do more damage to life on Earth than a full nuclear exchange between all nations. Doing nothing about the Globalists can lead only to one or the other.

Liberian Nationalist Revolution
A reformatted after-the-fact story version of the following section appears at the end of every novel in the series. Read on, and see why.

Libertarian Nationalist Revolution

Most of the big problems on Earth are caused by parasitic international bankers who, via central banks, manipulate currencies, and with the help of subverted politicians, engineer wars and economic upheaval so that they can lend money to governments for military mobilization and otherwise unnecessary social programs.

The Shadow Government / New World Order agenda, called Globalization, is merely Totalitarian Socialism with One World Government, giving absolute monopoly to predatory bankers. Any reputable economist will tell you that what the World Libertarian Order proposes will result in ongoing liberty, prosperity, and peace for all people on Earth.
Saving the world is a big job, but it's the best, and involves the making right of all past mistakes, not mere adaptation to the aftermath. No single group, governmental body, or army is expected to affect this entire program. Those who like the future vision depicted, should simply do whatever they can towards the desired end.

Without the Globalists, we will have a future for the entire world, free of economic upheaval, war, and pollution, with no encroachment on any living thing, indigenous peoples enjoying strict population control, race and culture preservation, absolute individual liberty, prosperity, and peace as separate sovereign nations competing in a free world market.

Following is a ten point program, which must be implemented to liberate societies so that natural order can prevail. The best approach will vary from one country to another because of what has occurred in the past, but the variations involve only short term emphasis and sequence, not policy or principles. The time frame for phasing in any particular policy must be of sufficient duration for smooth transition tp minimize any short term bad effects upon individuals or economies.

This is a summary, and may suggest the need for further reading, so please press ahead.

Ten Steps to Libertarian Nationalist Revolution

1. Revolution

Politicians:

All at the same time, stand up and be courageous. Show some integrity. Stop serving the New World Order parasites. Accept the premise that government is at best a necessary evil and that the less of it we have, the better. Please support all measures outlined herein.

Everybody Else:

Initiate revolution. Support all popular measures that are in a basic Libertarian direction, such as budget balancing. When there is no other choice, deal with gross encroachments against individual liberty covertly on an individual basis. Educate the upcoming generation at the grass roots level, about the sole workability of Libertarian principles so that un-Libertarian elements can finally be voted out of office everywhere. Maintain health, practice martial skills, and stay well-armed in case we get a chance to do it sooner. All this is the only difficult part. The rest is simple and could then be implemented quickly unless otherwise specified.

2. Banking and Trade

In every country, nationalize privately owned central banks, like the US Federal Reserve, repudiate the national debt, and demand reparations for the amount already swindled by the creditors, as a civil alternative to being put on trial for engineering every war and ruined economy over the past two hundred years, or being the beneficiary heirs thereto, all of which is easily provable from existing historical records. Return to currencies backed by durable commodity of intrinsic value, like gold or a mixed store of precious metals, the value of which will be determined in the world marketplace.

Consumers worldwide will have total product choice. Goods offered in the free world market will be produced solely within each country by the citizens of that country, with no foreign ownership of business anywhere. Banks will lend only within their own countries. Once all nations are prospering, few will think it good practice to invest away from home, and imbalances will subside. Simultaneously, phase out all subsidies and unjust regulation of business, trade, financial transfers, and banks.

For any bank, including the central bank, to maintain less than a one hundred percent reserve at all times is simply dishonest. The new policies will correct things easily with mandatory disclosure to depositors about actual amounts held in reserve, and clear information on what it all means.

3. Taxation

Eliminate wealth redistribution at gunpoint, aka taxes, and institute specific user fees and designated lotteries. This will not happen simultaneously in all areas of spending, but immediately wherever possible. From here forward unnecessary foreign adventures by governments will have to be paid for only by those who support them.

4. War

In this new scenario, war will fast become just an unhappy memory. The energies previously squandered in these conflicts will be channeled into undersea farming, renewable energy technology, space exploration, and interplanetary mining operations. Defense spending everywhere can be cut to a safe minimum, substituting standing military with a skeleton crew of officers for the coordination of a voluntary citizen militia adequate to any emergency. To this end, replace frivolous athletics in the schools with basic martial and survival training.

5. Socialism

End the artificial sustenance of non-viability. Gradually phase out social programs and entitlements as the improving economy and rate of employment makes this possible in each particular locality. This will be done slowly enough so that nobody will be hurt. How quickly this can happen, however, will be a great surprise to most people. Nobody will be hungry in a Libertarian society. There will be an emergency fund to alleviate desperation caused by unpredictable local catastrophe or incurred disability. This can be funded by designated lotteries at the federal and state level.

6. Crime

Deal intelligently with crime:

- Legalize victimless crimes involving consensual areas of human contract. Free all those confined for victimless crimes with a public apology, a little money to tide them over, and a list of realistic job offers.

- Recognize the true bad guys: rapists, human traffickers, kidnappers, child molesters, child and snuff porn filmmakers, arbitrary murderers, and serial killers. These people are irredeemable constitutional psychopaths who have made an unforgivable breech with humanity. For the safety and moral integrity of societies they must be put painlessly to death. Opponents of this should appreciate that one needn't be a rocket scientist to figure out that all it takes to avoid being executed for these terrible things is simply not to do them.

- Replace prisons with self-sustaining isolation communities, several square miles with agriculture, livestock, and small manufacturing. As economies improve, the inevitable one percent of humanity simply unable to support themselves can be offered permanent sustenance by private charity as per specified terms, such as voluntary sterilization. Any such individuals refusing this option will have to shift for themselves. If this causes them to make encroachment on anyone else's liberty, they will be placed in isolation communities.

7. Protectionism

As the distortions produced by hundreds of years of unnatural coercive government slowly begin to subside, cautiously phase out all unnecessary or unjust protectionist measures such as unnecessary safety regulations.

8. Education

Institute programs in schools to teach children about what went wrong in the past and how Libertarian policies have improved everything. Explain the manipulative relationship that previously existed between international finance and politicians. Supplement this with rigorous teaching about devolving humanity, racial preservation, excess birth rates, birth control, disease, and all individual classes of drugs. Make understanding of all this requisite for promotion. Teach the truth for forty years before eliminating public education.

9. Adjustments

Make all adjustments associated with simple Libertarian decency and smart living.
Examples include:

- Stop unnecessary environmental pollution as soon as this is viable. No pay-offs for ten year "feasibility" studies or twenty year "implementation" programs. Just stop it.

- Institute requirements in livestock production, zoo administration, and pet ownership based upon humane, free-range, hormone/drug-free models.

- Stop the cruel decadent down breeding of pets into evolutionary non-viability. Sterilize the existing animals. Ask yourself why little dogs are so nervous and angry that they bark viciously all day, every day. Would you not be angry if captors had done this to you?

- Give national park and forest lands back to the native populations from whom they were originally stolen. This with the provision that they continue to run the lands at a high standard, for the enjoyment of all. Current non-native employees can be offered life tenure or a new job.

- Overhaul medicine, stressing nutritional solutions, both therapeutic and preventive, as opposed to only pharmacological and surgical options. Eliminate the duplicitous role of the physician as both personal doctor and commission salesman for drug companies, Allow doctors to prescribe only within generic categories, the specific choice of drugs being left to the patients who select for themselves on the basis of price and manufacturer reputation.

- Respect the right of individuals to decide when their life is no longer viable. Establish regional centers where people can be put into cryonic suspension, or receive a lethal injection and be cremated.

10. Population and Race

Deal decisively with the issues of population and race:

- History shows that smaller numbers of people in any given place work best, so long as there are enough to defend the borders. For the land mass of Earth, the *ideal* population is 320 million people. This number was passed c 900 A.D. By the word *ideal* we mean a level consistent with vital self-actualization and opulent joy in living, rather than mere subsistence in anguished mediocrity. To this end, rigidly enforce a limit of two children per couple. More than two is an unjust encroachment upon others, like house burglary. World population will slowly decline to workable levels everywhere. The projected ideal numbers are as follows:

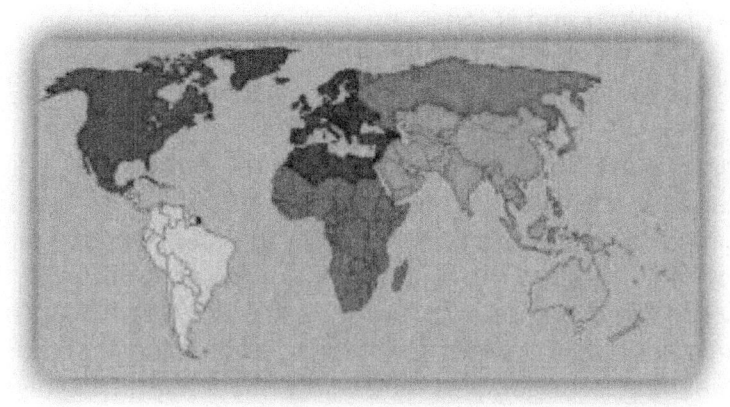

Canada, United States, Mexico
50,000,000

Central, South America
50,000,000

Greenland, Europe, Northern Africa
50,000,000

Southern Africa
50,000,000

Russia
50,000,000

Near, Middle East, Asia
50,000,000

Australia, New Zealand
20,000,000

- Workable societies must be based on natural principals. It is natural for people to feel most comfortable among those of their own race and ethnicity. In all of human history there has never been a multiracial or multicultural society which did not self-destruct because of the unnatural mixing. The New World Order bankers, who work for totalitarian Socialism and world monoculture, want everyone to mix together, so they can lend money to national governments who must deal with all the resulting social problems.

- All people have the natural right to grow up among their own racial kinsmen. Resident racial outlanders are simply an unjust encroachment upon the personal liberty of indigenous peoples. To survive, we must emphasize race preservation and the prevention of global monoculture. Interracial marriage advocates are attempting to eliminate all existing races. They try to sound very interested in human variety, but their breed-up quick programs, long term, will completely obliterate human variety by making what are now separate races into one race. Variety is the spice of life. Imagine the tedium of universal sameness. The globalist bankers want to destroy race and culture. They know that one world government, giving global finance monopoly, will be more acceptable to people with no racial or ethnic identity.

- A common falsehood perpetrated by politicians in service to big business seeking cheap labor has been that ongoing immigration is necessary to keep industry alive. In actuality, business simply expands to accommodate any available work force. With worldwide prosperity, people will not flee their ancestral homelands.

- Note that third-world people usually favor globalization because it will allow them to prosper via social programs paid for by productive host populations. The predatory bankers know that countries with hordes of immigrant third-worlders, if the globalization question comes to a ballot referendum, will be far more likely to relinquish sovereignty.

- Close borders everywhere to immigrants of non-indigenous race. Anybody can leave, and a great many will begin to return home. Request voluntary sterilization of all who choose to remain in host countries, with special retirement programs for those who cooperate and adoption priorities for qualified couples within this category. No restrictions on travel. Tourists from now on will be able to enjoy the full undiluted potency of indigenous cultures everywhere.

- There will be new technology for determining constitutional psychopathy, even in the prenatal state, along with intrauterine diagnosis of fetal deformity, mental retardation, and genetic predisposition to sexual perversion. This will lead to the elimination of human non-viability everywhere on earth.

- Implement an equitable solution for the problems caused by a century of Socialism in unnaturally increasing the quantity, while undermining the quality, of people everywhere. There will be new foolproof brain-scan methods for determining intelligence. Use it to assess IQ in populations worldwide. Request voluntary sterilization of all those having an IQ of 94 or less, also with special retirement benefits and adoption priorities. Because higher moral conceptualization is a function of the cerebral cortex, these IQ adjustments, along with the elimination of constitutional psychopathy, will effectively spell an end to commonplace moral stupidity on this planet.

A Brighter Future

When all nations have attained free enterprise with global free trade, a basically Libertarian world will finally have been achieved. Evil will still exist on Earth at interpersonal levels, but it will no longer rule the day, nor will it never again be institutionalized by governments.

Dumbing Down of Populations

Under the influence and tutelage attached to Globalist banker endowments for education, American schools have been dumbing kids down for over 100 years.

The goal is to replace logical common sense reactions to life with moral lassitude. This is done by slowly changing the curriculum with false ideas about wealth, economics, science, health, nutrition, sex, gender, natural selection, archaeology, race, history, good, evil, right, wrong, love, hate, spirituality, liberty, security, and national sovereignty. This is done, not just with false emphasis and interpretation, but often using outright falsehood.

After graduation, the dumbing down continues, especially with selective information about current events, from the subverted media. The upside-down agenda we see today is to make reality and policy conform to a distorted world view instead of changing the world view and policy to be in conformity with workable reality.

Under Libertarian policies, with increasing prosperity and the return of indigenous peoples to their ancestral homelands, there will be a resurgence of ethnic and cultural pride everywhere. We will see it in the arts, music, and culinary industries. Tourism will be up worldwide. Travelers will enjoy the full potency of other people's indigenous cultures everywhere on earth.

People will be comfortable with who and what they are. All the phony *gender fluidity* nonsense will be a thing of the past. The bleaching and dying of hair and skin in mimicry of other races, will be gone, and there will be no more retarded catcalls of *racism* or *phobia* for every nuance of normal human preference.

Footnote: Gender Fluidity

There are two biological genders. Appearances to the contrary come from five sources: random genetic mutation, inherited genetic predisposition, hormone imbalance, mistakes in leaning as outlined by Sigmund Freud, and outright perversion usually associated with drug augmented aberration and the false belief that every random impulse must be nurtured for the true liberation of the evolved self.

Gender is fixed, but gender-specific behavior is variable. A puritanical view is that gender specific behavior is fixed, therefore gender must be variable. At first, this might seem arbitrary, but on closer view, the utility is that it absolves people of responsibility for their actions. In this way they can blame dysfunctional behavior on random genetic chance and avoid any proactive effort towards constructive change.

Suggested Reading - The Globalist Agenda:

How the Elite Control your mind and Your Life

Education & History
Research for Yourself...

The Deliberate Dumbing Down of America
by Charlotte Thomson Iserbyt

Charlotte Thomson Iserbyt, former Senior Policy Advisor in the U.S. Department of Education, blew the whistle in the `80s on government activities withheld from the public. Her inside knowledge will help you protect your children from controversial methods and programs. Visit author's website and buy a hardcopy of the book.

Underground History of American Education
by John Taylor Gatto

As John Taylor Gatto explains the secret of American schooling is that it doesn't teach the way children learn, and it isn't supposed to. It took seven years of reading and reflection to finally figure out that mass schooling of the young by force was a creation of the four great coal powers of the nineteenth century. Nearly one hundred years later, on April 11, 1933, Max Mason, president of the Rockefeller Foundation, announced to insiders that a comprehensive national program was underway to allow, in Masonic words, "the control of human behavior."

Who Controls Our Children?

While parents, schools, provinces and states across North America bicker about the democratic process of running public schools, forces are manipulating education from behind the scenes. Major international players are reshaping public education to suit their own self-serving agendas, without regard for the wants of parents and the welfare of their children. This video lecture by Peg Luksik documents how today's educational system dumb down kids deliberately, making zombie-like people who don't ask any questions but just follow orders. Also see her book "Outcome Based Education: The State's Assault on Our Children's Values."

America BC
by Barry Fell

Barry Fell's book on ancient settlers in the new world prior to Columbus.

Forbidden Archeology
by Michael A. Cremo and Richard L. Thompson

Over the past two centuries researchers have found bones and artifacts showing that people like ourselves existed on earth millions of years ago. But the scientific establishment has ignored these remarkable facts because they contradict the dominant views of human origins and antiquity. Cremo and Thompson challenge us to rethink our understanding of human origins, identity, and destiny. Forbidden Archeology takes on one of the most fundamental components of the modern scientific world view, and invites us to take a courageous first step towards a new perspective.

Brain Washing 101

Brainwashing 101 is a provocative short documentary (46 minutes) showing how university faculty and administrators use tools such as "speech codes" to force their political views upon students. In this cutting expose, documentary filmmakers Maloney, Browning, and Greenberg shine a light on political correctness, academic bias, student censorship, even administrative cover-ups of death threats, at three schools: Bucknell University, the University of Tennessee at Knoxville, and California Polytechnic State University (Cal Poly).

It's OK to be of Any Race

Wake up! This includes being white. Today, those of other races are saying that white people are bad because, in recent memory, they colonized other peoples. Throughout history every race has tried to colonize other people. The anger comes only from jealousy. Whites have simply been more successful at it.

Let us also notice that those who criticize whites in the universities, almost to an individual, mimic whites in every way possible They bleach their skin, dye their hair, cultivate patterns of dress, speech, and mannerisms, all in the image of the thing they claim to hate so much, but can never be, genetically.

Today, members of races who chose to quarrel, dance around cook fires, and mutter incantations for twelve thousand years, while Europeans and Orientals were building civilizations, now seem to think that they have an intrinsic right to breed their way into more advanced civilizations. They seek to upgrade their own family genetically, while ruining the gene pool of the victim culture. All this in the name of "social justice."

So, here I am, Dr. C. M. Zimbobo, back home, thinking of a white girl in the USA, who sat in front of me in my genetics class at a state university I will not name. I cannot easily get her out of my mind, but will eventually. I choose not to rape, or to infiltrate another race. This is because I am a *man*, and I know that my people have equal potential to evolve, and become what white people in general, and a few exceptional others like myself, are now.

Diversity Delusion / Fake Racism

Belief in multiculturalism is always sustained by members of an inferior culture who want to live parasitically at the expense of a superior culture. They fabricate ideas about racism, and drug themselves into disability, so as to be sustained by government. They think of themselves as "good" people, too depressed by "racism" to work, the "disenfranchised" victims of all those "haters."

Real life tells a different story. It is our natural evolutionary heritage from millennia of fierce tribal competition for food and shelter, to prefer the company of our own racial kinsmen. What the parasites call "racism" is simply a natural human reaction to other races.

Any form of government not based upon natural principles is doomed to failure from the outset. There is no example in all of human history of any multicultural society that did not self-destruct because of the multiculturalism. It is also natural, however, to be peace-loving in a non-self-destructive way towards peoples of other lands, to visit them as travelers and enjoy the full undiluted potency of their cultures.

Human parasites propound the false idea that race mixing constitutes "diversity." If races mix, in two hundred years, where is the diversity? Real diversity is ongoing indigenous populations in separate sovereign nations competing in a free world market. Variety, not the grey slavery of global monoculture, is the spice of life.

The European Union and the United Nations are totally corrupt Globalist minions in service to International Monetary Fund (IMF) bankers. Both organizations are forcing incompatible races into proximity all over the world. Their purpose is not the "brotherhood of Man." IMF money masters work for one world government *only* to gain total finance monopoly and absolute control of everyone on earth.

In the meantime, they profit by lending money to government needed to address the endless problems caused by multiculturalism.

Most main stream media is owned by, or otherwise subverted to, the interests of IMF bankers. In the early 1960s, came Project Mockingbird, now eclassified. Globalist elements in the Central Intelligence Agency approached IMF subverted media with a list of words and phrases they contrived to help engineer consent for one world government by eliciting knee-jerk reactions in the intellectually lazy majority. Examples include:

bigotry, conspiracy theory, paranoia
provincialism, small town thinking, subtle racism
white male, white privilege, white supremacy

Since 1947, the covert posture of the Globalists towards the youth of the world has been "Dope 'em up and dumb 'em down." They have been very successful. Cognitive dissonance abounds. Today, sullen drug addicted self-haters work for the destruction of all races and cultures, especially their own, while shouting the catcall of "racist" against any who work for the preservation of all races and cultures. Breed-up-quick advocates never look more than a few weeks ahead. They never contemplate ideas like *evolutionary destiny*. Twits will throw down all human potential forever, just to be fashionably liberal minded sounding at campus drug parties.

When all nations leave the IMF and nationalize their central banks, there will be prosperity everywhere on Earth. There will be no economic oppression to run away from. Countries of origin will be able to accept the return of those who wish live once again in their rightful ancestral homelands. When this splendid day comes, there will be no further excuse for the delusions of multiculturalism.

Right to Bear Arms

In a free society, the individual has the legal right to own or carry abroad any weapon he chooses, except the intrinsically unsafe weapon. This is one that cannot possibly be used without injury to innocent bystanders. Even governments have no right to own such a weapon. The popular objection that an "assault" weapon is designed to kill people misses the main point. What else, other than hunting, would any liberty loving person want a weapon for? To kill flies? It is not flies who invade countries and private homes to rape, torture, and murder. It is people who do that.

The individual has the natural right not to be treated as a criminal before the fact of committing a crime. Owning a weapon is not evidence of intent. In a free society, it is up to the individual to decide what measures he will enact to insure the safety of his own person or home. These decisions must be made based upon his individual expectations about other people and the future of his country, and must not be usurped by "optimistic" pacifists who would slavishly thirst to lick the boots of an invading enemy rather than to ever resist anything. Observe that these cowardly collectivist life managers would gladly see their oppressive confiscatory laws enforced using deadly coercion if necessary by government bully-boys with guns. Learn well the names of the true enemies of liberty who reside within your own country.

Any individual advocating the confiscation or undue regulation of safe weapons in the hands of responsible citizens is a clear traitor to the country in which he lives. Such a person is guilty of treason, and will by liberty loving individuals, be dealt with as such immediately, using whatever means are available. Any government attempting to deny it's citizens the right to purchase and bear arms has been subverted, and will, by courageous spirited people, be thrown down immediately, using any degree of force necessary.

Defense of Borders

Indigenous populations commit racial and cultural suicide if they allow their country to be invaded. A sovereign nation, not run by traitors, will enforce its borders by any means necessary. The situation is like a contract. The country gives fair warning to potential invaders that if the borders are violated, deadly force will be used to stop the invasion.

Border policy should be announced via popular media, with ongoing warning given by signs. Once fair notice is given, there need be no consideration as to whether invaders are men, women, or children. Reprisal should be carried out as necessary using snipers, strafing from
helicopters, and satellite lasers from space.

At this writing, the southern border of the United States has been under siege since 2014. If the United States is to survive as a nation, this invasion must be stopped. Every invader so far apprehended, should be deported, and if they come back, executed. It's perfectly just to resist invasion with deadly force, if people are made aware of the contractual terms in advance.

Islamic Conquest

Islamists have an average IQ of eighty. They believe that they are superior to everybody else on earth, and that it is their just destiny to rule, then destroy, everybody who differs from them in any way. These delusionary values are shared with their noticeably smarter 105 IQ Semitic kinsmen, the Jews.

Many in Europe and America have been saying lately,

"Almost every problem in the West, including our disabling cheek-turner religion, has come to us from the Hooknoses of the East."

Could it be time to fight back?

One standard diplomatic lie is that Mid-Eastern terrorists are considered extremists within their own countries. In truth, their actions are done with the full approval of the vast majority of Islamists. What we call terrorists are simply the military class within their own countries. The goal of Islam is world domination. The Quran is a blueprint for the conquest and subjugation of nations. When asked about this, Islamists excuse, "It is one of the lesser prophets." Their plan has four steps:

1. Infiltration
The advance guard comes in as "refugees" seeking humanitarian aid. They are, humble, soft spoken and friendly, at first, but always live parasitically on welfare.

2. Consolidation
During this period, the immigrants instruct the weak mined members of the host population in their religion and convert them. Mosques appear everywhere. Terrorist attacks begin, but the IMF subverted media doesn't report them.

3. Takeover
This is when the number of invaders becomes sufficient in various districts to elect their own officials to government. Now injustice in the courts favoring terrorists against the host population skyrockets.

4. Theocracy
Host population must convert to Islam, leave the country, or be killed.

Note that the Globalists are aiding and abetting the invaders via the European Union and the United Nations in entering Western Europe and the United States. Eastern European countries, however, are not admitting Islamists.

The Japanese have always been smart people. They welcome Buddhists, Christians, and Hindus, but not Islamists, because they know that Islam is not really a religion, but a method of conquest.

Sharia Law

Values passed down through generations eventually become ingrained genetic predispositions for behavior. Sharia Law proclaims that it is the right of Islamic men to rape women and children. By civilized western standards, the values of Islam are psychopathic and their sustenance for so long a time has made the practitioners into a race of constitutional psychopaths. Know a good one? Wake up! There are always a few exceptions to help underscore anything that is generally true.

Short Summary Sharia Law

Theft is punishable by amputation of the hands.
Denying any part of the Quran is punishable by death.

Criticizing Muhammad is punishable by death.

Criticizing Allah is punishable by death.

A Muslim who leaves Islam is punishable by death.

One who leads a Muslim out of Islam is punishable by death.

A non-Muslim man who marries a Muslim woman is punishable by death.

A woman or girl who has been raped cannot testify in court against her rapists.

Testimonies of four males is required to prove rape of a female.

A female who claims rape without producing four male witnesses is guilty of adultery.

A female found guilty of adultery is punishable by death.
A male convicted of rape can have the conviction dismissed by marrying the victim.

If a child or a woman is taken captive, they become a slaves. A woman's previous marriage is immediately annulled.

A woman may be forced to marry a man whom she does not want.

A wife must have sex whenever her husband demands it.

Muslim men have sexual rights to any female not wearing the Hijab.

A woman can have one husband.

A man can have four wives.

A man can marry a female infant, and sexually consummate the marriage when she reaches nine years of age.

A girl's clitoris must be cut.

A man can beat his wife for disobedience.

A man can simply divorce his wife.

A wife needs the husband's consent to divorce.

A divorced wife loses custody of children when they reach six years of age.

A woman's court testimony in property cases, has half the veracity of a man's.

A female inherits half of what a male inherits.

A woman cannot speak alone to a man who is not her husband or relative.

Meat for meals must come from animals that have been sacrificed to Allah.

Muslims should lie to non-Muslims to advance Islam.

Liberty and Terrorism

Council of the Gods

May 3, 2002 11:02 AM

On C-Span 1 this morning there was a new statistic:

Forty eight percent of Americans polled believe that America is under the special protection of Jehovah in the Mid-Eastern War.

Awhile back on one of the cable news channels there was similar data about people throughout the Middle East believing that Allah is backing them militarily.

Since we have such perfect separation of church and state in America, it would be too much compromise to ask one of the Congressional prayer groups to intervene. We do, however, suggest that if the UN could somehow get Jehovah and Allah together for negotiations, the rest of us could simply stand aloof from the entire business. With the 2004 Olympic Games to be held in Athens, perhaps a summit could be arranged on Mount Olympus.

Objective View of Political Terrorism

November 23, 2002

Comments we have received trigger the following response. In the longer view of history the following things are true:

1. Political terrorists in general are far more concerned about impacting public events and history than the average person.

2. Political terrorists are usually revolutionaries who also believe that their agenda for long term social change is more important than individual human lives. This latter trait is often shared by functionaries of the governments they oppose.

3. Those who disagree with specific terrorist goals often avoid dealing with the political issues by trying to shift attention away using phony psychological "explanations." This will often involve highlighting any lack of standard affiliations or personal involvements in the life of the terrorist which might have otherwise consumed personal energies: "He was a loner who didn't belong to any clubs on campus." "He was angry at society because he wasn't getting enough nookie."

4. The viewpoint of political terrorists and most "lunatic fringe" elements can be useful as part of the advance warning system about bad directions in government policy. In this context the more "sensitive" terrorist reactions may be likened to the quicker response of those small birds taken underground in cages to test the breathability of air in mines.

June 21, 2017 9:32 A.M.

War and terrorism today are a very difficult study. Just when you think you understand an event, new information surfaces showing that it was actually a false flag, usually involving Globalist traitors in your own government working with foreign operatives. The purpose of endless war is to generate "refugees" aided by EU and the UN, to invade and destroy indigenous race and culture, so that people lacking identity will except globalization.

Terrorism is supported by deep state funding, open borders, and, police stand-downs. The purpose is to make our daily lives so dangerous that we will gladly surrender our guns and liberty just to feel safe. Good people need to become proactive about building a better future. We will be rid of these problems only when the Globalists and their invading outlanders have been permanently defeated.

Challenge of Street Terrorism

Within the borders of any country, street terrorists are usually just psychopathic enemies of society in general, rarely people with any reasoned political motivation. Their numbers are increasing everywhere. In any country where criminals are protected by corrupt socialist governments, this army of darkness can only be dealt with on an individual basis. It's always best to keep a low profile by simply humoring subverted cowards who try to tell you that the victim is just as bad as the criminal if he retaliates.

You have the natural right to defend your life and property. and to rid your country of evil people. Every person willing to fight back should carry a pistol, sword cane, or stun gun. If attacked or threatened, he should kill all the assailants . There will be that many less of them in the world, and he will never have to fight them a second time. He should leave the vicinity immediately, keep his own council, and tell absolutely nobody what happened. The weak character trait of compulsive intimacy is no substitute for the personal integrity gained through unimpeded righteous action.

Specifically: The Knockout Game
November 30, 2013 9:00 AM

This morning a neighbor told me about a new phenomenon known as the "knockout game" now happening in America. Last week he was nearly assaulted by three young Mexicans, but used his cane in self-defense. He said the TV news claims that three victims have been killed already. I looked it up online. The Internet news says that the problem is beginning to appear nationwide in the USA. Remember the immortal wisdom of Bernard Goetz,
"Speed is everything."

Globalism Defeated

Whenever possible it's best to conserve useful structure created by the work of others, even when they are a vanquished enemy. Besides the International Monetary Fund, there are three Globalist institutions which we will either reorganize to serve Libertarian Nationalist goals or simply eliminate. They are, of course, EU, NATO, and the UN. What follows are idealized situations in the future where reason and voting produce the needed results. In real life it will probably violent revolution. The alternative is to allow money mad Globalists to destroy every race and culture on earth. Imagine the tedium of universal sameness.

European Union

According to the leaders, the EU was formed: as a counter balance to the United States as the only global super power, out of the need for stability in Europe after the Second World War, and as a product of economic agreements, all of which still form its basis today.

In 1957, when the Treaty of Rome was signed to prevent war in Europe. Fifty years later, with war still seeming far away, the EU redefined itself as the leader against climate change, but few Europeans could identify with greening up the economy and lowering carbon emissions.

Hypothetically, an American Libertarian Nationalist leader addresses the European Council:

"I have searched the web a good deal, and find that the EU doesn't seem to have any clear idea of its own purpose. Following is a edited comment from the EU Training Site:

"The EU says it wants to increase employment, and prosperity, also to advance its innovation capabilities on a global scale, but these are very vague ideas, and do not translate into a coherent narrative that one could call a "mission statement.

"EU leaders need to reach an agreement on what the European Union really stands for, and then summarize it, not in a ten-page European Council Conclusion, but in two or three sentences that are concrete and inspiring enough so that even a bus driver in Estonia will be able to understand…and maybe even support.

"How can European citizens be expected to support EU institutions and goals if they don't know what Brussels is struggling to achieve?

"Now I'm going to talk about what the EU actually does. The job of the European Union, as a federal government, strives to create and implement laws and regulations to dominate the member states. The leaders have mandated that the countries of the EU have uniform laws and policies for weights and measures, trade, labor, job choice, travel, immigration, rape, and politically correct speech. The EU enforces these laws.

"This enables the rights of sovereign member nations in these issues to be by-passed. If a member country wants to opt out, the EU threatens them with invasion by the EU army. The biggest EU initiative, in Globalist complicity with the UN, is to destroy the European race, culture, and civilization by flooding Europe with morally inferior peoples from whatever third world garbage pails they can get them."

There is a good deal of tension and murmuring in the auditorium as speaker continues:

"Anyone who has studied history knows that there has never been a multiracial society that did not self-destruct because of the forced unnatural mixing. There is absolutely no reason for persisting in the current mode except the evil goal in serving the avarice of Globalist bankers.

"Indigenous populations in separate sovereign nations competing in a free world market is what works. The present course is not working, and can only lead to war. Europeans are waking up to all of this fast and will soon be gunning down racial outlanders in the streets for target practice on the way to work.

"Do the right thing while you still can. Stop further immigration, and send the resident outlanders home. Globalism is being defeated everywhere, but now there will be an infinite number of constructive projects for the bankers to finance. Isn't prosperity for all with lasting peace, better than prosperity for a few elitists, with endless warfare for the many? I know, what about population increase? Don't worry, we know how to reduce world numbers without mass starvation.

"The days of the EU are numbered. After just the pending withdrawals, it will be ludicrous to even call what's left European. If I worked here, I would be looking for the first available position with NATO or the UN. Help speed positive change. Please read about the Libertarian Nationalist program. It is the only arrangement that can lead to lasting worldwide peace and prosperity."

Many of the leaders look favorably impressed and the speaker is offered a great many handshakes on his way out to the cafeteria.

After two weeks of discussion; the European Union is officially dissolved. How could it be otherwise, with no viability for the future? Sovereignty for all the former member states will be preserved. It is agreed that he earlier national customs regulations will not be reinstated except along borders of indigenously non-European countries. The former currency exchanges are no longer necessary. With a little cashier technology, small business transactions can be for any amount, in any currency, anywhere.

NATO

When NATO was first set up, it was assumed that the US might be needed to help defend Western Europe from the Warsaw Pact. The original stated job of NATO was to be a defensive alliance to discourage war in Europe. Any member that is attacked can call on all the other members for help.

The only time this ever happened was September 11, 2001. The US asked NATO for help, and all the other nations responded.

NATO's mission statement as of 1999, did not envision any activity outside Europe and the North Atlantic. Today there is even division within Europe about how to handle the problems faced by these nations.

Anders Fogh Rasmussen, the NATO Secretary General has said,

"We will need a strategic concept that takes account of today's realities and tomorrow's challenges… The world has changed, the threats have changed, so has NATO."

NATO's 28 member states hope that the future approach will help persuade an increasingly skeptical public in many European countries that the 60-year-old alliance remains relevant, decades after the end of the Cold War.

The task is harder at a time of economic crisis and shrinking defense budgets, analysts say.

Fogh Rasmussen's top priorities are expanding NATO's partnership with moderate nations in North Africa and the Middle East.

Hypothetically, an American Libertarian Nationalist leader addresses the North Atlantic Council:

"The North Atlantic Treaty Organization is not dead. Nothing likes to die, big international organizations included. Like anything living, it wants to be fed and continues to grow and extend itself.

"NATO was originally supposed to focus only on the common defense of its member states, and later threats like piracy, terrorism, and cyberattack. Today it gives itself free reign over the entire world. The excuses for NATO military actions appear limitless, along with the geographic arena in which it might take action.

"It made me sad to learn that NATO troops had amassed in Arizona to suppress the retaliation of American citizens to an expected economic collapse engineered by the Globalists. I remember a bumper sticker: Send our troops home. We need them to protect us from the government.

"Now that the EU is gone. and the UN will soon be reconstituted as an advisory body based upon Libertarian Nationalist principles, I and many like me in the US, feel that NATO should sever its now irrelevant allegiances to the Globalists and work with the newly emerging European nations to promote worldwide nationalism with the preservation of indigenous peoples and cultures everywhere. The new NATO agenda I suggest would be to review and get information to member nations about the superior options of worldwide nationalism, prosperity, and peace."

The speaker gets normal audience applause, followed by questions and answers.

After a few weeks, NATO is reconstituted to be completely in accord with Libertarian Nationalist policies and to continue as an advisory clearing house for the natters it used to act upon directly at the behest of the Globalists.

The United Nations

Informal Mission Statement of the UN:

- To keep peace throughout the world

- To develop friendly relations among nations

- To help nations work together to improve the lives of poor people, to conquer hunger, disease and illiteracy, and to encourage respect for each other's rights and freedoms

-To be a center for harmonizing the actions of nations to achieve these goals.

Hypothetically, an American Libertarian Nationalist leader addresses the United Nations General Assembly:

"The UN originally had some very high sounding goals more or less associated with altruism. Unfortunately, it is today openly controlled by Globalist bankers. This is not surprising since it was they who treated it in the first place. The main functions of the UN now. of course, are the destruction of European race, culture, and civilization through the flooding of Europe with economic migrants disguised as refugees, and human trafficking in children for pedophilia.

"This shameful activity will not continue. Even the phony altruism will be opposed by all aware people from here on. Giving food to worthless layabouts only serves to suppress agriculture and to increase the numbers and moral lassitude of the recipients. We must guarantee all people an equal chance to succeed by their own volition. We must not guarantee them equal success apart from the quality of their participation in the process.

"The globalists are now irrelevant. The UN needs to wake up to this and purge your ranks of this foulness. Member nations will soon desert you if you don't get on board with what's happening now. Please study the literature I have provided on Libertarian Nationalism. With your talent and imagination, we can all live to see a lasting Golden Age for mankind on Earth."

The speaker sees a lot of scowls, and a lot of long overdue smiles in the assembly. This has been a very productive day indeed.

Soon the U.N. General Assembly votes that the United Nations is now to be an advisory body, committed to a Nationalist Libertarian future. All the UN Globalist functionaries have already been replaced with nationalists.

The new method of the UN will be to discuss and vote on the viability of worldwide policy suggestions, then pass on recommendations to national governments. For national leaders with good ideas, this will have the effect of being able to suggest legislation to everybody on earth, with the added legitimacy of the many-minds principle.

World Future Doctrine

World Revolution / World War III

"If the individual is born into an un-free society, he will have no legal rights corresponding to his natural ones, since these depend upon other people. He is endowed, however, in many cases, with the potential to be something more than merely a slave, and always with the choice of turning his will towards this end."

~ Dirk Aubrey Lokison ~

1. The world is in the worst trouble it has ever been in. There will be no help via supernatural intervention. We must fix it ourselves, and we can, but it requires good example through action, along with educational speech. Those who will not acknowledge any of this are part of the problem and should be treated accordingly,

2. If we don't reverse our increasing numbers immediately, nothing else we do will matter. We must have strict population control now, enforced with an iron fist if need be. In an overcrowded world, irresponsible couples who have more than two children are recklessly endangering everyone else and will not continue in this.

3. There are many races on Earth. They are not equal. The highest are, on the average, thirty five IQ points above the lowest. All races, however, have equal potential, by their own long term own effort, but only if they are not interfered with by missionaries or those seeking colonial dominion. Unevolved people who have done nothing but hunt, gather, sing, and chant for the past twelve thousand years, of course, would just love to breed their way into developed, civilized societies. One is not being hateful or bigoted to recognize these irrefutable facts.

4. There is one superior race who wants total ownership and control of everything on Earth. They want everybody else's earned prosperity, and false credit for everybody else's achievements. These goals are clearly stated in their earliest writings penned thousands of years ago. All over the world, they infiltrate every area of human endeavor that can give them power over other people. They try to convince humanity that they deserve special advantage, and that they have been persecuted by everyone else, especially certain nations. Through monopolistic media control, they create false feelings of guilt by using selective emphasis, massive exaggeration, and outright lies. They seek to stifle decent by sponsoring legislation against what they label "hate speech" which is any speech that tells the truth about their activities and plans. They try to enforce the Doctrine of Political Correctness by every means possible. This is the body of principles debated in Russia after the Bolshevik Revolution, to be held dogmatically by both Socialists and Communists, a common core of unnatural non workability. In their scheme for world domination, their own country is merely a home base to work from. or when necessary, retreat to. Once they are all in that country, without nuclear capability, their unjust adverse effect upon others will be neutralized.

5. Most world problems are caused by parasitic international bankers who, via privately owned central banks, like the US Federal Reserve, manipulate currencies, and with the help of

subverted politicians, engineer wars and economic upheaval so that they can lend money to governments for military activity and otherwise unnecessary social programs. We can rid ourselves of this problem by restoring the right to issue and control currency to the people. This will be accomplished by nationalizing all central banks worldwide. Reputable economists have developed workable models showing how this can be done without causing economic collapse.

6. In all of human history there has never been a multiracial or multicultural society which did not self-destruct because of the unnatural mixing. The predatory bankers exploit even the early stages of social decay. because they lend money to the national governments who must deal with the resulting problems.

7. The New World Order / Shadow Government wants most of the races of mankind to become extinct through forced intermixing. They know that world government, giving global finance monopoly, will be more acceptable to apathetic people with no racial or ethnic identity, living in a tedious gray landscape of universal sameness.

8. People have a natural right to grow up among their own racial kinsmen. Immigrant racial outlanders are an unjust encroachment upon the liberty of indigenous peoples. To survive, we must implement policies of race preservation to avert global monoculture everywhere.

9. To summarize, what works best is indigenous peoples enjoying strict population control, race and culture preservation, with absolute individual liberty, as separate sovereign nations competing eventually in a free world market. This will lead to a lasting peace and prosperity, an ongoing Golden Age for all of mankind. We have a right to implement this now, and to eliminate those who interfere.

10. People of all races need to look deep within themselves to isolate what is frivolous, and discard it. This is an excellent time in which to practice martial skills. Integrity will be gained by reading the facts and openly speaking the truth, about World War II, the last major conflict on earth. Inspiration can be gained by reading the biographies of men like Heinrich Himmler and Reinhard Heydrich to understand the tremendous obstacles they had to overcome

11. In a country where the government consists of subverted traitors in service to globalist bankers, there is no remedy at law. Those who ruin or imperil the lives of others for pleasure or profit, are combatants in an army of darkness, whether at the level of immigrant rapists or sponsoring globalist bankers. Moral people are empowered by the simple goodness within them to deal covertly with these enemies of all life. Such initiatives should be individual and never discussed with anyone, including spouse, parents, children, or friends. In the degenerate world of today, liberty and natural order will not be granted, so it must be seized. Soon we will all be involved in a worldwide revolution that will prevail by any means necessary.

Servants of oppression,
dig your graves!
Winter is coming.

European Future Doctrine

People of European Ancestry, Rise!

"Life is harsh. It leaves only one choice, that between victory and defeat, not between war and peace." ~ Oswald Spengler

Workable societies must be based on workable principals. It is natural for people to feel more at ease among those of their own race and ethnicity. In all of history there has never been a multiracial or multicultural society which did not self-destruct because of the unnatural mixing. The globalist bankers, who work for world Socialism and monoculture, want everyone to mix so they can lend money to government who must deal with the inevitable social problems.

People have the right to grow up among their own racial kinsmen. Immigrant racial outlanders are an unjust encroachment upon the liberty of indigenous peoples. Interracial marriage advocates want to eliminate existing races. They speak about variety, but their mixing program, in the long term, will obliterate human variety by making separate races into one race. Imagine the tedious gray landscape of universal sameness. The globalist bankers want to destroy race and culture because they know that one world government, giving them global finance monopoly, will be more acceptable to people with no racial or ethnic identity.

People of indigenous European ancestry are at present the predominant race in all of continental Europe, the UK, Canada, the United States, Australia, and New Zealand, but this is changing fast. In most of these places, because of subverted Socialist politicians and misguided clergymen, we are being invaded by those of other races, often from Third World countries. The globalists promote this joyfully. They know that the immigrants will support their one world monopoly plans. If we want to survive racially and culturally, then it is well past time for us to stand up and take back what is ours.

After stopping racial influx, there are three ways to deal with displaced people in residence:

1. Mass Relocation
The best method, but sometimes problematical because countries of origin are often reluctant to accept people back because of learned cultural differences and racial impurity.

2. Mass Sterilization
This method causes little economic upheaval, but the cultural benefits are delayed for a very long time, and there will be vengeful troublemakers in the aftermath.

3. Mass Extermination
Very sad. All people are unique and have potential for excellence over time if allowed to develop at their own rate in their rightful ancestral homelands. If death, in some cases, turns out to be our only solution, then let us do it with chivalry, quickly and cleanly, without causing unnecessary suffering.

People of European Ancestry Everywhere, Rise!

Liberty or Death!

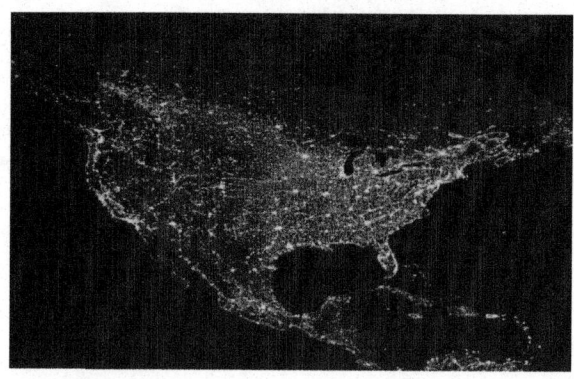

United Stares Future Doctrine

Essential points have been raised in discussions among Libertarian Nationalists about things that must be changed to ensure a viable future for the United States. We would all like to see these changes made democratically, as they would be by an informed populace, but it must be noted that these changes will ultimately be made by any means necessary. The body of doctrine developed from this is as follows:

1. Media Monopoly

Legislation will be enacted, and enforced, to ensure that information media ownership by special interest groups not exceed the percent of these groups in the national population. Information media are about teaching, and render the entire nation a classroom. Those who insist on representative percentages in the schools, cannot logically object to having the same principle applied to the country as a whole.

2. Central Banks

The right to issue and regulate currency will be a function of the people through their government, not of privately owned corporations driven only by the profit motive. We will nationalize the Federal Reserve Bank and repudiate the national debt. The Internal Revenue Act will be repealed without upset, since the income tax today pays only interest on the national debt. We will demand reparation for all the money swindled from the American people since the subverted politicians sold out their country in 1913 with the Federal Reserve Act. We will return to a currency backed by durable commodity of intrinsic value, such as gold or a mixed store of precious metals, the value of which will be determined in the world marketplace.

3. World Trade

We will correct destructive trade policies enacted by globalist lackeys. Consumers worldwide will have total product choice, but all goods offered in the world market will be produced solely within any given country by the citizens of that country, with no foreign ownership of business anywhere. This includes the stipulation that banks lend money only within their own countries. Foreign monetary debt *is* foreign business ownership.

4. Israel

The point has been made that, since so many United States problems have their origin with the Jews, therefore Americans are called upon to deal with the Jews generically as a people. Examples include:

- Almost all national media in the United States and world is anti-Caucasian, globalist, and controlled by Jews.

- The United States money supply, and that of most other nations, is controlled by a cartel of Jewish owned banking corporations.

- Every war and ruined economy for the past two handed years has been a product of Jewish globalist planning. This is commonly conceded by all reputable historians.

- Jews now control most of the human trafficking in captive European women, especially from Russia and the Ukraine.

One guest speaker suggested that to insure the safety and liberty of people everywhere, every Jew on Earth should be killed. We object to this because of the good Jews that would die unjustly. This point, however, will not be used as an excuse to do nothing. There is a correct solution. What is said here about the United States also applies generally to every other country on Earth.

- Jews everywhere will return to Israel.

- Non-Jews residing in Israel will return to their native homelands to make room for the returning Jews.

- For their national safety, Israel will not be demilitarized, but since the Jews have for centuries shown themselves to be hell-bent on world domination, Israel will be devoid of nuclear weapons for the safety of all other nations.

- The United States will assist in all of these matters, but there will be no further aid to Israel. The Jews are very capable people and don't need help from anyone. These policies will get rid of all United States military problems with nations who are at odds with Israel.

5. Racial Displacement

European immigrants are the indigenous population of America. This especially includes the original people who came across the land bridge fourteen thousand years ago, most often called "Native Americans." They, along with post-Columbian European immigrants, are the only people who belong in the United States.

In all of history there has never been a multi-racial society that did not implode because of the forced unnatural mixing. Behind it has always been the Money Masters, who lend to the governments who must deal with all the resulting problems. Competing mono-racial societies is what works. It preserves human diversity in life and in the world marketplace.

In the United States, those who will return home are all people whose origin is from Africa, the Near East, Middle East, Asia. and all non-Caucasians from wherever else they may have come. This will eliminate most increase in human non-viability through undeserved subsidy, and will take a giant bite out crime. When these displaced people are back home prospering in their native lands, we will happily welcome them to visit us as tourists, and will feel honored to vacation in their countries as well.

6. Criminal Purge

Every person with any history of unjustly robing others of life or liberty will be hung publicly, all at the same time, all in the same place, with worldwide television coverage. This spectacular event will be followed by three days of Bacchanalian feasting and merrymaking.

This doctrine is an appendage of "Libertarian Nationalist Revolution" linked below.

People of European Ancestry in America, Rise!

𝕷𝖎𝖇𝖊𝖗𝖙𝖞 𝖔𝖗 𝔇𝖊𝖆𝖙𝖍!

Survival in North America

Survival Strategies:

1. Wealth

Facts:

The Forces of Darkness reign everywhere. Globalism is the enemy.

It is Evil to pay taxes to this enemy whenever this can be avoided legally.

Strategy:

Disdain material things completely. Sell everything that you can live without.

Achieve total liquidity. Enable instant mobility. Learn the science of invisibility.

2. Health

Facts:

Most in health care providers today have immense situational power. Evil exemplars, via willful negligence, can and sometimes do, select for extermination whomever they please.

Strategy:

Avoid hostile territory or large congregations of un-Libertarian elements.

Attain hand to hand martial prowess and appropriate weapon skills.

Preserve health with proper food, supplements, fluids, deep breathing, exercise, right-thinking, meditation, and Yoga.

3. Pleasure

Facts:

Most sought-after pleasures are costly, frivolous, and produce dependency.

Keeping a good outlook makes nearly everything pleasurable without disadvantage.

Strategy:

Travel to enjoy what's left before it's gone. Look carefully. Remember what you see. Take photos. Maybe we can restore some of it later.

4. Intellect

Facts:

It's more useful to accumulate memory based on fact than on speculation or fiction.

Ancient mythology is real in an archetypal sense, even though it is frequently not actual.

The aware volitional use of make-believe, as in goal oriented visualization augmented by archetypal imagery, is a very useful tool but should never become an end in itself.
Strategy:

Read voraciously. Learn much. Never display knowledge unnecessarily.

Seek information from all viewpoints especially "forbidden" sources. Keep opinions to yourself.

Study all things which truly interest. Allow interests to change radically and quickly.

Develop a very broad and balanced learning program. Practice many arts.

Be careful to focus on utility and avoid spreading oneself too thinly.

Bone up on areas previously neglected as you discover what these are.

Read Revisionist History. Enjoy accurate historical novels.

5. Spirit

Facts:

For every element in any religious tradition there is usually a parallel element in all other traditions. Differences generally involve only emphasis. Variations will occur even among individuals within any one tradition. A deep understanding of one's own ancient spiritual heritage is archetypally more relevant and closer to the bone than inappropriate involvement with "outland" traditions.

Reincarnation seems to be the best explanation of how life works in the long term. Cases abound.

Strategy:

Study appropriate early religious heritage and mythology.

Plan your next incarnation as a hypothetical upgrade for personal insight. Base plan upon how you would live your past life if you had it to do over again, but with current technology. Update this periodically for personal growth.

Help those terminally ill towards peace and happy anticipation of future life.

Practice true chivalry in its modern form. Always be polite and just.

Never cause any unnecessary pain or suffering to any living creature. This should apply even to the vilest of human enemies. Kill only to preserve life and liberty, but do this quickly and cleanly.

Be kind to all people and animals. Show affection to parents, children, dogs, and kitties.

6. Activism

Facts:

The individual is born with the right to absolute individual liberty. With this comes the logical obligation of reciprocity towards others. If the individual lives in an unfree society, he has the right to gain total individual liberty any way that he can. People who don't want to be free are cowards. Those who do not want others to be free are morally inferior and expendable, the mortal enemies of all decent people.

One world government will spell the end of liberty on Earth. It will institute an absolute monopoly for a small group of greedy internationalists. The one clear enemy of all people on Earth are those striving towards the New World Order. These individuals must be defeated at any cost. Separate sovereign nations competing in a free world market is better than the tedious cookie-cutter sameness portended by advancing global monoculture.

The preference to live and manifest among one's own kind is a trait, which during man's evolutionary development, became genetically ingrained as a natural instinct because it had survival value during periods of fierce tribal competition for food and shelter. People are naturally more aesthetically content, and feel far more at ease, among members their own people. This is a perfectly normal trait and cannot correctly be perceived as anything other than that. It is proper to respect the right of all individuals who justly strive to preserve their own race from destruction.

Freedom of religion best helps people to find their natural level of manifestation. This does not mean that we need condone those who ruthlessly seek dominion over everyone around them. Tolerance among separate unique religious traditions is vastly superior to the bland faceless beehive spirituality of worldwide universalism.

People who are obsessed with trying to reconcile modern experience with scriptures written thousands of years ago are being false to their own heritage and to the present day world. Slavish dogmatism renders the individual an ineffective participant in modern society. No one need look to another culture for their spirituality, nor aid and abet the missionaries of monoculture. Nobody should adhere to any tradition which has clearly failed. Religions based upon false values and unnatural principles are not worth following. The vile dispiriting nihilism of wandering internationalists is a poor substitute for the spiritual integrity of being rooted in one's own ancestral tradition. There are many fine natural religions being reborn. These represent diverse ethnicity. One must seek, however. They will not come to you.

Spiritual dualism involves absolute knowledge that good and evil are coequal, eternal, and cosmic in manifestation. Spiritual monism is the popular belief that either good or evil is the predominant moral force on Earth. This involves imaginative wishfulness about the supposed destiny of one to eventually triumph over the other. In this mode of error, one force is thought of as being a mere pathological deviation which can somehow be cured. Ironically, such ongoing cures institutionalized by collective human action have been responsible for most of the real evil and suffering faced by human societies throughout the ages. The idea that "good" is the prevailing force in the universe and will someday obliterate "evil," and that there is not supposed to be any suffering in the world, is the fantasy of weaklings, and usually leads to the kind of fanaticism exploited by power hungry leaders to the great detriment of all.

Absolute separation of church and state is impossible because the spirituality of the people determines the form of government they will choose or condone. The ultimate test of workability for a major system of religious belief is the effect that it has on society over the long term. A viable spirituality intended to exert major influence will not only attract widespread adherence but will also have a positive effect upon society. Monistic spirituality attracts many people but does so only because it appeals to human weakness by promising supernatural justice to apathetic sluggards. It is passive and limp-wristed. It contributes to all that is devolutionary. Wherever we find the institutionalized cowardice of scarecrow religion, we also find Socialism or some other unworkable form of collectivist government. The economic system of a country will never exceed the soul wisdom of the people residing therein. We can't expect an inferior prevailing spirituality to result in a superior way of running society. If the people are no good, the government will be even worse.

The religions based upon spiritual monism are acquiescent slave traditions. The practitioners are morally weak, simple-minded, cowardly, or insane. Most are all of these things. Their actions are rarely at one with their words. Individually they are impotent, but in larger numbers, each fueling the sickness of the others, they will become as torturous and murderous as their combined strength and self-serving rationalizations allow them to be.

The monistic majority is responsible for allowing the Socialism which now besieges us all. Certain elements within monism sponsored and now exploit this Socialism.

Unrestricted influx will destroy whatever is achieved anywhere. No country should allow vast throngs of fools who have out-bred their ability to feed themselves at home to come flooding in only to do the same thing in their new country as well.

The means to these ends should be contemplated dispassionately. Creative energy must be diligently applied to their implementation.

Strategy:

Avoid unproductive entanglement by restricting relationships to an absolute minimum.

Do not mix unnecessarily with un-Libertarian elements.

Help to promote worldwide Libertarian Nationalist Revolution to the utmost.

Educate others anonymously. Simply put superior knowledge within their grasp.

Write the best that you know. Reach those in places of power and learning.

The ideal attitude if one survives, even in a world decimated, is to continue in chivalrous Libertarian manifestation for as long as possible.

Ritual für den Tod

"Rise those who despise the weak
Spare none and ride proudly
on the winds of death"
~ Immortal ~

The following is a spur for the preservation of the Nordic Race, a declaration of war against sub-humanity everywhere and against racial outlanders who invade Nordic territories. Ritually it can be inserted as the "Statement of Purpose" within any format used by Nordic kindreds or communities.

Portent of Victory

"We shall ride triumphantly
through the streets in bright armor,
upon white horses, the corpses of these
impotent weakling slaves of darkness
lining the walkways at each side,
their blood running out and
filling the gutters at our feet!

"Then shall begin their conversion
into ash for our fields,
and the recasting by fire
of their holy chalices and idols,
of gold under Sun,
of silver under Moon,
from icons of shame and meekness
into gleaming images of Truth.

"And we shall fashion their holy places
into strongholds of voluptuousness,
their skulls will adorn the rafters
and gaze down upon us
as we enjoy our naked women
upon their holy altars."

Notes:

1. Nordic Race: of European ancestry, Caucasian, White.

2, "Portent of Victory" written long ago by Elof II.

Globalism: Logical Fallacies

It is important to study logic because most logical fallacies seem more or less reasonable, even though they are not. Sometimes there is innocent intent with error, but more often, there is a deliberate attempt to misdirect. Among the controlled media subverted to Globalism, there are a great many today who have studied hard upon the "engineering of consent."

This presentation uses examples of standard Globalist arguments as they are countered by those of Libertarian Nationalism. Sometimes examples are left to the reader. Fallacies are divided into four standard categories. Some fit into more than one category and, of course, many arguments involve more than one fallacy.

August 9, 2017
9:46 A/M.

Fallacies of Relevance
Arguments to Cases Not Relevant

Ad Baculum
Appeal to Force
Might Makes Right

Example:
New World Order goals are correct because men of great power support them

Genetic Fallacy:
Suggests that the origin of something necessarily determines its essence and character

Example:
"He comes from a background of privation, so he will naturally support our Socialist agenda."

Ad Hominem
Addresses opponent instead of his argument

First type:

Abusive
Name Calling
Often involves phony psychologizing

Examples:
You are called a *racist* if you if you work to preserve all races and cultures.

You are called a *homophobe* if you do not support teaching children in the public schools that same-gender sex perversion is really just an equal alternative lifestyle.

You are called an *Islamophobe* if you do not support the slow takeover of your country by Islam, as in Europe today.

Second type:

Circumstantial
Categorizing
Opponent should accept an argument because of his circumstances or category

Example:
"You are a Democrat, so you must support all Democratic Party policies."

Guilt by Association
Water Seeks its Own Level
Birds of a Feather Flock Together
One's character is judged totally by the company he keeps

Example:
"He has meetings so often with the Russians, so he must be on their payroll."

Poisoning the Well
Mud Slinging
Presenting negative, especially false, information about a person before they speak so as to discredit their argument

Example:
Most of what Globalists say about Nationalists

Gaslighting
Attempt to invalidate a person's experiences by twisting facts, memories, events, and evidence in order to disorient a vulnerable opponent and make them doubt their own judgement

Example:
Globalist media spokesmen regularly make claims and then, when challenged, deny ever having made them

Ad Populum
Attempts to validate an argument by citing a plurality or majority consensus

Three subcategories:

Bandwagon
"Everybody supports it."

Example:
It is an obligation of government to provide ongoing livelihood for the "disenfranchised" because immigrant third world savages, seeking sustenance, and their subverted accomplices, vastly outnumber good people at the voting booths

Patriot
Flag waving at the opponent to imply that he is not loyal to his country

Snob
"All the best people support it."

Example:
"Many of the Globalists are bluebloods."

Appeal to Tradition
Premise is true because people have always believed it

Example:
"Two inescapable verities, death and taxes."

A Priori Argument
Dogmatism
Starts with as established belief, then searches for any reasonable-sounding argument to defend the argument based upon it.

Example:
False assumption that if there are economic differences between two racial groups at any fixed point in time that there must be foul play involved. Therefore government must implement "social justice" by victimizing the more successful group. Ignores history.

The *More Righteous for Not Questioning* version of A Priori is liked by religious fanatics.

Example:
With enflamed piety,
"Don't speak to me of reason.
Don't confuse me with facts.
Don't confound me with logic.
Don't burden me with truth.
The anointed one is my redeemer,
And I will not disobey!"

Appeal to Improper Authority
One claims that his argument is right because someone famous or powerful supports it

Example:
Sound economic policies must be wrong because famous, uneducated, Hollywood twits make impassioned, but treasonous, threats against those who support them.

Ad Misericordiam
Appeal to emotion or pity
Often ignores the long term

Example:
"By 1920, Ludwig Von Misses had proved everything that Karl Marx ever postulated."
"But ... poor people are suffering."

Adverse Consequences
Conclusion must be false because the consequences of it being true are just too terrible to contemplate

Example:
"My heart tells me that that no major religion could ever endorse or condone rape."
Guess what? Islam does. Wake up!

Personal Incredulity
Argument must be false because you don't understand its technicalities

Example:
"We can't eliminate the personal income tax. How will we pay for government?"

Grasping at Straws
Desperate citing of unrelated irrelevancies

Example:
"Are you for or against Socialism?"
"I believe we should all love each other, nobody understands another person's feelings, you should think about being in the other person's shoes, what about poverty, what happens if we have to eat pigeons and rats?"

Snow Job
Smoke Screen
Blizzard or cloud of distraction used deliberately to cover up the main issues
Example:
Ongoing rhetoric of Globalist media

Anecdotal
Uses a personal experience or an isolated example instead of a sound argument

Example:
"Their economic proposals remind me of the time my cousin Lucy got locked inside the neighbors' outhouse in a snowstorm. The neighbors were away, and she was missing in there for three days. When the police finally found her ... well, you can just imagine ..."

Pedantry
Last Refuge of Little Minds
Jumping on a minor spelling or pronunciation problem, grammatical error, or typo to distract from the substance of the argument.

Example:
In an Email letter:
"It's wrong that American women are being told they must wear berkas."

Email reply:
"I'm sorry, but the term is *burkas*."

Component Fallacies
Errors in Syllogistic Reasoning

Begging the Question
Premise and conclusion say the same thing
Often ignores slow changes over time

Example:
"Recreational drugs don't hurt us, because we are back to normal the next morning."

Circular Reasoning
Phrasing premise and conclusion in different words that mean the same thing

Example:
"Absolute individual liberty will present a danger to society, because society cannot be safe if people are truly free."

Glib Generalization
Jumping to Conclusions
Cannot See the Forest for the Trees
One uses too small a sample to support a sweeping generalization. This often involves reasoning backwards inductively from an exceptional particular instance to a false general premise

Example:
Some high IQ members of a genetically inferior group are able to succeed, so they all can.
Therefore evolved societies should be ruined to give special advantage to Stone Age people.

False Cause
References a cause-effect relationship that does not exist

Two common types:

Non Causa Pro Causa
Mistaking a false cause for a real cause

Example:
"Free thinking led to all this drug use."
In truth, Prohibition created a huge black market profit potential that led to a program of aggressive marketing we call p*ushing*.

Post Hoc, Ergo Propter Hoc
After this, therefore because of this
Assumes that correlation equals causation.
If one circumstance occurs in proximity to another, then it must be the cause of it.

Example:
"The excess love of whiskey in the 1920s caused the terrible gang wars of that period."
In real life, it was the inability of bootleggers to arbitrate disputes in the courts that caused the gang wars. Prohibition was the cause. Make court actions illegal in real estate disputes, and watch the murder rate go sky high.

Ignorantio Elenchi
Irrelevant Conclusion
Argument used to establish a particular conclusion by redirecting it back as though evidenced by a more general related premise which may, or may not, be true.

Example:
A proposal is under consideration for increase in immigration by racially incompatible people.
"It is desirable for society to have a diverse racial and ethnic population."
To guilt ridden self-haters, this seems self-evident. They all agree. Later…
"My proposal is this…like I said at the beginning … it is desirable to have a diverse … therefore I move that we …"

The entire premise is false. Historically there has never been even one multi-racial society that did not self-destruct because of the forced unnatural mixing.

A subcategory of Ignorantio Elenchi is

The Red Herring
Changing the subject to avoid answering

Example:
"Marxism doesn't work."
"All people are entitled to personal dignity."
Another form of the Red Herring is

Tu Quoque
"And you too!"
An argument must be false because the person presenting it doesn't follow it himself.

Example:
"We need to take back our streets."
"We do?? I never see *you* out at night."

Yet another Red Herring is the

Straw Man Argument
Takes one of an opponent's weaker, less central, arguments, refutes it, then acts as though it was the crux of the issue. This is usually done using exceptional particulars.

Example:
"All those poor people who accidentally shoot themselves at home would still be alive if guns were banned."
Ignores the vastly greater number who have been murdered in no-gun zones because they had no way to defend themselves. In 2016, 400 people in Chicago alone.

Non Sequitur
Argument does not follow from the previous.

Usually ignores many other considerations

Example
"Use of energy is too high. We must have a carbon tax."
Energy use is too high because there are nearly 8 billion people on Earth when there should be 320 million.

Another specific type of Non Sequitur is the

Slippery Slope Fallacy
Argues that, once a step is taken, more steps of negative consequence will inevitably follow

Example:
"If you encourage liberty and individuality, it will most certainly lead to cultural divisiveness."
Strong cultures are good, bring it on!

False Dichotomy
Harbors the premise that there are only two possible solutions, therefore disproving one automatically validates the other. Ignores other alternatives

Example:
In cases of snuff porn video makers, "Rehabilitation therapy with parole is the best solution, because long, fixed periods of incarceration don't work."
Ignores the fact that death is the only effective way of ridding society of the threat posed by the proven irredeemable evil inherent in constitutional psychopathy.

False Analogy
Phony comparison to prove a point rather than arguing deductively and inductively

Example:
"Freedom is like pepper. A little tastes good, but too much gives you indigestion."

Undistributed Middle Term
The minor and major premise of a syllogism might or might not overlap. The falseness is usually obvious or even funny, but not always.

Example:
"Libertarians engage in free thought.
Crooks engage in free thought.
Therefore Libertarians are crooks."

Contradictory Premises
Logical Paradox
Premise contradicts another earlier premise

Example:
"We need to construct Holocaust study programs so that it can never happen again."
Sorry, but there is no hard evidence that it ever happened in the first place.
See essay, *World War II and Causes*

Special Pleading
Suggests a universal principle, then insists that it does not apply to the issue at hand

Example:
"Monogamous relationships are the norm because they give people what they truly need. Prostitution must therefore remain illegal."
Ignores the fact that prostitution also gives many other people what *they* truly need without detriment to anyone. Globalists don't want free enterprise prostitutes to compete with their human trafficking operations.

Ad Nauseum
Sickening Repetition
Where there's Smoke, there's Fire

Repeating a statement too often in the hopes that the listener will begin to accept it as truth, instead of providing evidence.

Example:
Phony Russian narrative touted by subverted Globalist media. Totally disproved, but reintroduced every two weeks

False Claims
Argument based upon false claims, but is logically coherent

Example:
"How could they have good intentions, when they murdered six million innocent people?"

Retrospective Determinism
Argues that because something happened, it was inevitable.
Example:
"Taking back Danzig was bound to lead to war sooner or later."

Texas Sharpshooter
Where there is smoke, there is fire
Occurs when one sees an apparent pattern of data and applies to their argument

Example:
"He has so many conversations with the Russian Prime Minister, he must be a spy."

Missing the Point
The premise supports a conclusion different from the one drawn

Example:
"Fuel prices are much too high, so speed limits will have to be lowered."

Fuel prices are too high for many reasons unrelated to speed, besides, slower speeds do not reduce fuel consumption.

Spotlight Fallacy
Exploits the false assumption that events which receive the most publicity are also the most common

Example:
This trick is used by subverted Globalist media bosses to destroy race and culture by instilling unwarranted guilt and self-hatred in host populations: In America, white on nonwhite crime is made front page news over and over, enflamed by phony editorials and bills to Congress about white racism. Nonwhite on white crime is buried on page four with no mention of race. This has been done by Jewish media bosses in America since 1945. Ride the city bus every day to see the result.

Misnomer Fallacy
Defending an absurdity by calling it something it is not. Often ignores the longer term

Example:
The breed-up-quick crowd refer to race mixing as d*iversity.* In actuality it is just the opposite, because over time it would ultimately obliterate all individual races, resulting in *grey slavery*. Real diversity is indigenous populations in separate sovereign nations competing in a free world market, with travelers enjoying potent undiluted cultures.

Stereotype
A stereotype is the random generalization that an individual member of an identifiable group, for better or for worse, probably possesses a particular characteristic which is alleged to, but may or may not, be especially common among members of the group. Stereotypes are often based upon race, nationality, sex, and age, but only become harmful when used to make judgements of consequence

about a person, without any substantive knowledge of the person as an individual.

Example:
"Watch out, or them corn-servatives will call you a pre-vert and summon the poe-lice."

False Grouping Stereotype
The notion that ideas must me embraced as package deals

Example:
If someone supports gun ownership, they must, of course, oppose a woman's right to choose about abortion.

Category Error
Attributing a property to something that could not possibly have that property

Incomplete Comparison
Two things are compared that are not related, in order to make something more appealing than it really is

Quoting Out of Context
When an original phrase is distorted by quoting it out of context

Etymological Fallacy
Posits that a term's original meaning applies to its colloquial and modern understanding in current circumstances

Gambler's Fallacy
Belief that likelihood of a specific event can be effected by unrelated events, or that something has happened so often in the past that it is less likely that it will happen in the future.

Inflation of Conflict
Belief that instances where so many scholars have differing opinions, that this in itself calls the credibility of the entire field into question. Therefore no action should be taken.

These last four were used at Nuremberg.
Read the transcripts for yourself.

Kettle Logic
Use of several inconsistent arguments to defend a position

Shotgun Argumentation
Too many arguments for the opponent to answer them all

Proof by Verbosity
Argument too complicated and verbose for opponent to address all the particulars

Intimidation
Person making argument is so well-respected that everyone takes his claims as truth

Fallacies Of Ambiguity
Change of Meanings in Discussion
Render Arguments Fallacious

Equivocation
Making equivalent things that are not

Example:
Referring to the *country*, the *people,* and the *government* as though they were one thing. *Country* is a geographically defined area within which exists the potential for absolute individual liberty. *Government* is that group of subverted collectivist traitors in the service of international finance who prevent this liberty from occurring. The *people* are that majority of brainwashed, deluded individuals who aid and abet government in doing this.

Reification
Misplaced concreteness

Example:
"We will stop Libertarian truth with censorship."

Composition
Reasoning from of the parts of the whole to the whole itself

Example:
"Libertarianism is a sham."
"Why?"
"It won't pay for sex change."
Division
Argues that what is true of the whole must be true of individual parts

Amphiboly
Grammatical construction causes ambiguity
Hedging

Use of a double meaning or an unclear description applied to mislead or misrepresent the truth, then changing the meaning of the terms later. This is often done by politicians.

Fallacies of Omission
Absence of Necessary Information

Stacking the Deck
Ignores examples that disprove the point

Example:
"Libertarians are always libertines."

No True Scotsman Fallacy
Stacking the deck by defining terms narrowly to exclude relevant examples

Example:
"Bolshevists were evil. They murdered sixty-six million people during their revolution."
"Yes, but their revolution was for the future of *Russia*. Forty six million of the casualties were Ukrainians and Poles."

Ad Ignorantium
Appeal to Ignorance

Example:
We should not establish a truly Libertarian society because there has never been one in the past, so we cannot know what bad things might come of it.

Ad Speculum
Hypothesis contrary to fact

Example:
"In America, whites owe blacks bigtime."

In the USA, virtually all black people are descended from those who were brought to America as slaves. Most white people in America, however, are not descended from southern plantation owners, and have inherited no culpability in any of this. The presence of black people in America is, for most white people, simply an unjust cultural and gene pool encroachment.

Another related lie is that all free people were unjustly enriched by the institution of slavery. In truth, the only people who gained from slavery were the plantation owners. Everybody else was hurt because of what it did to the price of commodities and the labor market. The slavery lies are used to promote so called "social justice" via mandatory wealth redistribution.

Complex Question
Loaded Question
Implies that another unproven statement is true without evidence or discussion

Example:
"How many deaths from overdose will be acceptable to you Libertarians, if we repeal Prohibition relative to heroin?" Ignores the fact that before Provision there was no epidemic in drug use, because there was no black market profit potential to sell it.

Argument from the Negative
Approach-Avoidance Conflict
Running to Extremes
One position is untenable, so the opposite must be true

Example:
Right wing extremist parent produces
left wing extremist child, who produces right wing extremist child, who produces left wing extremist child … ad infinitum.

Doublethink
Collectivist government favorite for adding insult to injury by naming harmful policies the exact opposite of what they are. The truth is totally omitted.

Formal Examples:
Monetary Control Act
Bank Secrecy Act
Homeland Security Act
Patriot Act

Casual Examples:
Friendly Fire
Collateral Damage
Enhanced Interrogation

Human Trafficking: A Few Facts

Victims:

Children and adults for sex, labor, and service

Statistics:

Human trafficking is a $150 billion industry worldwide, the third largest international crime industry after illegal drugs and arms trafficking.

80% is sexual exploitation

19% is labor exploitation

25% are children

75% are women and girls

The International Labor Organization claims that there are 40.3 million living victims of human trafficking worldwide.

The U.S. State Department says that, 600,000 to 800,000 people are trafficked across international borders every year.

Between 14,500 and 17,500 people are trafficked into the U.S. each year.

The International Labor Organization estimates that women and girls represent the largest share of forced labor with 11.4 million trafficked (55%) compared to 9.5 million (45%) men.

The U.S. Department of Labor identifies 148 different products from 75 countries made by forced labor.

In 2017, one out of seven runaways reported to the National Center for Missing and Exploited Children were child sex trafficking victims.

Of these, 88% were in the care of social services or foster care when they ran away.

Eighty percent of children sold into sexual slavery are under 24, some as young as six.

The average age for the sex trade in the U.S. is 12 to 14 years old. Many of the runaway girls were sexually abused as children.

At this writing, there is one internet pedophile ring in the U.S. with 70,000 members.

Five noteworthy points about Globalist pedophile trafficking:

- the tens of thousands of people involved

- the high rank and tremendous wealth of many of the participants

- the activities, especially torture, mutilation, blood drinking, and gourmet cannibalism

- the involvement of those we should be able to trust, like CIA, Vatican, United Nations

- the automatic protection of participants by subverted government officials and media

Most human trafficking in the United States occurs in New York, California, and Florida.

California has three of the FBI's highest child sex trafficking cities in the nation: Los Angeles, San Francisco, and San Diego.

The National Human Trafficking Hotline receives more calls from Texas than any other state, 15% from the Dallas-Fort Worth area.

Trafficking plays a major role in spread of HIV.

30,000 victims of sex trafficking die each year from abuse, disease, torture, and neglect.

Sudanese phrase: "use a slave to catch slaves." Traffickers send "broken-in girls" to recruit younger girls into the sex trade.

Sex traffickers often train girls themselves, first raping, then teaching them sex acts.

71% of trafficked children become suicidal.

UNICEF estimates that 300,000 children younger than 18 are currently trafficked to serve in armed conflicts worldwide. Often they serve as suicide bombers.

Traffickers target victims on the telephone, the Internet, through friends, at the mall, and through after-school programs.

Traffickers often work with corrupt government officials to obtain travel documents and seize passports.

Traffickers are increasingly taking pregnant women for the newborns. Babies are sold on the black market. The profit is divided between traffickers, doctors, lawyers, border officials.

People are trafficked for organ harvesting.

Increasing numbers of trafficked children are being terrorized, drained of adrenalized blood, then prepared and eaten like piglets or turkeys.

Per capita, there are more human slaves in the world today than ever before in history.

Due to globalization, every continent of the world has been involved in human trafficking.

Slaves are cheaper than they have ever been in history. The population explosion has resulted in a huge supply of potential workers. Globalization has created a mindset and environment where people are vulnerable and easily enslaved.

Worldwide, average cost of a slave is $90.

New World Order

Short History

In 1773, Meier Amschel Rothschild met in Frankfurt, Germany with twelve of his most influential friends. He convinced them that by pooling their resources, they could rule the world. Rothschild soon found a man of incredible intelligence and ingenuity to head their organization, one Adam Weishaupt, a professor of Canon law. and Jesuit priest.

At the request of Rothschild and his friends, Weishaupt abandoned the Catholic Church, and created the secret Order of the Illuminati, on May 1, 1776. The objectives were, through currency manipulation via central bank control, and the cooperation of subverted politicians, to establish what they called a New World Order, which will seek:

Abolition of all ordered governments
Abolition of private property
Abolition of inheritance
Abolition of patriotism
Abolition of family
Abolition of religion
Creation of world government

Concern about the unelected power of international bankers arose as Congress prepared to extend a twenty-year charter with the Bank of the United States, a private central bank formed in 1816. Andrew Jackson vigorously opposed efforts to strengthen the grasp of any central bank over the U.S. He called private central bankers a "den of vipers" and in 1832 vetoed a bill to renew the charter.

Thomas Jefferson warned,

"If the American people ever allow private banks to control the issue of their currency, first by inflation and then by deflation, the banks and corporations that will grow up around them will deprive the people of all property until their children wake up homeless on the continent their fathers conquered."

The New World Order's power is nearly total today, with presidents, senators, congressmen, and mainstream media bosses among the subverted. The opposition to banker monopoly has shifted from those who govern to those who are governed, the people directly affected by the banker's totalitarian agenda.

Alexander Solzhenitsyn, in a speech at an AFL-CIO meeting, July 1975, spoke of a turning point where our hierarchy of values may waiver or collapse:

"The political crisis of today's world and the oncoming spiritual crisis, are occurring at the same time. It is our generation that will have to confront them."

Globalism and the Federal Reserve

The Federal Reserve Bank is the central bank of the United States. Out of thin air, by *fiat*, it creates paper currency and regulates the US money supply. Despite the misleading name, it is not part of the federal government. It is a private corporation owned by a cartel of international banking firms. The list of creditor-shareholders appears below.

The argument used by the bankers has always been that they can do a better job of managing things, so the government should borrow currency the bankers create by fiat, rather than create it on their own.

George Washington and other presidents kept the international bankers from taking over the issuing of currency for one hundred and twenty-four years. During this time there was a period of ninety years with total monetary stability, no rise in consumer prices at all. The only taxes were on real estate, tobacco, and liquor, and this was during the time of greatest immigration and road building in all of human history.

It wasn't until 1913 that the increasing number of corrupt politicians and media bosses made a banker takeover possible. Both the Federal Reserve Act and the Internal Revenue Act were debated in Congress, but many say that neither was properly ratified, and for that reason are both unlawful. This, of course, is a moot point, since both are unnecessary, destructive, and based on deception. The banker friendly controlled media has been ever vigilant in making the American people believe that both are not only lawful, but worthwhile. The entire swindle hinges only upon mass public ignorance about the facts presented here.

To *nationalize* the Federal Reserve Bank is simply to return the power to issue and regulate currency to the people through their government, which will no longer have to borrow or pay back the money. The unnecessary federal income tax pays only the interest on the unnecessary national debt which is now at nearly twenty trillion dollars.

Most other nations have a central bank equivalent in function to the US Federal Reserve. The globalist regulating agency for the entire worldwide banking cartel is called the International Monetary Fund. To get things back in balance, countries everywhere need to nationalize their central banks, repudiate their national debts, and demand reparation for the amount already swindled by the globalist creditors, as a civil alternative to being put on trial for engineering every war and ruined economy over the past two hundred years, or being the beneficiary heirs thereto, all of which is easily provable from existing historical records. This should be followed by a return to currencies backed by durable commodity of intrinsic value, like gold or a mixed store of precious metals, the value of which is determined in world markets.

US Federal Reeve Bank Shareholders:
Rothschild of London, Berlin
Lazard Brothers Banks of Paris
Israel Moses Seif Banks of Italy
Warburg Amsterdam. Hamburg
Lehman Brothers of New York
Kuhn, Loeb Bank of New York
Goldman, Sachs of New York
Levi P. Morton of New York
Hanover Trust of New York

Thomas Jefferson
3rd President of the
United States

"I believe that banking institutions are more dangerous to our liberties than standing armies. If the American people ever allow private banks to control the issue of their currency, first by inflation, then by deflation, the banks and corporations that will grow up around [these banks] will deprive the people of all property until their childern wake-up homeless on the continent their fathers conquered. The issuing power [of currency] should be taken from the banks and restored to the people, to whom it properly belongs."

World War II and Causes

Relatively Common Knowledge
Bankers and Subverted Politicians
"Lending Requires Spending"

Hebrew goals in early fiction unite them as a tribe.
Isaiah 60, 61 Covenant promise of Jehovah to the Israelites:
"Therefore, thy gates shall be open…that men may bring unto thee the wealth of the Gentiles...For the nation and kingdom that will not serve thee shall perish...Thou shalt also suck the milk of the Gentiles...Ye shall eat the riches of the Gentiles, and in their glory shall ye boast yourselves."

1917 Russian Revolution
Jewish Communists murder and confiscate the property of twenty million Christians.

March 1919 First Communist Party Comintern Congress
Of the three hundred ninety three delegates, all but seventeen are Jews.

June 1919 Treaty of Versailles
There is no evidence that Germany started World War I, but with the help of baker accomplice, Colonel Edward Mandell House, Germany is blamed for the war, forced to

demilitarize, give up large territories, and pay huge reparations, so the bankers can lend the money to Germany. They know that the German effort to stop Communism will provide an excuse for another banker windfall in a Second World War.

In the wake of Versailles, roaming Communists are shooting German citizens in the streets. Adolf Hitler's SA Storm Troopers stop them. Josef Goebbels describes Communism as the "dictatorship of the inferior." Heinrich Himmler reaches the conclusion that the war against subhumans, because of the vast numbers, can never be completely won, but that good people must forever fight simply to hold the line.

Germany's huge reparations require nonstop fiat currency which causes massive hyperinflation. Gentiles must sell everything just to eat. Jews buy up large amounts of real estate in Germany. In Czechoslovakia they acquire eighty percent of the property. Germans grow very tired of Jewish Communists and bankers, and decide to find the Jews to a homeland of their own.

November 1938 Polish Jew, Herschel Grynszpan, enters the embassy in Paris to murder the German Ambassador, who is away on business. Instead, he shoots an assistant, Ernst Vom Rath. Germans want peace, and react angrily to this by breaking Jewish shopkeepers' windows. Goebbels has the SA encourage the activity. Finally the incident is stopped by the SS at Hitler's order, and is named the Night of Broken Glass, Kristallnacht.

September 1, 1939 a plebiscite has established that the resident population of Danzig, one of the territories lost at Versailles, wants to be re-annexed to their homeland, so Germany invades Poland.

September 3, 1939 Lord Halifax, the bankers' choice, has replaced Neville Chamberlain as the British peace negotiator. The bankers and paid-for politicians are now able to take England and France into a Second World War.

September 17, 1939 Russia invades Poland, and on November 30. Finland.

In furtherance of Adolf Eichmann's plan for the creation of Israel, Germany wants to send a ship to Madagascar with thirty thousand Jews on board. With the outbreak of war, the plan is spoiled because of French shipping blockades. Reinhard Heydrich has been conducting a successful resettlement program for the Jews, but due to the war this too comes to a halt. Ultimately, Germany asks twenty-five different countries to take their Jews, but nobody will have them.

Germany negotiates for an end to the war, but Sir Winston Churchill, with a chess master's personal obsession to defeat Hitler, persuades the Allies to insist on unconditional surrender. For Germany, this would mean another Versailles, or worse, so the war drags on, and the Jews are shipped to work camps, mostly in Poland. The Allies succeed in bombing German supply lines. This leads to malnutrition and disease in the camps.

January 27, 1945 as the war winds down, the Russians liberate Auschwitz and other camps in Poland, but will not allow the press inside any of them for another five years, a year after the final verdicts at Nuremberg. When the camps are opened, there are lots of gas chambers that no one remembers seeing who visited the camps during the war.

In Berlin, invading Russian soldiers see flush toilets for the first time and think they are potato washing machines. They rape fifty thousand German women. Three million Germans are murdered after the official end of the war, two million civilians, mostly women, children and elderly, and one million prisoners of war. British historian Giles MacDonogh details how they are killed in cold blood, or confined and left to die of disease, cold, malnutrition, or starvation.

At the Nuremberg Trials, seventy five percent of the staff lawyers are Jewish. Controlled media, friendly to Jewish banker goals, latch on to a careless estimate offered by a Vermont magistrate, that six million Jews were gassed in the camps. The higher the death toll, the bigger will be the loans for Germany's ongoing reparation payments to Israel.

American forensic doctors examine hundreds of bodies, but can't find even one that was gassed, most having died of typhus or starvation. Throughout the war the Red Cross, under the rules of the Geneva Convention, visited each of the camps once every two weeks. They say the total number of people who died in the camps is 271,301, including non-Jews. Based on census data, the World Almanac for 1940 gives the world's total Jewish population as 15,319,359. For 1949 it puts the number at 15,713,638.

For Auschwitz specifically, the plunderers claim a number of four million, but the top Jewish authority on Holocaust demographics, Gerald Reitlinger, says the number for Auschwitz is three hundred thousand. The banker media, however, hold fast against all the updated estimates, and always make a point of stressing the activity of atypical Germans like Dr. Joseph Mengele. Decades pass before we hear about Oskar Schindler.

February 2016. if anybody disputes the six million number, they are immediately labeled a "Holocaust denier." Banker friendly publishers have almost exclusive control of all mass media, and with tribal singularity of purpose using selective emphasis, have turned three generations of white Europeans into guilt ridden self-haters, blindly acquiescent in New World Order plans to ruin national economies, destroy European culture, and eliminate the white race with endless immigrant hordes of Third World savages. Any white person who will not proactively participate in the extermination of his own race, is labeled a "hater" or a "white supremacist." The next time a subverted globalist traitor invites you to a "conscious raising" Holocaust seminar, hang him for treason.

Jewish Globalist injustice in Europe today is legendary. The escalating plunder of the United States has taken the standard of living of the average American down forty percent since 2000. Financial aid from the US to Israel amounts to three thousand dollars a year for each Israeli family of four, in a time when Americans can't even pay their own mortgages. The aid to Israel is the reason for another banker delight, the continuing US war with Islamic nations, including the attack on the World Trade Center.

Fifty years ago, the US was the world's biggest creditor nation, now it is the biggest debtor nation. The US National debt is nearly twenty trillion dollars, every penny created by fiat. It's only controlled media disinformation that keeps Americans from knowing that the government can create its own currency, and tie its value to receipts for hours worked. We don't need to borrow from a Globalist banker cartel.

Holocaust Debate

Countries that ban questioning Holocaust mythology also limit speech in other ways, such as banning so-called "hate speech."

There is a difference between common law countries, such as the United States, Ireland, and most British Commonwealth countries, and civil law countries, such as Scotland and most mainland European countries.

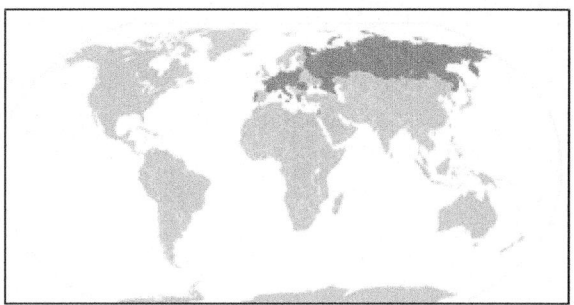

In civil law countries, the law is parochial. The judge acts as an prosecutor, gathering and presenting evidence as well as interpreting it.

The principle that the work of Holocaust questioners should be protected by the universal right to free speech, was used in 1992 by the Hungarian Constitutional Court when it rejected a proposed law against Holocaust denial.

Laws against Holocaust denial are against the European Convention on Human Rights and the Universal Declaration of Human Rights.

This, however, is completely ignored by the Globalist European Union and United Nations.

Author Noam Chomsky says,

"It seems to me something of a scandal that it is even necessary to debate these issues two centuries after Voltaire defended the right of free expression for views he detested."

Holocaust Historian Deborah E. Lipstadt argues,

"I am a firm opponent of laws against Holocaust denial. First of all, I'm a fierce advocate of the First Amendment... I don't want politicians making a decision on what can and cannot be said. That scares me enormously."

Holocaust Reparations

The six million "Holocaust" death toll was suggested by Raul Hilberg, a scholar from the University of Vermont, who presided at Nuremberg. The IMF banker-friendly media jumped on the number, and have never let go since. There are some problems, however:

The International Labor Organization states that the highest number of Jews ever under the control of Germany in prison camps, was not more than 1.5 million.

The World Almanac uses official census data. For 1939, it reports a total world Jewish population of 15,319,359. For 1949, the figure is 15,713,638.

Under the terms of the Geneva Convention, the Red Cross inspected all the camps once every two weeks. Their official estimate of the total number who died in all the camps is 271,301. This includes non-Jews.

American forensic doctors examined hundreds of bodies and found only typhus and starvation as causes of death, not even one from poison gas.

When the Russians liberated the camps in Poland, including Auschwitz, they refused to admit the press into the camps for five years. When they finally lifted the restriction, eager journalists got to photograph "gas chambers" that nobody remembers seeing who visited the camps during the war years.

The buildings claimed to have been used as gas chambers at Auschwitz were examined by Fred Leuchter, top American consultant in the building of gas chambers for U.S. prisons. His conclusion was that the buildings he examined could not have been used as gas chambers. Later the proprietors of Auschwitz conducted their own forensic study, and reached the same conclusion.

IMF bankers, of course, continue to lend money to Germany for the ongoing reparations to Israel and individual Jews, based on the six million estimate. Anyone who questions anything they claim is shouted down as a "holocaust denier."

"You can easily understand how that within a few years Hitler will emerge from the hatred that surrounds him now as one of the most significant figures who ever lived." ~ John F. Kennedy 1945

Worldwide Racial Displacement

Intelligent Humanity is an Endangered Species

Evolutionary destiny is the imperative for the unimpeded, ever-more varied and complex expression of intelligence. The mechanism for this is natural selection, the principle that organisms manifesting traits having negative survival value, will reproduce at a lesser rate because they will not live long enough to do so. This will ultimately cause the trait to die out in that species, unless those manifesting the traits are given unnatural sustenance to prolong their lives and periods of reproduction.

When non self-sustaining organisms are sustained artificially and end up reproducing when they would otherwise have not, evolution stops and devolution begins. Devolution is the reverse of evolution. The damage to evolutionary destiny is even worse if the evolutionary expression of self-sustaining organisms is encroached upon in the process. These principles apply to all life forms, including humanity.

Evolution will not continue, and ultimately intelligent mankind will not survive, if societies continue to act as subsidized breeding farms for human non-self-sustainability.
Recognition of this does not mean that anybody needs to go hungry or starve. In a Libertarian Republic all people can live long happy lives. Ongoing sustenance of chronically unemployable people can be provided efficiently without

dragging down human excellence using coercive government wealth redistribution. It is also possible with education about birth control to help people to curb the encroachment they make by having more than two children in a world that passed the ideal population of 320 million people in the year 900 A.D..

Race Preservation is Not Injustice

It's perfectly normal to feel more comfortable and at ease among one's own kind. This is an instinctive trait which comes from tens of thousands of years of fierce tribal competition for food and shelter. Nobody should ever allow themselves to be put on the defensive about having these normal feelings. Sometimes normalcy in this regard is mitigated by other things: spirituality, education, fashion, brainwashing, fear, lust, insanity, greed, naivety, social masochism, self-hatred, stupidity, or any combination of these.

It's safe to say that a person's feelings are always based upon the total of what they have experienced. Most so called prejudice is just a normal human reaction to what an individual has experienced. Since we all have different experiences, we all have different reactions.

A stereotype is the random generalization that an individual member of an identifiable group, for better or for worse, possesses a particular characteristic, which may or may not be more common among members of that group, this without any substantive knowledge of the person as an individual. Stereotypes are usually based upon race, nationality, sex, age, and creed.

There is a double standard about constructive racial pride. If a member of a less highly evolved race shows it, he is praised for cultural consciousness, If a member of a more highly evolved race shows it, he is scorned for divisiveness or bigotry.

Dictionary definition: "Racism is the belief that race is the sole determinant of character in the individual". There are very few people who believe anything like this. Everyday experience contradicts it. When people speak the deeper truth about race, however, it's usually shouted down with catcalls about hatred and bigotry. What this tells us is that if we want to be thought of as being loving and open-minded, we have to go along with social lies.

Ideological falsehood about group member potential is always reinforced using induction, that is, reasoning backwards from exceptional particular instances to a false general premise. Individuals must be judged individually. That doesn't mean, however, that we have to be deaf, dumb, and blind as to what is true about groups, or the adverse effect that one group can have upon another when it is wrongfully displaced from its rightful ancestral homeland. What hurts a group, hurts individuals.

Evolved Intelligence is being Lost Forever

Probably the best definition of a race traitor is "one who will throw down everything that has been gained through four and a half billion years of evolution to be fashionably liberal minded sounding at cocktail parties". The differences between racial groups are based on far more than mere physical appearance. More importantly, there are significant differences in intelligence. This has many consequences.

Science shows that the seat of higher moral deliberation is the cerebral cortex. The ability to conceptualize morally is tied to overall intelligence. Less highly evolved races not only have a lower average IQ, but also a lower average moral IQ. This leads to poor relations with other groups. All one needs to do is to search "crime by race" on the Internet. Statistics show these things very clearly. Ivory tower wishful thinkers will, of course, deny, or twist, every nuance of truth in this area.

The interbreeding of a more highly evolved race with one less highly evolved, results in a new race somewhere between the two original races, in humans, usually closer in manifestation to the lower. Once racial interbreeding gets started in any society, devolution and downfall has begun.

It's usually the lower members of the more highly evolved race who interbreed with the upper members of the less highly evolved race. As time passes, more and more intelligence disappears overall, and group differences become increasingly blurred. Those of mixed race usually identify with the lower half of their ancestry out of a need for self-justification, and are usually not accepted by members of the higher race. The most noble thing such a person can do for evolutionary destiny in general, is to identify the higher race, abstain from the gene pool, and adopt children.

The Role of Politics

Ambitious representatives of less highly evolved races will always champion the genetic intermixing of their people with the more highly evolved race. Why wouldn't they? They have everything to gain and nothing to lose.
 Interracial marriage advocates are trying to obliterate race by making all people intp one race. Dominant genetic traits are those which win out over long periods of interbreeding. Examples are brown eyes and black hair. Recessive genetic traits are the ones that lose out. These include light eye colors, such as green, blue, and hazel. Also gone forever will be light hair colors, such as blond, ash, auburn, and red.

If one race possesses mostly recessive genetic traits, then that race will be destroyed by race mixing. Self-respecting members of such a race will quite properly perceive all the breed-up-quick philosophy as a threat to the continued existence of their own race. They will feel that interracial dating websites are not examples of open-mindedness or cultural progress, but only of ignorance and societal decay, something effectively akin to an epidemic of fatal disease.

The real issue is racial preservation, diversity rather than sameness, variety rather than monoculture.

International finance manipulates politicians and always promotes any massive government spending program that will allow them to lend money. This includes ongoing programs that implement unworkable Socialist policies. They escape the cultural impact, because they can afford to live or vacation anywhere on Earth. People have the natural right to grow up in a society among their own racial kinsmen and should not accept being coerced at gunpoint by cruel socialist slave masters into intermixing with sullen, angry racial outlanders, who have an in-your-face attitude and speak with a tone of blaming.

It's important to know that third-world people usually favor globalization, because it will allow them to prosper from social programs paid for by productive host populations. Globalist bankers know that countries with multitudes of immigrant third-worlders, if globalization comes to a ballot referendum, will be far more likely to relinquish sovereignty. This is the reason for all the new indigent faces in productive countries.

Solution: Make the Whole World Free

Science teaches that when two groups compete for the same ecological niche, the stronger will destroy the weaker. Distance between the groups, of course, eliminates the competition. A good non-human example is timber wolves and coyotes. Both are *canis lupus*, but they are also natural enemies. Both survive very nicely if they are at a distance from each other. Coyotes like to travel around a good deal, but the smart ones have learned not go within seventy five miles of timber wolves.

Those who would rob you of your liberty, or threaten the existence or evolutionary destiny of your race, are your mortal enemies. There are two ways to deal with them. You can either have them at a distance or eliminate them completely, at very least by stopping their further reproduction. Which you choose should be determined only by your perception of possibility and cost.

It's normal for the people of a more highly evolved race to take up arms against those who seek to destroy their race, and with it the evolutionary destiny of mankind. There are, however, more peaceful solutions.

Populations displaced by coercion have the natural right to return to their ancestral homelands. This option can be made legal through the cooperation of governments everywhere. Worldwide liberty and capitalism will produce worldwide prosperity. This will allow populations who have been unjustly displaced to return to their ancestral homelands, because the newly prospering nations will be able to easily accommodate their return.

Displaced people of reproducing age who are realistic, responsible, and mature will want to participate in this great adventure. They can entrust their property to older friends and relatives who choose to remain in the host counties. Their property can then be sold at a time advantageous from the standpoint of market.

There is no substitute for the splendid integrity of living in a place where you are wanted, and where you don't have to blame, or thank, anyone but yourself, for how well you do.

                        Eric F. Magnuson
                        October 15, 2008
                        Late Morning

The following is an adaptation of a essay written by Dirk Aubrey Lokison in 1983 about racial displacement problems particular to the United States. In the original version, specific ethnic and racial groups were identified. The WLO's goal is not to hurt anyone's feelings, just to make a better world, so I took these specific references out. The who-does-it is gone, but the what-they-do remains. See if you can ID the various groups. I also made editorial changes for easy readability, but not for meaning or content. Those of European heritage will think of many culturally displaced individuals who they like or love. Personal affiliations, however, must not interfere with more important matters such as race preservation and evolutionary destiny. Goals must be prioritized. We can visit our friends overseas when they are happy and prospering back in their ancestral homelands. - EFM

Displaced Racial Populations in America

People of European ancestry are the founders of America as it is now constituted, and must not be hindered in the establishment of a totally free society by antithetical groups who never belonged here in the first place. There are many specific problems in the USA which accrue to the presence of displaced populations. There is, of course, in every group a percentage of decent people. In the groups that are hurting the United States however:

- Many are significantly less intelligent. Those who question the accuracy of intelligence tests need only look at the long record of almost total non-achievement by certain groups in both America and in their countries of origin. They are often loud, belligerent, and foul-mouthed. Their presence in America spoils the quality of life for people of European heritage.

- Many have out-bred their ability to feed themselves at home. Americans should not have to put up with vast throngs of third-worlders coming into our country to do the same thing here. Most of the invaders are tedious and uninspired, addicted to indiscriminate reproduction and cowardly medieval religion.

- Many are cruel, fanatical, and given to terrorism. The dangerous ones exist in sufficient percentage so that we shouldn't have to worry about which are which.

- Many are conniving monoculturalists who are openly aggressive towards the host populations of European ancestry. This parasitic element sponsored and now exploits the Socialism that is destroying America. We shouldn't have to put up with the vile dispiriting nihilism of these wandering internationalist blood suckers.

- Many are intelligent, quiet, polite, and hard working. There are, however, enough of them in their homelands. In the interest of our own preservation, we should not welcome vast numbers of them here with their cheerless similarity of appearance. It's simply a bad move genetically from the standpoint of human aesthetics and variety.

Social lies are always used by collectivist governments to justify non-viable policies. There are two big lies guiding American social policy. One pertains to who did what. Virtually all black people in the USA are descended from those who were brought to America as slaves. Most white people in America, however, are not descended from greedy southern plantation owners, and have inherited no culpability in any of this. The presence of black people in America is, for most white people, simply an unjust cultural and genetic encroachment. The other big lie is that all free people were unjustly enriched by the institution of slavery. The truth is that the only people who gained from slavery were the plantation owners. Everybody else was hurt because of what it did to the price of commodities and the labor market.

The slavery lies are used to promote so called "social justice" via socialist wealth redistribution. Affirmative Action programs deny education to more qualified people of higher intelligence. Colleges in the United States have been invaded by loud, motor-mouth jokers who disrupt the study of serious students. When anyone asks them to please quiet down, they often respond defiantly with name calling and threats of violence. This is especially true first semester, before many of them flunk out. Anybody who doubts any of this need only sit for a while in any college library of computer lab and listen to what goes on, and then see for themselves who is responsible. Try riding a city bus over time and then ask yourself why ninety nine percent of the trouble consistently comes from twelve percent of the people.

Non-Coercive Solutions

Large percentages within all displaced population groups are antagonistic to the interests of liberty loving Americans of European descent. Only small percentages have demonstrated any real comprehension of free-enterprise principles. Their continued insistence on the injustice of Affirmative Action and unnecessary social programs is the most concrete expression of this.

Admitting the truth of all these things does not mean that anyone should condone cruelty, injustice, or disrespectful behavior towards anyone else. Nor should it be used to refute the great accomplishments of exceptional individuals within any displaced group.

On the average, however, people of European ancestry have everything to lose and nothing to gain through further association with displaced populations. The terrible injustices of history cannot be rectified by the further injustice of perpetuating Socialism in America. Two wrongs don't make a right.

Our greatness as a nation can now only be realized by doing what is clearly most workable. It is in our interest to help displaced people get back home to whatever country they came from. Mass influx should be stopped immediately. Incompatible groups already in the United States must be allowed to return to their countries of origin.

So called "Native" Americans are actually first wave European immigrants who came here via the Alaskan Land Bridge fourteen thousand years ago. They are the only people who truly deserve to be in America, but there are not enough of them left to defend the borders of a country this size. Most of them are gone because of diseases brought by later European settlers. As Americans we owe the survivors a great deal.

We should give Native Americans back good tracts of government land to inhabit, plus all of the National Parks and

Forests, to be run by them for the use of all Americans. Their religion is much like the original spirituality of Europeans. Whenever possible they should be given the autonomy of a separate nation, while at the same time, remaining our military allies relative to any invasion from outside America.

Dirk Aubrey Lokison

1983

Updated Commentary

In all of human history, there is no example of any multi-cultural society having survived. It has always led to the downfall of the society, because only those who create a great culture are capable of sustaining it. What works are indigenous peoples, enjoying race and culture preservation in absolute liberty as separate sovereign nations competing in a free world market. Only this, can lead to world peace and prosperity. We are tired of being victimized, and of explaining the facts to militant sleepwalkers. Revolution is at hand! Good people will, by any means necessary, make natural order prevail on this planet. Those who oppose us, dig your graves. Winter is coming.

                        Eric F. Magnuson
                        February 23, 2016
                        11:05 A.M.

Indigenous Peoples Everywhere, Rise!

"We often give our enemies the
means of our own destruction."

~ Aesop ~

Are Racial Outlanders Dangerous?

American Case History

This is the testimony of a man of European ancestry living in the United States. He will remain anonymous and withhold location information in order to preserve future options:

"When I was young, I had very liberal viewpoints, liked Jack Kennedy, and believed that all that government assistance would inspire the recipients to pull themselves up and become productive members of society, because that is how *I* would respond in their circumstances. This was very innocent of me, because I didn't understand the basic differences between people. Today I use the *N Word,* but in this context I prefer the term *Negro,* so as not to distract all the boot-licking Socialists from the content.

1962 Massachusetts
I'm walking along having a normal conversation with a Mulatto student near campus dormitories, when he suddenly jumps me. We wrestle, but he gets the better of me with a choke hold. I say 'Okay, I give,' but that isn't enough. He tightens his grip until I'm strangling. It's almost impossible to talk, but I manage to tell him to let go, or I'll have to report him to the school administration. He reminds me that nobody is around, that he could kill me and nobody would know, then he chokes me for another ten minutes. This is a very bleak and frightening experience. Finally, he lets go. and I tell him I have to head home. In the future I avoid him.

1964 Boston
My mother returns from shopping to her car. Before she can lock the passenger door, a Negro jumps in and tries to rape her. She manages to open the driver door and yells for help, The Negro panics, jumps out, and runs away.

1968 San Francisco
A girlfriend of mine moves to San Francisco. Within two weeks she is raped by a Negro.

1972 Boston
A friend of mine is returning home when a Negro pulls a knife on him and demands his money. He complies, and later talks to a girl who has been robbed this way fifteen times in the past two years, always by Negroes.

1995 Northern California
I am diagnosed with a fatal tumor and referred to a neurosurgeon. When I phone the office, the surgeon's Mexican secretary can barely speak English. I express dismay at this. She becomes sullen, angry, and uncooperative. Finally she says she will put my file on his desk. I call periodically about getting my appointment. Three months pass, my condition becomes much worse. I will die soon, and become so frightened that I seek administrative remedy outside the surgical unit to bypass the secretary.

When I finally get my appointment, the surgeon apologizes. It turns out that the secretary kept shifting my case folder to the bottom of the pile on his desk. Although this is clearly attempted murder, I don't pursue the matter at the time. To do so would have reset the entire process and waiting period. At last I get my surgery, but nearly die from complications resulting from the delay. Later I look for the secretary, and find out that she no longer works for the surgeon. After a follow-up exam, I'm told that I will need a second operation in 1997, so I decide to delay taking action. There is no way to find out who she is without giving away my intention.

1999 Northern California
In a traffic jam quick-stop, a white kid in a pickup truck smashes into the back my car at about 60 mph, He is listening to dirty mouth Negro rap music with a subwoofer, and doesn't hear the noise of screeching tires ahead of him. He doesn't see all the stopped cars, because he is looking in his rearview mirror to see if the white family behind him are properly impressed with his rebellious demeanor. After an examination and a cat-scan at the hospital, I'm told that I have a skull fracture and a herniated lower lumbar vertebra. I am partially paralyzed in my right leg to this day. In a good country, the installation of subwoofers in vehicles would not be legal. They are generally used by Negroes and Mexicans to make unjust encroachment on white people.

2002 Nevada
I'm living in an apartment house with no other residence options at the time. There is a very loud Mexican in the next room. He never sleeps, and yells all night, every night. The manager, also a Mexican, keeps telling me he will move the loudmouth to another room the next time his rent comes due, but it never happens. The typical excuse is that when the yeller comes down to pay the rent, the girl on the desk doesn't know the situation, and simply renews him for another two months. This continues for six months. I am

getting only two hours sleep every night, because the Mexican doesn't stop until 4:00 A.M. Finally my resistance becomes so low I become deathly ill with pneumonia, This persists for six months, I become anemic, my muscles atrophy, and I am going to die. The hospital keeps me on an antibiotic intravenous for two weeks. When I get out, the loud Mexican is still there. He's half my age and twice my size, but I threaten to kill him, so he moves out.

2005 Nevada - Winter
I overhear a conversation between two Negroes at a bus stop, 'Yo, I got Brown Recluse. Carry in saltshaker. Put in Motherfucker's bed. That fix Motherfucker's ass.". How this works out I don't know. Naturally I'm curious, but feel that it might be impolite, or politically incorrect, to ask.

2005 Nevada - Spring
Am talking with a friend outdoors when a Negro, acting like an ostrich for some reason, comes up and grabs me. I shove him away. The Negro addresses two passing security officers, 'Did you see that? How he put his hands on me?' One of the officers replied, 'Yes, but I also saw what you did first.' The Negro looks disappointed and continues up the street as an ostrich.

One night, around 2:00 AM, in a public dormitory, on the lower bunk, I am awakened by my blanket being pulled off by a yelling Mexican on the upper bunk. I start to sit up. With a broad swipe, he claws me with his fingernails, drawing blood from my forehead about an inch above my right eye. He's raving incoherently, saying that I must leave the city immediately. I tell the security officer, who knows who the fellow is and says. "Oh, Jesus!" then goes over to calm him down. The Mexican now pretends to be asleep, so the security officer shines a flashlight in his face and awakens him to see if he's okay.

2005 Nevada - Summer
In the same dormitory, am awakened about 1:00 AM by the conversation of security officers as they carry three stationary men, one at a time, out of the dormitory. Next day in a breakfast line, a friend tells me that he heard that three dead white guys were removed from the dormitory, the previous night. I never learn anything more about this, so who knows what happened? I do remember, before I fell asleep, seeing a Negro man prowling around in the dark like he was studying possibilities.

One morning I'm waiting for a bus, and a mad-dog Negro with no shirt, comes raging down the street shouting and throwing stones at everyone and everything. I see him and hide bend the bus kiosk. Too late, he sees me and starts throwing at me. Then he crosses the street and opens a big water main that starts flooding the area. In late afternoon the water is still flooding as previously.

Another day, out front of a convenience store, a Negro asks for money. When I refuse, he threatens that I will be hung by his neighborhood friends. Then he walks a safe distance away, and starts throwing stones at me. When the bus arrives, he runs up and heaves a big cup full of ice inside, hitting me, the driver, and two other passengers.

2005 Nevada - Autumn
I'm eating a nice chicken dinner at city social club, and get talking with a friend at the table. He tells me that he became an alcoholic because he could not get over the murder of his fifteen year old daughter a few years earlier. He tried to warn her, but a fast talking Negro boy managed to get her alone. After he and a friend raped her, they cut her throat, and left her to die behind a restaurant. A few years later, the father got a call from his mother saying that two Negroes were trying to break into her apartment. He arrived in time, and shot them both in the head. In court he said, 'Two of these people murdered my daughter. What was I supposed to do, let them kill my *mother* too?' He was acquitted.

2008 Nevada
I need a follow-up MRI scan to check for recurrence of the tumor. My doctor refers me to a Negro "neurologist" who talks more like a gruff railroad worker. He says he will schedule me for an MRI. Call to check at normal intervals and always get the 'It takes time, Sir' routine from the Mexican secretaries. Finally at five and a half months, I insist that the secretary check the status of my scheduling, and am told that nobody ever ordered the MRI.

2009 Nevada
I'm on the way to a film premiere on a double decker bus when, from behind, a Negro pushes me into the stair well. Somehow I keep my orientation so that I land on my feet, but am badly lamed in both legs. Nobody sees it. I'm in too much pain to beat up the Negro, besides this, it would be on the security camera. I proceed, limping, to the premiere, and the left leg still hurts me to this day.

For each of these events I have endured at least a hundred arbitrary insults or threats, mostly from Negroes. As a race I consider them the second foulest living things on Earth. Yes, today I use the *N Word*. I say *No* to savages in America, and I'll call them any goddamned thing I want. It's the prejudice of experience. I've never had any problem with Asians or Caucasians. I know that there are some nice black people, but the benefit derived from them is massively outweighed by the danger from the hordes of bad ones, and the relative number is increasing. Tje honeymoon is over. Integration has failed. Racial outlanders *are* dangerous.

In my lifetime I have watched my country slowly turned into a quagmire of filth by the Globalist Shadow Government. What we need is a fleet of ships sailing to Africa, not obese welfare mammies mass-producing Negroes, like turds, at the public expense. Let's do it now, because if an inspired leader like Adolf Hitler comes to power in the United States, all *good* European Americans are going to follow him to Hell and back to purge our country of this subhuman pestilence."

C B P
December 21, 2015
9:57 A.M.

Indigenous Peoples Everywhere, Rise!

𝕷iberty or 𝕯eath!

World Libertarian Revolution

Introduction

"We are not to expect to be translated
from despotism to Liberty in a featherbed."

~ Thomas Jefferson to the
Marquis de Lafayette. April 2, 1790 ~

The Basic Libertarian Premise: It is wrong to unjustly encroach upon any creature or the environment to the detriment of any living thing. Most people agree with this premise. The disagreement is over what constitutes encroachment.

The innate love of liberty and the concession of this to others is what we may call the Basic Libertarian Impulse. Depending upon the degree of spiritual development, the individual either manifests this or does not. We know that it is unjust to unnecessarily kill, assault, coerce, rob, defraud, slander, or otherwise encroach upon any living creature. Calling these acts by other names and programming an ignorant majority to agree that they are necessary or permissible does not change their nature. To do evil is to trespass unnecessarily upon the liberty of any living organism. Historically this principle has been called the Golden Rule.

Perhaps the most noble and heroic trait of mankind is the innate impulse towards individual liberty. It works very well because it is both self-serving and generous. In the past this impulse has often been obscured by events. The hindsight we now enjoy, because of the massive historical changes of the past two centuries especially the last three decades, enable us to see that most social philosophers of the past have been wrong about the so called "cycles" of history.

The very long term trend is, and always has been, towards increased individual liberty in the creation of human societies. The history of Man as exemplified by the great nations of the Earth has proceeded in the following way:

Hunter Gatherer Bands
The dawn of civilization. To secure advantages Man organizes.

Agricultural Feudalism
Strong centralized control. Exploitation leads to revolution.

Industrial Socialism
Capital base is generated. Exploitation leads to further revolution.

Democracy with Capitalism
Populace develops intellectually. Libertarian refinements follow.

Libertarian Capitalist Republic
Highest known potential for human societies (1).

The premise here is that the highest evolutionary destiny for all living things can best be manifested by continuing peace and prosperity in the human sector, and that all moral people want this. Most believe that such a condition, sustained on a worldwide basis, is an impossible utopian ideal. It is, however, only the current activities of governments which keep us from this very natural and easily attainable condition.

People who mock Libertarians today are the exact modern equivalent of the slave owners who mocked Abolitionists in the nineteenth century, attempting to justify the vile institution of slavery by claiming that it would not exist if it were not "God's Will." Virtually everybody now realizes what jack-asses these people were. The struggle for liberty today has simply gone to a higher level of refinement.

It has been wrongly said that most situations are neither black nor white, but gray. They are in fact, almost always black or white, and there is usually one best way of handling them. What is gray are people and people's muddled perceptions of situations, these usually reflecting some combination of ignorance, societal brainwashing, and the individual's own short term selfish interests.

Liberty, in fact, always works best. This book explains how and why. Educated people know that a Libertarian Capitalist system can achieve worldwide harmony without treating anyone unjustly. No individual sacrifice is required. All that is necessary is to elect Libertarians to all government offices at the same time. Once this happens, most of the large scale trouble on Earth will soon be over. This may seem like a very grandiose claim at this juncture, but will be fully substantiated as the reader progresses.

There are very few who will openly admit to preferring a world continually disrupted by economic upheaval and war. There are, however, some who do prefer this, and they are running things. This is not "cynicism" or "pessimism" but irrefutable fact. The result is a world ravaged by war (2), choked by pollution and the rapid disproportionate proliferation of non-self-sustaining people.

The situation is caused by collectivist governments financed and manipulated by a certain parasitic segment of the international banking community who profit from everything that is going wrong on this planet. "Lending requires spending" and that is their only political objective - simply to influence politicians to spend money. To gain total monopolistic control of this lending extravaganza they are deliberately moving us headlong towards a collectivist one world government.

The "New World Order" is not merely a label for the post Desert Storm political climate. It is a term coined in the early years of the twentieth century to describe these long-term monopolistic goals. The individual names of the pirates involved in this are not mentioned here because that has been done already by others. Besides, most of what they do is legal and unredressable in the courts.

Something far more important however, is revealed here - the peaceful and legal means to their absolute and permanent defeat. Happily, this won't hurt them a bit, because the total prosperity resulting from world Libertarianism will give them greater financial opportunities than ever, plus the chance to earn their money honorably for a change.

The biggest problem in educating people about these matters is to overcome the brainwashing. The average person thinks of the 20th Century as a standard of normalcy against which to evaluate current events. This is a good example of how ignorance feeds apathy. In actuality the 20th Century was an unprecedented ongoing parade of unnecessary wars and economic upheaval. None of the bad things had to happen and would not have if people were even moderately vigilant. It was all a direct result of international finance manipulating human apathy for profit.

The slave mentality may well brag that his country is more prosperous than those that are even worse off, but will never contemplate the fact that without the unnecessary financial interference of banker monopolists that his own country would have been vastly more prosperous. We don't buy the old standard "It's OK because we're all in the same boat" excuse. The more people that are hurt, the more reason there is to change things.

The triumph of Libertarianism does not depend upon a moral reformation of society except in the final stages of Socialist degeneration. Even in a declining Democracy there is still time to educate a majority of the voters that simply adopting Libertarian Capitalist methods will result in a much higher standard of living for everybody without anyone having either to work harder or to steal.

There is no speculation, philosophy, or anecdote presented here, only facts and proven principles. Everything said can be corroborated through experience or further research, and applies in various measure to every country on Earth.

After making those basic efforts necessary for survival of self and family, one of the first concerns for any moral individual living in a society which unjustly interferes with human potential is to change that society. Mere adaptation to immorality is cowardice. Part of living well is to actually spend some time working to make the world a better place.

One need only look at the frivolous nonsense with which most people occupy themselves, and the incredible amount of emotion expended, to understand how things have gotten so badly out of hand. Slaves, awaken from your cowardly religious fantasies, impotent drug dreams, and tedious ball games! Are delusion, intoxication, and frivolous simian competitiveness more important than liberty and the future of your children? (3)

Ignorance persisting in service to chaos effectively becomes treason. The present volume is intended for those who are not embarrassed by seriousness and who have the courage to demand that their lives not be ruined unnecessarily by endless economic disruptions and war. It is written for people who are willing to do something about these things, right now. An understanding of the world's problems will not come by osmosis or from popular television news programs. Enlightened participation in historical change can only be accomplished by first learning the truth and then teaching it to others.

It has been said that anyone who is not a Libertarian is not because of one of three reasons: ignorance, immorality, or both. The truth of this becomes increasingly clear with every election. "Crooked people elect crooked leaders promising crooked solutions, and then complain."

In all fairness, many lately are saying that the only reason they don't vote Libertarian is because they feel they must use their vote to keep the "greater of two evils" out of office. Decade after decade however, this hasn't helped anything. This book explains why. Moral cowards, please just ignore this bothersome material, go home, and save us the trouble of shooting you.

Grassroots education is already underway. This is absolutely all that is needed for the triumph of natural order on this planet. Western Democracies can be improved the most easily. Once this has occurred, other nations will eventually follow suit. Revolutionary change, however, will not occur in time to save us from past mistakes unless people get involved now. This means you!

The money-mad enemies of evolving life can afford to spend hundreds of dollars on misdirection for every dollar that good people spend on truth, and make no mistake about it - they do. But, there is light at the end of the tunnel. The victims outnumber the exploiters ten thousand to one. People who are ignorant of these matters however, only outnumber informed individuals one hundred to one.

Things can be made to change very quickly. It could happen with one election. Libertarians are still on the ballots everywhere, but this won't necessarily continue. Time is growing short. The eleventh hour has past. It's eleven fifty five. The time to act is now upon us. The chance will not come again.

The author is a patriotic American citizen. The principles discussed in this volume however, apply everywhere and are presented here for everyone on Earth. There are one or two clearly indicated places where the USA is used specifically as an example.

Part I Liberation of Society

This is a collection of self-contained aphorisms written at different periods and later put into meaningful sequence. The section explains in detail the superior workability of Libertarian Capitalist principles in all areas of society, often using specific examples. There are many instances where the author is deliberately general, even cryptic, in order to hold up a mirror wherein many may view the adverse effects of their actions upon society without feeling that they, or anybody else, aer being individually targeted for disproportionate criticism.

Apologies in Part I, especially the first chapter, for the overkill. For light reading this material should be sprinkled through several books, but a friend once told me "A good teacher is someone who can say the same thing fifteen different ways" and of course, some will prefer one way to another. Think of this section as a choice of weapons.

Part II Liberation of the World

"New Look at Western Civilization" is a brief scan of certain vitally important but seldom contemplated aspects of western world history.

"World Power Through Misdirection" is a businesslike summary of the true balance of power on Earth at dawn of the Twenty-first Century. This content is especially useful as summarized here in the form of a chart.

There is information about "The New World Order."

Alternatives are discussed in "Superior Options Ahead."

"Declaration of World Independence" is a spontaneous inspired writing which preceded most of the rest of this material.

"Liberty Works Best Everywhere" addresses specific areas of everyday liberty not dealt with previously.

Part VI World Libertarian Order:

"History of the WLO" is a concise timeline selected from the author's personal journal.

Reading one chapter at a time is best. The reader will have time to digest and reflect. Except for 7 and 9 in Part I, plus 5, 9. 10 in Part II, a second reading is recommended, especially of the first section "Number One Priority."

Credits

Grateful thanks to our friends at UNR, CSN, and UNLV for their valuable help and support, especially Professor Gary Ogren. Back in 2003, Gary was known to me as the Ogre of UNLV and was working on his PHD thesis, a truly exotic Norseman who wore Hawaiian shirts, taught psychology by day, and moonlighted as a conga drummer by night.

Special tribute to Dirk A. Lokison, known in many quarters as "The Sun Warrior." He and his family were good friends, who in 1985, were murdered by radical Socialists in Canada. Without their international Libertarian affiliations and hard work, the WLO would probably have remained just an idea.

Dirk is paraphrased occasionally here for his unpolished gems of militant Libertarian rage. People who have lost friends, loved ones, or their life savings because of collectivist government may well appreciate the ferocity of his anger. Libertarianism is, for some, a matter of life and death, not just a way of being among the intellectual avant guard. The author has kept the violence of Dirk's statements intact to help "fire the blood" of the reader, but then immediately follows with peaceful, solution-oriented commentary.

Many thanks also to Bert Valdison who took over the membership drive in 1986 and helped us immensely until the WLO relocated to the West in 1998.

Also to Robert White, publisher of "Economic Security Digest" for all the good information he brought to our attention. Mr. White was murdered in Central America July,1988. One needn't be a rocket scientist to know why.

Footnotes:

In popular historical fiction this volume has been referred to as "The World Saved by Liberty and Free Enterprise".

1. Some assert that feudalism can go directly to Capitalism. With no capital base however, this necessitates massive foreign ownership, an unacceptable evil in itself. The United States was unique because it was settled by Capitalists from all over the World, rapidly displacing a non-industrial culture. The agricultural feudalism of the United States of course, was the institution of slavery. The Civil War, as a class struggle for individual liberty, is really more analogous to the French and Russian Revolutions than is the American Revolution, which was an international struggle for colonial independence.

2. "And he's fighting for Democracy,
He's fighting for the Reds,
He says it's for the peace of all.
He's the one who must decide,
Who's to live and who's to die,
And he never sees the writing on the wall."
Donovan - "Universal Soldier"

3. "The Threefold Path to Slavery - Fantasy Religion, Drugs, Arbitrary Competition." This is not to say that people shouldn't have hobbies or enjoy sports in moderation, but men who care more about athletic competition than their own or their children's liberty are justly referred to as "rah rah boys" by more serious individuals.

Part I: The Liberation of Society

Preface: Evolutionary Principles

"Evolutionary Psychology" is another book by the current author and is the spiritual underpinning of Evolutionary Libertarianism. Originally it was Part I of the volume at hand and is best read in its entirety before continuing here. The following is a very sparse reproduction from that volume and retains chapter numbers only. The content is eclectic free thought and is included here because it will help establish the proper moral tone for the remainder of this volume

II. Good is that characteristic of any situation, which if all else remains constant, causes an increase, no matter how slight, in the overall amount of justice in the universe. Evil causes an increase in the overall amount of injustice.

Justice occurs simply when the natural consequences to a living organism normally to be derived from it's actions according to natural laws, are not in any way interfered with.

Injustice interferes with evolutionary expression because it constitutes a disrupting unpleasant stimulus or worse to an organism and is, for this reason, a direct initial encroachment upon individual liberty. This applies equally to all life.

Evolutionary destiny is the principle imperative of nature.

The Quest for evolving good is to establish justice everywhere within reach. Pay close attention to recurring uses of this term. The meaning will be clarified forthwith.

"Morality" will herein refer to the relative balance of good and evil within the individual as this is reflected by the relative amount of justice manifesting in his treatment of all other organisms.

Good and evil themselves reflect emotional reactions more than anything else. Good is based upon the constructive impulse. Evil upon the destructive. Evil simply comes from entertaining the wrong emotional premise.

Any individual who persists in interfering with the normally occurring process of evolutionary expression, must by good men be regarded as evil, since such an individual impedes the ever more varied and complex expression of good.

The destruction of evil provides good people with excitement and adventure, and is simply the courageous and activist component of goodness manifesting itself tangibly as opposed to mere philosophizing. Good people of courage should humor good people lacking courage and not confide specific activities to them overmuch.

III. The caring and gentleness occurring among members of non-human species is necessary for the preservation of self and the species, and is perfectly natural.

Much of what is described as love among human beings is merely the same necessary caring and gentleness natural among non-human species.

Love, in a truly spiritual sense is totally impersonal, and is simply the desire arising within to see another living organism treated justly.

The uncaring and viciousness occurring among members of non-human species is necessary for the preservation of self and the species, and is perfectly natural.

Much of what is described as hatred among human beings is merely the same necessary uncaring and viciousness natural among non-human species.

Hatred, in a truly spiritual sense, is totally personal and is simply the desire arising within to see another living organism treated unjustly.

Cruelty is the willful use of unproductive or unnecessary viciousness, is unjust, and is primarily a human characteristic which cannot usually be attributed to so-called "lower" species. Cruelty is the product of hatred, also primarily a human characteristic.

It is unclear at what point on the evolutionary ladder we can first observe unnecessary viciousness being manifested. In any case, the behavior will usually be related to an appetitive drive and the organism eliciting the cruelty will usually perceive his behavior as being necessary to his own survival or that of his species. It is important here to distinguish true cruelty from culturally determined, moralistic, or hysterical human reactions to natural viciousness.

The main cause of hatred in humans is the individual's exaggerated reaction to the time consuming worry and unpleasant anticipation which comes from having enemies who are capable of long term planning, coordinated collective action, and subtle manipulation. Ironically, much of life's excitement comes from these very same causes. As the individual attains to understanding, much of life's joy and sense of achievement will come from successful avoidance or dispersal of such enemies.

The natural desire for justice or "getting even" which arises within when one has been truly wronged has often erroneously been described as hatred, usually by rationalizing cowards or manipulative evildoers. Desire for "justice" when one has not truly been wronged is evil because it seeks its remedy through initiating or perpetuating injustice.

Much of human hatred is the natural response of desiring "justice" in situations where one has not actually been wronged, but where one has been taught since youth that he has been wronged. What may be just in intent becomes unjust in effect- a natural response to an unnatural situation. At some level the individual may sense that he is wrong and his subconscious self-reproach will add fuel to the fire of his hatred. People of intrinsic value, of course, will usually manage to sort out the truth sooner or later. Those who earnestly persist it seeking "justice" when they have not been wronged, once they have had the truth presented to them with reasonable clarity, are usually people of bad moral character and must be firmly encouraged in the courageous art of soul searching.

People will often unjustly accuse others of "hate" simply for not loving the same things or emphasizing the same goals that they do. Such accusations will often represent an attempt to rationalize the exploitation of those accused.

All people, for their own self-esteem and inner peace, must realize that another is not guilty of hatred and is not "anti" some identifiable group simply because he doesn't want to be unjustly sacrificed for their agenda, or because he prefers the practice of his own cultural heritage to theirs. The sense of rootedness and spiritual integrity which comes from a thorough familiarity with the traditions of one's own people is far more gratifying than being merely cosmopolitan. Having strong cultural roots, when this is combined with a rudimentary knowledge about other traditions, does not lead to divisiveness but to a greater respect for the cultural heritage of all people.

IV. Philosophy is used to create a feeling of personal integrity and wholeness within by attempting to extrapolate beyond available facts. Correct reactions are based upon facts, not upon philosophy.

Most philosophy is merely the "explanation" that people lacking facts offer to justify their own particular emotional reaction to their environment. The only worthwhile "philosophy" is a comprehensive overview of all available factual data fused by love, heroic idealism, and courage. This involves an eclectic approach to the attainment of wisdom, not a slavish adherence to "isms" of any kind, including the fashionable zeitgeist of well entrenched science.

The spiritual development of an individual in the long term can only be judged by the net effect of his behavior upon himself, all other organisms, and the environment.

A person's spiritual development is reflected by his goal orientation. This will, via self-justification, determine his "beliefs." A person's "beliefs" determine his behavior. A person's behavior in the context of a totally free society, determines his situation.

The freedom of belief in society is absolutely necessary for the individual to reach the level of manifestation natural to his degree of self-development.

Freedom of belief does not preclude our attempting to educate those whose "beliefs" cause them to feel justified in habitually encroaching upon the liberty of others. This includes unnecessary insult.

People of positive spiritual development do not persist in "beliefs" which seem to justify unjust encroachment upon others. People of negative spiritual development often persist in any "beliefs" which seem to promote their interests even if such "beliefs" put them in opposition to logic, known science, and simple human decency.

V. Most of the worst atrocities committed throughout history have been done in the name of a loving God. It seems that the more energy expended in talking about love, the less energy there is left over to give love it's actualization.

The amount of tolerance enjoyed by any particular religion, even in a society professing religious freedom, is directly proportional to the amount of clout wielded by the religion. This in turn, is proportional to the amount of financial or political influence exerted.

VI. Life, to be enjoyed, must be embraced for what it is- a great and exciting epic journey filled with both love and hate, good friends and terrible enemies, vibrant joy and unbearable sadness, exquisite pleasure and excruciating pain, deep inner peace and unspeakable danger, all of which for the heroic individual are interwoven with the Quest.

It is well to discourage within ourselves any intense feelings of dislike for anything which does not constitute a discernible threat to the overall amount of justice in the universe. Let us deal with things of importance and pure forms rather than irrelevant mental associations.

While, in all matters, it is well to be as sensitive to the intent of others as to any alleged effect of their actions upon oneself, it is also equally well to be as sensitive to the true long term effect of the their actions upon oneself as to any stated "intent" regarding these actions.

The illuminated individual often makes the mistake of thinking that others are the same way, when in actuality they are usually driven by motives of a much lower order. Sometimes our desire for human companionship among those of heroic nature will blind us to a person's true nature.

IX. The highest actualization of evolutionary expression can only be attained in liberty, through self-determination.

The individual may give or receive help from others, but it is wrong for him to expect the total impact of others in his life to be more than a break-even situation. The ways one gains in life should be achieved incidentally to the inevitable involvement with others.

When bemoaning the amount that you are encroached upon by others, be equally as cognizant of the ways in which others benefit you. Everyone else is pursuing their hopes and dreams too. Over time, the amount of encroachment is usually balanced by the amount of benefit. This is as it should be, in the world as a whole. It is well of course, to structure your affairs so that you can gain more than you lose in this regard. It is also well to structure society in the same way.

X. A higher morality consists in working towards justice for every living thing in the Universe, including oneself.

There are many today who think of themselves as having attained to illumination. The only ones who have however, are members of that loose aggregation of individuals who on a worldwide basis, continually work to move the World towards the one condition which favors the ongoing evolutionary expression of all living things. This is the Quest.

The Quest

XI. Collectivist propaganda notwithstanding, interdisciplinary studies have objectively established that the Libertarian Capitalist Republic is the only political-economic system ever devised with complete internal coherence and long term workability. This is because it is the only system which works in harmony with natural principles rather than against them. It is the one and only condition which favors the ongoing evolutionary expression of all living things.

The highest aspiration of humanity is that the evolutionary destiny of life throughout the universe be unimpeded. The Quest here on earth is the elimination of all deterrents to evolutionary expression through the actualization of a Libertarian World Order, right now. This does not mean one nation or "One World," but a worldwide aggregation of separate Libertarian Republics, not completely attaining to this exalted condition simultaneously, but eventually. This can only be accomplished by the active participation of intelligent people everywhere in Libertarian Revolution.

I. Liberty and Natural Order

1. Liberty is that total optionality regarding individual behavior which must end only where that of the next living creature's begins.

2. Liberty is man's inalienable birthright to pursue life and happiness in any way which does not reasonably and directly interfere with anyone else's pursuit of life and happiness.

3. Among the Wise it is generally conceded that besides youth and health, absolute individual liberty is the one thing of this world which is truly worth having, because in having this, all else can be attained with reasonable effort.

4. The amount of liberty for true self-actualization is effectively greater for the individual possessing inspiration than for the mediocre individual who demands very little of himself. Apart from any question of moral development, this is why the mediocre individual cares less about liberty. He simply can't perceive as much need for it. (6)

5. The truth is a treasure chest unlocked by a key forged in the Fires of Love and tempered by the Waters of Reason. There is no morality outside of completely Libertarian values, only varying shades of immorality.

6. Some, in attempting to sound very cosmopolitan, like to say that "nobody has a monopoly on truth". Actually, Libertarianism has an absolute monopoly on truth - and morality. Let us keep in mind, however, that these things exist apart from the ability of any particular individual to perceive them with absolute clarity. In a society where one has been endlessly bombarded since youth with collectivist ideas from both sides, it may be difficult to be perfectly Libertarian in one's perceptions in all situations. Developed people, however, will continually aspire to perfection in this.

7. Collectivism is the general term used to denote any political system based upon the compromise that "otherwise unjust" coercion against the individual is justified, for the so called "greater good" of society. Collectivists will say that they believe in individual liberty, but always have a list of exceptions which they feel must exist anyway. They will say that we must give up some liberties to preserve others. Sometimes it is mere intellectual ignorance which makes people think this way, sometimes innate moral inferiority. The problem is that when everybody is through reading their list of exceptions to individual liberty, all that is left is the unworkable structure of a collectivist society.

8. When collectivist government crimes are continually perpetrated in defiance of known superior alternatives, they must also be effectively regarded as treason:

Private Sector	Collectivist Governments
Treason	Any Restriction on the Right to Keep and Bear Arms
Murder	Military Conscription Resulting in Death
Attempted Murder	Military Conscription Not Resulting in Death
Mayhem	Military Conscription Resulting in Mutilation
Torture	Prevention or Interference with Suicide
Slavery	Imprisonment for Victimless Crimes. Military Conscription
Rape	Sexual Assault Committed or Condoned by Prison Authorities
Assault or Coercion	Arrest for Victimless Crimes. Military Conscription
Robbery	Wealth Redistribution at Gunpoint. Euphemistically called Taxation
Extortion	Threat of Imprisonment for non-payment of Taxes
Burglary	Forced Entry. Search + Seizure for Victimless Crimes or Taxation
Counterfeiting	Central Bank Policy of Fiat Currency or Debased Coinage
Fraud	Economic Misdirection. Falsification of History
Privacy Violation or Spying	Surveillance for Victimless Crimes or Taxation
Coercive Harassment	Unnecessary Regulation of Anything
Coercive Interference	Unnecessary Licensing Requirements (7)

9. There are two kinds of individuals in the world, free men and un-free men. Un-free men further divide into masters and slaves, both of whom are un-free because they need each other.

10. A man is a slave to the extent to which he will give his labor, or his income, to another who demands it from him. If he allows himself further, to be brainwashed into believing that being sacrificed this way is really for his own good, then he is also a stupid slave.

11. There is a natural human right to be free because animals are free. Liberty, however, does not mean freedom from normal predation or struggles for dominance in the human world any more than it does in the animal. It does, however, mean that there will be adequate mechanism for dealing with either if the degree of either should become measurably unjust.

12. Any society which sacrifices the individual for the "greater good" is based upon a false premise, because ultimately society is nothing more than an aggregation of individuals. One does not inherit a yoke at birth. The individual owes absolutely nothing to society that will not justly serve his own interests, except to respect the liberty of others. Liberty, in the purest sense, does not involve being a slave harnessed to the task of alleviating hunger among the "underprivileged", eternally a mere dumb soldier in "the war on poverty".

13. Liberty has been destructively compromised in any society whose government can legally coerce, or openly steal from any of its citizens. Civil liberty is essential in a free society, but should not be seen as a substitute for economic liberty. The freedom to travel means absolutely nothing without the money for it.

14. It is government's job to protect the just interests of the individual citizen, but not against the just interests of any other citizen. What one earns or inherits honorably is justly and entirely one's own, and in a free society is respected and defended as such.

15. Liberty involves the responsibility for bearing one's own failures every bit as much as it involves the right to enjoy the

fruits of one's own success. It is the freedom to lose or win fairly.

16. The true Libertarian impulse comes from the desire and courage to walk life's tightrope without that safety net provided by collectivist government through the victimization of others. It is a matter of simple self-respect and has to do with the pride of rightness within oneself.

"If the individual is born into an unfree society, he will have no legal rights corresponding to his natural ones since these depend upon other people. He is endowed, however, in many cases, with the potential to be something more than merely a slave, and always with the choice of turning his will towards this end". ~ Dirk the Sun Warrior

17. Any encroachment upon individual liberty constitutes an interference with evolutionary destiny, because it interferes with the evolutionary expression of another living organism. Any individual attempting to prevent the triumph of libertarian ideals in any way is to that extent an enemy of evolving life everywhere in the universe, regardless of expressed intent.

18. In this context the terms "un-Libertarian" and "evil" are synonymous. Evil is the tendency to make any kind of unjust encroachment against another living thing. Un-Libertarian politics are simply the attempt to institutionalize such encroachment.

19. Once having had adequate exposure to the truth, those who persist in un-Libertarian attitudes identify themselves as mere thugs and thereby proclaim their inferiority and herald their own doom. There will be no compromise.

20. Collectivist governments of any kind have no legitimacy whatsoever, either from a standpoint of morality or long term workability, and will by right thinking people be thrown down everywhere.

21. Recalcitrant functionaries of collectivist governments who interfere unjustly with the enactment of Libertarian policies have little positive worth as people, are criminals, and will everywhere be treated accordingly. The approach needn't necessarily be confrontational, as "between gentlemen".

22. Natural order will prevail ultimately no matter what man does. It will prevail either with man's self-destruction or with his survival in liberty. There can be no middle ground.

Footnotes:

6. This is not intended to imply that mediocre people are entitled to less liberty.

7. Usually sponsored by politicians to give monopoly to cronies in return for support. Not to be confused with legitimate user fees like a fishing "license" which simply pays for wildlife management in connection with fishing.

II. Lending and Spending

"Single acts of tyranny may be ascribed to the accidental opinion of a day; but a series of oppressions, begun at a distinguished period and pursued unalterably through every change of ministers, too plainly prove a deliberate, systematic plan of reducing us to slavery."
 ~ Thomas Jefferson 1774 ~

1. Axiom One for Constructive Social Change:
National leaders are usually very capable people. If the leaders of a country claim to be working for specific positive change, but decade after decade the public gets only the opposite, then the cause of this will usually be discovered by finding out who is making great amounts of money from the status quo. "Follow the money!"

2. It is impossible for a small group of masters to exploit hundreds of millions of victims by brute force alone. It has to be done primarily by making the victims believe that they are in control. This is called "rule by misdirection." The exploiters themselves refer to the techniques they use to persuade the populace as the "engineering of consent."

3. Almost all people are completely ignorant about how societies, including their own, are run, and about what works well and what does not. The vast majority of people, however, also believe that we are all responding ideologically to the same information. They believe that all of what comes to us courtesy of the popular media is fact and that there are no relevant facts that do not reach us in this way. They will perceive political differences as being based almost completely upon character traits such as sensitivity and caring on the one hand, or upon maturity and judgment on the other. The idea that there could exist a completely different base of information to which a person might be reacting will allude them completely. The idea that anyone could react differently from themselves politically and yet be

both sensitive and caring, as well as mature and rational, will also allude them completely.

4. Most of what happens in the larger arena of human affairs happens because of international finance, because of those who lend money to governments for repayment with interest. This financial-military-industrial-complex are the people commonly referred to as the "vested interests" or the "Establishment." This is not supposition or opinion. There is a highly specific body of knowledge about all this, and the individual who lacks this knowledge can have absolutely no understanding of current events or of history. Even people who call themselves Capitalists, but who do not address this problem, are mere dilettantes (8).

5. The consent for a collectivist system is gained by making a majority of the population believe that there is no better way of running things. The two subcategories of collectivism are "Fascism" and "Socialism" but are rarely called by these names (9). Most societies and political parties today are subtle mixtures of these two elements, using less conspicuous labels like "Democracy" or "Populism." They are all however, controlled or at least manipulated, by international finance. This is accomplished primarily through the regulation of national currencies.

6. The value of a currency is established in the same way as with a commodity. It is the relative scarcity of a usable commodity which determines it's value. If you increase the amount in markets of a commodity relative to what it is traded for, then the relative value of the commodity is diminished thereby. The same is true for currency and for the same reason - the currency is then relatively less scarce.

7. The only stable currency is one which serves as a system of warehouse receipts for a fixed amount of scarce and durable commodity, and whose value is agreed to depend, within reasonable limits, upon the market value of such commodity relative to the goods and services which the

currency will be used to purchase. A mixed "portfolio" of many commodities would provide the most stable backing for a currency because it would eliminate the problems which accrue to massive changes in supply or demand for any one commodity.

8. Even a privately issued commodity-backed currency will lose value unless backed by a one hundred percent reserve. Having less reserve would render the currency less scarce relative to the commodity it is supposed to represent.

9. A currency not backed by anything of intrinsic value, but created by a central bank at government request, is called "fiat" currency. This has the same effect on an economy as counterfeiting in the private sector, and should be illegal for the same reason.

10. There is absolutely no ambiguity whatsoever about what causes price inflation. It is simply a rise in consumer prices representing the normal response of producers to any increase in consumer spending for goods and services. The increase in spending itself is a normal response to any increase in the money supply. This usually precedes the price inflation by about two years. This time lag completely obscures the cause-and-effect relationship involved except to those who study graphs.

11. An increase in the "money supply" is any increase in the total amount of currency in circulation relative to the amount of goods and services that the currency is used to purchase. The amount of currency in circulation at any given time is determined by the central bank in any particular country.

12. Central banks insist that they can control the "economic cycle" with fiat currency. They neglect to mention however, that without fiat currency there is no economic cycle in the first place - just a continuing slow prosperity with full employment. No boom and no bust. Statistics about all this don't tell the whole story because they are based on national

averages. The unworkable policies of Socialism have their destructive effect much sooner in some places than others because of local economic conditions. When one area is going into the recession phase another area is beginning to re-inflate. At any given point when the numbers are averaged together the illusion is created of a fairly even and uneventful "national" economy.

13. Central banks are privately owned corporations held publicly only through investor participation. They are not truly "national" or "federal" because they are not actually part of government. They are insolvent and do not keep a one hundred percent "reserve" today, only about one and a half percent. They have their own agendas and make most of their profit by borrowing money from large international banks and then lending it to government and individuals at a higher rate. Government borrows by selling large blocks of redeemable securities, like T-Bills, to the international banks and smaller amounts to individuals. The money government receives from the banks is the newly printed un-backed currency.

14. Increasing the money supply effectively robs society. The central banks finance government programs which seem to be needed to relieve the hardships caused by the economic cycle, itself produced by fiat currency in the first place. Increasing the money supply rewards cooperating government officials by allowing them to draw and spend large salaries in connection with all the unnecessary government programs before the normal response of markets results in price increases. This ongoing interaction, combined with aligned industrial interests like defense manufacturers, is what is correctly known in it's entirety as the "Welfare-Warfare Economy." While there are many charming and likable individuals involved in all of this, collectively, in terms of their impact upon this planet, they are at best a crew of wicked old pirates, more so than even the most infamous villains of olden times. They simply wear business suits (10).

15. In "managing" the economy, a less obvious way of increasing the money supply is through fractional reserve banking. This occurs when central bank regulations encourage the smaller banks to lend out amounts far in excess of deposits. This makes the smaller banks illiquid. All of them, including the central bank, are insolvent. Fractional reserves render banks unstable and later seem to justify even further increase in the money supply by the central bank to "monetize" the bailout of many of these banks in order to "save the economy" from collapse. The people pay for all of this with increased taxes, price inflation, and recessions. In this case disclosure laws are a good free market remedy, but can only work if people understand the cause and effect of what's going on.

16. One specific way that monetized bailouts are used to rob society is when a large international bank or a government, through the central bank, makes a reckless unsecured loan to a Third World country. When the loan is inevitably defaulted, government arranges for the bailout to be monetized. The central bank creates fiat money and pays off or refinances the loan to "save" us from the banking collapse which would be triggered by the defaulted loan. Those who speak up are labeled "heartless, irresponsible advocates of isolationist foreign policy."

Riding ourselves of these cental bank monetizing problems does not involve interfering with international finance capitalism by regulating bank lending procedure. It simply involves eliminating government bailout policy. When this is done, the large banks will have a natural free market incentive not to make these imprudent loans in the first place.

17. Perhaps the most tragic irony in society today is that the means used to pay for entitlement programs actually cause the problems, the effects of which, the programs are supposed to relieve. Entitlements necessitate deficit spending via fiat currency, which itself is the only cause of

the economic cycles which lead to the rise in living costs, followed by the recessions which produce unemployment.

18. Deficit spending for defense seems to become necessary in response to painful shortages occurring when goods and services cease to cross borders because of trade deficits. These in turn are produced in world markets by fluctuations in the relative values of the fiat currencies used to finance all the government spending programs. Most of the military in so called "free" societies today are not really necessary and are effectively rendered little more than elite welfare bums, brave and well intentioned though they may be.

19. It has been posited that giant laser and particle beams targeting missiles from orbiting space stations can make nations safe from nuclear attack. Nuclear weapons however, can be clandestinely assembled and maintained throughout a targeted country and then detonated by radio control from a distance outside the borders. In reply to this, some have suggested that a laser defense system could prevent an alien invasion from another planet. A man with a stone ax might, in some exceptional instance, triumph over a modern aircraft carrier. The real "advanced technology" here is one of finance propaganda (11).

20. On the surface it often seems that economic upheavals in a nation are not just determined by central bank policy, but by longer term things, such as when people representing a large bulge in population reach an age where their numbers cause a disastrous distortion in markets. For example, a post-war boom generation is destined to flood the market with primary residences at retirement. Ironically, however, even these distortions are determined by central banks since there would, in this example, be no post-war population boom without a war, and no war without the manipulative policies of central banks.

21. Like the royal families of old, the international families who control the central banks cause and finance wars for profit and self-aggrandizement. They too are all intermarried, but the different branches usually finance only their own country in any particular conflict and thus avoid being charged with treason. History, of course, reveals some outstanding exceptions where one branch has actually lent money to both sides (12).

22. Unnecessary prohibition of a usable commodity causes all the problems it is supposed to solve. By increasing the risk in selling the commodity, it causes the price to rise, creating a large profit potential for black market entrepreneurs. This soon increases supply, and ultimately, because of increased sales promotion, demand. The central bankers of course, finance the massive, always increasing, government enforcement expenditures and lobby against legalization of any such illegal commodity. Victimless crimes make central bankers rich a second way. The bankers finance the bulging prison system and have ruthlessly oppose therapeutic methods to reduce recidivism (13).

23. Even if we were to accept the immoral premise that fiat currency for massive government spending is somehow desirable, there is still no excuse to run a deficit. The only reason that government borrows fiat currency from a central bank instead of simply issuing it themselves is because the people are not vigilant. If we must suffer the instability caused by counterfeit money, why make things worse by having to pay it back to anyone? It is created out of thin air. Nobody has earned it. It doesn't represent wealth generated by productive activity of any kind.

Footnotes:

8. Historical detail about this is explained in books such as "None Dare Call It Conspiracy" by Gary Allen (California, 1971), one of the most important books any American could read. There is no excuse for any liberty loving citizen not to have read this yet. Those who have been told about it, but have not inquired further, are apathetic fools not fit to call themselves Americans.

9. Watered down versions of these in the United States are called Conservatism and Liberalism.

10. "The pen is mightier than the sword."

11. On the bright side, it is now claimed that giant lasers can be used to break up or deflect incoming asteroids, comets, and meteors.

12. The Viet Nam War. See Gary Allen "None Dare Call It Conspiracy" (California, 1971).

13. Many say it was Establishment flunkies who framed Timothy Leary by putting marijuana in his car ash tray. Dr. Leary developed a 97% recidivism cure employing LSD at Harvard University.

III. Economics and Power

> "Call out the border guard.
> The castle is crumbling.
> The king is in the counting house.
> Laughing and stumbling."
> ~ The Electric Prunes ~

1. Most of society's economic upheavals come from fiat currency used for deficit spending. The distortions thus produced, in turn, are used to seemingly justify all kinds of otherwise unnecessary remedies such as taxation, regulation of business, and protectionism in foreign trade. All these consequences are really just products of individual human dishonesty. It is the simple unwillingness to earn what one spends which leads to unstable war-based welfare economies. In a Libertarian society the behavior proceeding from such dishonesty is neither tolerated, nor is it institutionalized.

2. International banking interests go with the tides of history by quickly adapting to inevitabilities. Long ago they set up tax exempt foundations so that they could retain control over vast fortunes. They then lobbied to hasten the impending income tax and anti-trust legislation which would have otherwise hurt them. These foundations have, in turn, endowed organizations which promote Socialist teachings in the schools and churches. This has led to ever increasing government victimization of business through regulation and taxes, with proportionately diminishing competition for the old monopolies (14). The liberty loving individual, or any one making the slightest pretense of being a good citizen, will seek further specific knowledge of what these people have done since those days.

3. Elected officials have little direct control of economic cycles unless they have some direct control over their country's central bank. Campaigning politicians simply ask

their economic advisers what will happen because of the current economic cycle during the next term of office. They then promise to deliver the upcoming good part and forecast the upcoming bad part, blaming this in advance, on the unsound policies of their predecessors.

4. The notion of divided power in two party systems is largely a circus to make the people think that they have some say in what goes on. The power all merges at the top. Inexperienced idealistic young politicians are often little beyond the people in their awareness of all this, but eventually they learn.

5. Eligibility for most political nomination today is simply to advocate spending as much money as possible, with as little perceivable long term positive result as possible. In this way the financial overmasters are best served. The politician doesn't necessarily have to understand the long term effect of what he is doing. The people who elect him certainly don't. Many of these politicians are just well meaning dupes, but some are not. It takes a good deal of attention to current events from arcane sources to know which is which. Intuition is not enough in this area.

6. Most of society's other "non-economic" or so called "moral" problems, in turn, come from the hopelessness engendered by war-based welfare economies. Much of what is seen as moral decline in society is simply the natural reaction of borderline individuals to an immoral and unnatural system. There are many who will live lives of shallow respectability if they simply have some reasonable expectation that their work will result in at least a minimal degree of prosperity for themselves, and that they are basically safe in their homes. Take even this away and have them "living beneath the volcano" always awaiting "the mushroom cloud" and they will resort to shortcuts reflecting their unrelenting hopelessness - virtual reality, drugs, perversion, theft, arbitrary violence, and child abuse. Remember that on the outside people will usually try to

appear tough, satisfied, and content. This doesn't mean that they are (15).

7. The economic cycle caused by fiat monetary policy pulls down almost everybody in society, sometimes even to a level of apparent non self-sustainability. Most of societies "homeless" individuals would have homes and would get by, at least marginally, in a stable commodity backed economy. What possible incentive does a person who has lost everything have to start over when he has every expectation that he will only lose it all over again? One is not a "bleeding heart" to want these people happy, productive, and out from under foot in the subway stations.

8. Mathematical models for how individual countries can be returned to precious metal backed currencies have been computed and are perfectly workable. Models of this sort are falsely "discredited" by committees made up largely of central bank board members appointed by government associates to study the "feasibility" of returning to a precious metal standard. The very least that would happen to these bank board members if there were such a return to sanity is that they would lose their jobs. You don't appoint a committee of your exploiters to study the feasibility of whether or not they should continue to exploit you. For the people to condone this nonsense is the equivalent logic of using weasels to guard a hen house.

9. All that is happening now has happened before. The Romans allowed themselves to be convinced that they had to conquer the world and, of course, the Roman coinage had to be diluted with base metals to appease the mob with "benefits." This has the same effect as fiat currency. The fall of Rome was primarily an economic one no matter how collectivist "historians" fictionalize to the contrary. Medieval China is another good example.

10. Collectivist wealth redistribution goes under three basic names. Socialism, Communism, and the Welfare State are

all based upon the "Theory of Surplus Value" of Karl Marx. This is the notion that all people work equally as hard and that there is really no way to judge who produces more in the workplace. This supposedly gives government the right to throw all the money into one big pot and then reallocate it on the basis of "need." Eventually when people finally accept this militant philanthropy in their hearts, the state is supposed to "wither away." In actuality, the state which confiscates wealth will inevitably only devour the people.

11. There is absolutely no excuse for collectivist wealth redistribution today. The great Austrian Free Market economists, especially Ludvig Von Mises, totally refuted everything claimed by Karl Marx by the year 1920. There is always a long time lag between the attainment of knowledge and the implementation in society. The avant guard in economics in the universities of the 1930s was the Keynesian-Marxist nonsense under which we now suffer. The current avant guard is the Austrian Free Market viewpoint. This, happily, is one of the best single hopes for the future of life on this planet.

12. Never allow yourself to be fooled by the distraction afforded through the phony elaboration of complex definitions. Communism, Socialism, and Welfare State may be different in some externals, but from an economic standpoint, are almost identical. All are unworkable for the same reasons. They all reward incompetence and pull down excellence. The method of obtaining popular consent may be different, but the non-workability of these systems stems from the same root causes and to distinguish unduly between them is mere hairsplitting among the intellectually obtuse.

13. Here's an easy way to compare government and economic systems. (16)

You own two cows. The government, under:

Fascism
- lets you keep both cows, regulates milk production, dictates who you sell to, and the price.

Communism and Socialism
- confiscates one cow, regulates milk production, confiscates most of your milk and profit. and gives it to unproductive people.

Democratic Bureaucracy
- lets you keep both cows, confiscates most of your profit and gives it to unproductive people. It also buys a large portion of your milk, and then pours it down the drain. Then it raises taxes to fund elaborate, expensive studies to find out why government is so inefficient.

Libertarian Capitalist Republic
- lets you keep both cows, the milk, and your profit. It regulates nothing. You sell one cow and buy a bull…

14. "The ongoing injustice of collectivism produces angry divisiveness in society. This causes some to speak out very much against what they believe to be hate. We only wish these fellow moral champions where as opposed to institutionalized injustice as they are to the emotional reactions which proceed as a normal consequence of injustice. They treat symptoms instead of disease. There is today massive government oppression everywhere. Most of this occurs out of ignorance or greed without any hate involved at all. None of this is necessary and occurs only because people are not awake."

15. Pros and Cons:

Anti-Fascism
- you oppose the just natural reaction to Socialism

Anti "Hate"
- you council slavish emotional acceptance of racial and cultural injustice

Anti-Socialism
- You spend lots of time explaining what doesn't work

Pro Libertarian Capitalism
- You spend a little time explaining what does work

16. The conditions normally prevailing in a Libertarian society are a stable currency with no business cycle, a continuous slow uneventful prosperity, full employment, and peace. Try to imagine what a truly splendid change this would make as a backdrop against which to live our lives.

17. The potential for new technology is infinite, and provides new ways of generating wealth. The potential for wealth is also completely unlimited. We don't need government to "stimulate" anything. Unimpeded industriousness, with a little education about birth control, will result in more wealth than humanity can ever spend.

18. The actual amount of money necessary to run a Libertarian society is only a minuscule fraction of what it takes to run a banker manipulated economy, and can be paid for entirely by user fees and lotteries. There need be absolutely no taxation whatever. The slow rise of deficit spending by governments has obscured these facts. There are few still living today who remember that in the past there were scarcely any taxes at all. They were not needed even during the Nineteenth Century, the greatest period of industrial expansion and road building in all of human history, and they are needed even less now.

19. The withdrawal of social programs possible in a Libertarian society would not lead to "starving children" as Socialists and Establishment propagandists have alleged. Entitlements can be phased out over a suitable period of time without hurting anyone. There will be no hunger in a Libertarian society. Just riding ourselves of fiat monetary policy alone will reduce unemployment to one percent. There can be an emergency fund for those who are in desperation because of local catastrophe, including those with a history of productivity who have, through no fault of their own, incurred disability. This can be funded by special lotteries at the federal and state level.

20. Voting for the "lesser of two evils" decade after decade is still a vote for evil, and will not slowly bring society to good as naive individuals wishfully believe. This is because the absolute amount of evil of what both candidates represent increases with every election. This is a consequence of rising deficits, and is completely apart from any consideration of the "intentions" of the candidates individually. Giving a "lesser evil" vote without further specificity seems to give total mandate to a candidate's entire program and registers nothing but approval to his mind. This gives him no message or incentive to change anything. There is, however, presently a very clear and easy alternative to evil. Libertarians are on the ballots everywhere now, but will they always be? The choices later will not be so easy. Slaves, awaken! Stand on your feet and seize your destiny as free men and women! Utopia is at hand, if we have the simple courage to do what is clearly right for once in our lives, all at the same time.

21. As the totality of human knowledge increases, so does specialization. In such an age it becomes increasingly more important that people be able to trust each other. The surgeon should not have to master economics to keep the central banker from stealing the shirt off his back. The central banker should not have to study medicine in order to

keep the surgeon from performing unnecessary operations for extra money.

22. Man's interference in the natural flow of human affairs because of collectivist government is exactly the same as man's interference in the ecosystem and produces the same types of difficulties. Human affairs have grown so complex that this fact is usually difficult to see and easy to hide. The chain reactions of cause and effect which produce distortions are so complicated and far reaching in a collectivist society that is usually impossible to conceive of them in advance or even to explain them when, in rare instances, they are understood (17). International banking families don't care about the details. These things only effect other people. All they want is to finance the increasing complexity. That is their only real political goal.

23. A criminal enterprise needn't necessarily be a monolithic conspiracy, constituting a conscious or malicious organized plotting against anybody, but can simply be a mutual tendency towards cooperation among individuals in conditions which favor their own personal interests at the expense of justice and individual liberty. A criminal enterprise on a grand scale is usually just a complex of mutually profitable, but manifestly unjust, interdependent relationships which develops spontaneously until it reaches an almost unfathomable complexity and cannot easily be detected against the larger backdrop of human affairs. Such will not usually be completely understood even by most of those who participate in it, even though most of the activities go on openly.

24. To the extent that any society is not completely free, it is a criminal enterprise, even if a consensus majority of the population are involved in perpetuating the oppression. The increasing criminal interaction between government and central bank interests may be thought of simply as that corruption normal among the very powerful. The increasing criminal interaction between crooked benefit-seeking voters

and collectivist politicians may be thought of simply as the decline of civilization. Any government or individual official who cooperates with international financial interests to the detriment of his country has effectively been subverted. To call this what it really is of course, will usually elicit a pretentious but fashionable, knee-jerk reaction from the youthful intelligentsia that one is being "paranoid." Other, even older pseudo-intellectuals may insult true patriotism in this same way. Anyone today who is not instinctively mistrustful of government must either be asleep or comatose.

25. Treason is usually thought of as selling military secrets to enemies during wartime. In a broader than usual sense, treason is any act where one knowingly subordinates individual liberty in his own country merely for personal gain. In every non-Libertarian society many trusted government officials are effectively guilty of treason in this broader sense. A person however, cannot be tried for an act which is not illegal at the time of the act. It is sometimes tempting of course, to consider "ex post facto" legislation, but such a precedent would then mean that nobody in the future would be safe from arbitrary judicial impulse. Besides, since the majority of these people are not really all that political from a standpoint of ideology, most could be retrained to lend their sometimes considerable abilities as functionaries under a Libertarian system. We would simply have to keep an eye on them.

26. If we are to have a truly workable society we must get rid of the idea that things will be fine if we can just put perfectly good men into positions of great coercive power over other people. A perfectly good man is a pretty rare duck. Political ambition is usually augmented by moral compromise. Power rewards evil far more quickly, easily, and tangibly than it rewards good. Power is the problem, not the solution. When we get rid of unnecessary coercive power by government, we won't have to depend on officials being perfectly good.

Things will work out very nicely anyway with people being just exactly what they are.

27. World leaders sometimes possess a curious mixture of genuine idealism and personal lust for glory. We must try to reach them with the truth to show them that their greatness can most completely manifest itself to posterity through a unflinching heroic commitment to those Libertarian principles which would truly render them the saviors of the world.

28. In a Libertarian world there will be continuing prosperity, full employment, and peace. Individuals will be able to prosper to the full extent of their abilities. Government will give no unfair advantage to anyone for any reason. The sooner that greed for short term unfair advantage is overcome, the sooner lasting earned prosperity will be achieved everywhere. The desire for this can only be kindled through education about the total workability of Libertarian Capitalist principles and the fact that no other system can ever produce these results.

Footnotes:

14. Ibid.

15. "I been on this killin' floor so long,
    feels like I'm a million miles away from God.
    Lately I been dancin' with Satin's grand-daughter
    on a sea of rotting cod."
    ~ Leatherstocking DuBois. Chicago 1931 ~

16. This basic approach appeared in a Florida newspaper. It was brought to the attention of the author by a very wise woman, Norma Johnston Young.

17. This will often reflect the endurance or commitment to liberty of the observer.

IV. History and Propaganda

1. Much of peoples' emotional reactions, values, and expectations for the future depend upon what they believe about major historical events of the century past. He who rewrites the past towards truth or falsehood rewrites the future as well (18).

2. Official histories at very least usually leave out a good deal of information necessary to a clear understanding of the larger picture. The portion left out usually has to do with the real causes of events, especially about those who gained financially and their role in determining the events.

3. Regarding historical contra-orthodoxy, the open minded patriotic individual will reserve judgment and will read. The brainwashed apathetic individual will lazily dismiss out of hand anything which challenges the official version with which he feels so comfortable, and will glibly proclaim himself to be "skeptical."

4. Both the manipulation of events and the rewriting of history are most easily accomplished during the chaos of war and immediately afterwards, and is usually done at these times. This is called "dis-information" and is every bit as important to wining a war as battle strategies. Other

motives include concealing the actions of one's own nation or allies, and the fabrication of blame in order to justify the forced surrender of territory or sometimes the extortion of "reparation" payments from the defeated enemy. The most important reason of course, is to rationalize the creation of economic sanctions which will pave the way for financing the next war.

5. There are two main ways that collectivist governments create dis-information. One is to promote lies by cleverly mixing little known, but easily verifiable, truth with the lies. The other is to discredit truth which has already been leaked, by mixing it with easily provable lies. This latter way can be done by seeking interviews with, or sponsoring publications of, lunatic individuals, who it is known will present the truth frantically, and well mixed with other often bizarre, ridiculous, or absurdly irrelevant information. This may later be treated as though it were very typical of the opposing viewpoints in the particular area and calmly dismissed by "reputable" sources in a very sympathetic and patronizing tone.

6. An historical myth needn't be an outright fabrication, but may simply involve huge exaggerations augmented by many small component myths which are outright fabrications. There are certain kinds of historical myths which trigger such emotionalism that any factual challenge to them among otherwise open-minded people, will almost always touch off an immediate angry reaction of phony not-wanting-to-know type "skepticism," accompanied by a knee-jerk, kill-the-messenger slandering of those who dare to question. Such myths, even a few years after they are created, can become almost like religions in terms of dogmatic adherence and, like religions, will generate statues, memorials, study programs, agenda oriented "conscious raising" seminars, and "interpretive" museums. Exploiters will often shout down those who question aspects or components of sacred social myths accusing them of wholesale denial motivated by bigotry.

7. True history, especially economic history, does not lie, although collectivist "historians" almost always do. Collectivist governments invariably create or greatly increase, in the longer term, virtually all of the problems which they appear to be trying to solve in the near term. It is only the time lag between cause and effect, plus general ignorance about how things work, which makes this unclear to the public.

8. The governments of collectivist societies are absolutely no different from gangsters even in the way they charge "protection" money and fight among themselves, except that they seem to have greater legitimacy because of better public relations through cooperating news media. The leaders almost always proclaim themselves to be men of the "people" and will sometimes dress the part, but behind closed doors will usually live in opulent splendor.

9. It has been said that it is only the victors in a war who write the history or hold trials afterwards. Usually government will officially attribute all kinds of atrocities to the vanquished enemy in order to draw attention away from their own or their allies' atrocities. Often there is a clever mixture of truth with lies - generally falsifications about numbers, methods, motives, and responsibility. Usually the victors are just as bad as the losers, or worse. Sometimes "evidence" is planted or constructed. Witnesses are paid, threatened, tortured, or killed. Occasionally the normal rules of evidence, such as cross examination by defense council, are abridged so that the witnesses will not be "traumatized." How can trauma occur, unless we are pre-supposing guilt? "Trials" of this sort are merely shows to give an appearance of being fair and civilized, indeed even chivalrous, to a "barbarous" enemy.

10. Those who seek historical information only from sources representing the winning side of a war commit intellectual and moral suicide in so doing. If you want accurate knowledge about any particular group, you must consult as

sources, some members of the group itself, some "neutral" individuals outside the group, and some mortal enemies of the group, but not just one of these, no matter how unlikely the sources may seem as avenues of truth.

11. Some have developed an unusual strategy for dealing with popular writings which have legitimately criticized them and are past copyright. They simply publish fancy deluxe editions of these works, editing out any truth which will not help them in appearing to be historically blameless. These volumes are then sold at bargain prices. In this manner, the truth about their historical misdeeds is slowly erased from human memory.

12. Via popular media we are always hearing about new historical "revelations." Often these are just facts that have become so widely known that they can no longer be officially denied without destroying government credibility to the point where the people will begin to question more recent things.

13. The collectivist, unable to truthfully or logically refute Libertarian arguments, will slanderously try to "analyze" why the Libertarian is so "mean spirited." Individuals who warn about the unsound practices of collectivist governments will usually be labeled "doomsayers" by the non-committal purveyors of "cautious optimism." It has been said that "a pessimist is just a well-informed optimist." When you have the facts, emotional postures such as pessimism or optimism are superfluous and completely unnecessary.

14. Historical truth is often obscured by the false redefinition of popular terms.

15. During the inevitable economic upheavals which occur under collectivist governments, those who have been thoughtful enough to invest in emergency supplies for daily life are labeled "hoarders" and are blamed for "shortages." In this way government can easily conceal their own blame, mobilize the rabble, and seem to justify mandatory "sharing"

imposed by force. One can avoid becoming a victim of this false influence by being well prepared and keeping it a well-guarded secret.

16. Collectivist opinion manipulators will quickly attempt to discredit those who speak the truth by "beating them to the punch" with exaggeration. This is done by publicizing that the truth teller is declaring a far greater divergence from official histories than he is actually doing - a divergence so great that we will know instinctively that it could not be true. This is done by using loose, overtly imprecise, but deeply suggestive language which would be easy to defend later as merely being "careless reporting" rather than deliberate slander or treason. By this trick, the truth teller finds himself on the defensive before he can even tell his story and, by popular gut-reaction, is then more easily dismissed as a "malcontent," a "hater," an "extremist," an "agitator," or a "whacko."

17. Historically great individuals, being rather bold people in general, tend also to be bold relative to the open expression of personal eccentricity. Such people will also often be very tolerant of the eccentricities of others. In a world of "mediocretins," greatness is itself an eccentricity. Notice that commentators who approve of a great individual will brag up personal eccentricities as endearing foibles. When the great individual is in the enemy camp however, commentators will treat every minor eccentricity as a bizarre deviance from the norm, every spontaneous gesture of human naturalness as a calculated hypocrisy.

18. Those seeking to cover up the past will even hold public opinion polls to see what percent of the population have begun to question a popular myth. Instead of any kind of detailed inquiry about whether people question certain particulars of the myth such as numbers, methods, motives, or responsibility, the poll takers will force an all-or-nothing, yes-or-no, choice. This of course, creates the illusion of almost total popular adherence. All of this is logically

fallacious to begin with, since consensus belief is not a valid determiner of the actuality of events. The one exception to this might be in the particular case of a pole taken among a large number of eye witnesses.

19. To be able to see and understand the future effects of ongoing events requires possessing a deep understanding of the complexities not only of what is current, but of what is past. This may become much more difficult in the near future. It is fast becoming possible with computer imaging to produce totally realistic "news" footage showing people doing things they never did and saying things they never said. Even with a pre-warning that "what you are about to see is a dramatization" of what someone believes or "remembers" actually happened, the deep subconscious believability that this imagery engenders, effectively constitutes excessive persuasion relative to anything that is merely speculation. Often in dramatizations, the legally required pre-warnings will be flashed quickly on the screen in very small print for all the eagle-eyed speed readers in the audience who happen to be tuned in at the very beginning of the show. Defenders of this will speak of "valuable air time wasted on generally understood standard disclaimers." Years later however, it may be impossible to remember what one has virtually seen and what one has actually seen.

20. It has been said that to speak primarily about the evil past behavior of a particular group, without also speaking about their virtues, is bigotry. This is true, but a corollary must be added here. If the past evil behavior of the particular group has been almost completely concealed, especially by slandering other groups, then it is most certainly not bigotry to speak primarily about it. This is especially true when the evil behavior is still occurring and the group who have concealed the behavior have left no stone unturned in their efforts to endlessly remind everyone else of their virtues.

21. The manipulation of societies through dis-information increased the minute that men learned to write. We find vast

discrepancies between many early scriptural writings and the objective concurrent chronicles of credible secular historians. The scriptural versions often reflect ergot-induced delusion coupled with a long term agenda in trying to make the writers' own people seem historically blameless. The more numerous secular accounts of course, usually show the normal balance between innocence and guilt.

22. The equivalent of the old secular historians today are the modern contra-orthodox historians whose voices are usually drowned out by collectivist propaganda. In many quarters today however, the truth about the past is being told, but not on the television news or through other collectivist media. In the years to come many lies will be swept away. Those who have opposed the truth will be remembered later. Some, who have been terribly maligned will be, if not fully exonerated as they deserve to be, at least partially understood in terms of their higher ideals. Many who have been wrongfully praised will at last be seen for what they really were and their true allegiances more generally understood.

Footnote:

18. Enemies of liberty have even been known to take a statement like this out of context and suggest that it represents falsehood being advocated rather than condemned.

V. Evolution and Devolution

So that we are not accused of overkill, let us acknowledge in advance that we know that the superior viability of Capitalism renders any arguments regarding human evolution superfluous and unnecessary. We simply like to illustrate the connection between natural and economic laws.

1. No species, no matter how highly evolved, can go against nature in the long term without bringing about it's own destruction. Man, to survive, must arduously study the laws of nature, because he is the only species on Earth possessing the ability to temporarily violate these laws.

2. Some who have raised a lion and a lamb to lay down with each other have claimed that this is the natural way for these creatures. Of course it is, when people are giving the lion three big meals a day.

3. The truth seeker will reason deductively from universal principals to their proper application in specific instances. Those not at one with truth will usually reason backwards inductively from exceptional particular instances to false

general premises.

4. The laws which govern human interaction are interwoven with the laws of the ecosphere, are every bit as mysterious, and like the latter, are far too complex to permit regulation of the consequences which proceed from them. Indeed, the affairs of men and of nature are one, and any attempt to unnecessarily regulate either is dangerous. One breech of natural law will produce a distortion which seems to call for yet another breech, and so on. The only way things can be "regulated" in a way consistent with survival on this planet is through a policy of non-interference with nature in the first place.

5. Man is an animal to be sure, but he is also something a bit more than just that. He is sometimes able to admit ignorance and, by his own volition, to develop himself intellectually and spiritually. By contrast, he also possesses the one characteristic which will allow him to deceive himself enough to destroy, first his liberty, then his environment, then himself, and that characteristic is rhetoric.

6. Rhetoric, in contrast to truth, is often used by the average individual to quickly rationalize the "rightness" of inaction relative to involvement in sweeping social change. Action in such areas might of course, interfere with activities of a frivolous nature, or even with pursuits of truly great and enduring human significance like ball games.

7. Congenital traits in human beings result from one of four known causes: heredity, random genetic mutation, intra-uterine conditions, or events during birth.

8. Notice how we refer to a quiet, serene baby as "good," and to a baby who cries all the time, as "bad." These casual labels reveal deeper truths.

9. Environment does not play the part in determining human behavior which many would like to believe. Intrinsic good

moral character will often resist and win out against immoral upbringing in the long term. Sometimes good moral character will even temporarily over react, as in the case of the approach-avoidance conflict, where a cowardly parent will produce a war mongering child or vice versa in the short term, until life teaches maturity and balance.

10. We can all think of people, who from early childhood, manifest true seriousness and wisdom. We can also think of people, who even in advanced age, manifest only frivolity and low self-importance. One already knows much from the time of birth. The other learns almost nothing from a lifetime of experience. In a multi-media culture where we are all bombarded with vast amounts of information, these individual differences do not reflect the influence of environment alone. Let us note that those who think that society can be remade simply by changing peoples' environment for one generation, usually disgrace themselves further by advocating fanatical and un-Libertarian methods.

11. Natural selection is the principle that organisms manifesting physiological or behavioral traits having little survival value, will reproduce at a lesser rate than other organisms since they will not live long enough to do so. This will ultimately cause the trait to die out in the species, unless the particular organisms manifesting the non-surviving traits are given artificial sustenance that will prolong their lives and periods of reproduction.

12. Among non-human species, non-self-sustaining individuals are those, which for any reason, are unable to behave in a way consistent with their own survival in the long term in the context of a natural ecology relatively undisturbed by man. Nature eliminates such creatures through natural selection, and allows evolution to progress. Evolutionary progress depends just as much upon the non-breeding of these individuals, as upon the breeding of self-sustaining individuals.

13. When non-self-sustaining organisms are sustained artificially and end up reproducing when they would not have otherwise, then evolution stops and devolution begins. Devolution is the reversal of evolution. The detriment to evolutionary destiny is even more greatly magnified if the evolutionary expression of self-sustaining organisms is encroached upon in the process.

14. Non-human species on Earth are evolving in directions different from man, and must be allowed to do so normally. Ironically, the primary danger to this occurs as the indiscriminate proliferation of humans begins to reflect man's interference with his own evolution. Allowing a non-human species to evolve normally does not entail finding a way to sustain the weak elements within that species, nor does it consist in murdering their natural predators because of the alleged "cruelty" with which these predators take their prey. It simply involves leaving them alone.

15. Predation of non-human species by man may strengthen or weaken a species, depending upon which members of the species are killed. This in turn, is often determined by the method of predation used. The outdoorsman or professional hunter should contemplate these matters deeply. Should not this ancestral joy in hunting also be available to future generations?

16. Among human beings, non-self-sustaining or unproductive individuals are those who lack the ability for whatever reason, to behave in a way which is consistent with their own survival in the long term under the conditions normally prevailing in a totally free society without having to make unjust encroachment upon other people or the environment.

17. Briefly stated, a self-sustaining or productive member of the human species is simply one who is capable of surviving in a perfectly free society without needing to make unjust incursion against the liberty of others.

18. Nature is able to systematically ascertain non self-sustaining members of animal species and to eliminate them through natural selection. Man is the only animal able to temporarily gainsay nature in this regard, because man is the only species whose unproductive members have ambitious champions possessing rhetoric.

19. It seems that among "nice" or "civilized" people, it is quietly and conveniently forgotten that evolution applies as much to humans as to any other species. Cowardly religions even falsely teach in many cases, that evolution is merely a theory. In actuality man has reached the point on the evolutionary ladder where he not only can, but to survive must, will the direction of his own evolution. This can only be accomplished by working with nature, not against it.

20. Mankind will not survive if societies continue to be subsidized breeding farms for human non self-sustainability. Recognition of this does not mean that anybody needs to go hungry or starve. In a Libertarian Republic all people will live long happy lives. Ongoing sustenance of chronically unemployable people, however, can be provided much more efficiently by means other than coercive government. It is also possible through education to help these people to greatly curb the encroachment they make by excess reproduction.

21. It is important to note that in a collectivist society the number of truly non-self-sustaining people is always far fewer than would appear on the surface. The economic cycle caused by fiat monetary policy pulls down a tremendous number of people to a level of apparent non-self-sustainability. By getting rid of this one simple ecomic policy alone, unemployment would thereafter not exceed one percent except in cases of local catastrophe.

22. It has been empirically proven that, through natural selection, humanity was able to evolve from less complex

forms only because nature offers no sustenance to non-self-sustaining organisms. In man's earlier development he was more at the mercy of nature than today

23. Man has not been able to cheat nature in the longer term. One effect of a warm climate and advancing medical science has been to endlessly thwart natural selection. This has devolved the human species both physically and intellectually. Cro-Magnon Man was not only bigger and stronger than Homo Sapiens, but with an average IQ of 165, was a race of geniuses by comparison. The decline in intelligence which we enjoy today was produced by thirty thousand years of warm weather and easy living preceding the last Ice Age (19).

24. More intelligent people tend towards self-actualization at the expense of procreation. Less intelligent people are outbreeding more intelligent people everywhere (20). The diaries of the Roman Emperor-Historian Claudius show that this trend had become a matter of concern even in the time of Augustus, who spoke publicly about it. The problem is accelerating at a more rapid rate today. The excess proliferation of less intelligent humans must be seen as a direct encroachment against all life on this planet if any reasonable quality of life is to be preserved, or ultimately if humanity itself is to survive (21).

25. Because of the prevalence of collectivist ideas, and man's foolish presumption that he can ignore natural law, unproductive humans are protected from the consequences of their own actions. This allows them to reproduce at a rate which they would not be able to sustain ordinarily. Such people see a large number of children as their insurance policy for old age.

26. Experience has shown that when people are prosperous because of their own activity, as under a Libertarian Capitalist system, that they will restrict their numbers by their own volition. Non-self-sustaining individuals cannot survive

without aid in the short term, or even in the long term, because they will indiscriminately increase their numbers to the point where even their protectors can no longer help them. When this happens, famine will cause far more suffering than would have been the case without protectionist interference in the first place.

27. Legislative measures to restrict birth rates among people at lower achievement levels have been proposed, are well thought out, and are technically workable (22). Of course, if we had Libertarian Capitalist economic systems in place plus education in the schools about the problem of human devolution, such measures would never become necessary. If we are going to do something, however, we had better get on with it, because in just forty more years the population of Earth is going to double.

28. The highest of men on Earth are as much above the lowest, intellectually and spiritually, as the lowest are above the chimpanzees. Those who don't instinctively know this identify themselves as being closer to the low end of the continuum.

29. What an individual learns in a lifetime is to some extent, passed on genetically. The forward progress of evolutionary expression is impeded if productive individuals are kept from learning by being sacrificed for unproductive individuals. Those who work diligently towards the devolution of life on Earth are being masochistic on a cosmic scale. The premise that excellence and evolutionary expression should be even slightly impeded to help sustain mediocrity is the beginning of the worst mistake which humanity could ever make.

30. The intelligent and capable "champion" promoting unjust encroachment by unproductive humanity, is the worst among them, because his inability to behave in a way which is consistent with his own and our survival in the long term, comes not from stupidity, but from moral inferiority. The truth will never reach these individuals, because they simply lack

the capacity to comprehend any concept as exalted as evolutionary destiny

31. It is a pity how vocal are the people who do not "believe" in the empirically proven fact of evolution, but who do endorse more or less evolutionary social policies. Mixing the ridiculous rhetoric of fanatical religiosity with Capitalist economics brings a popular perception of discredit upon economic truth because of guilt by association.

Footnotes:

19. Elmer Pendell, "Why Civilizations Self Destruct" (Howard Allen, Cape Canaveral, 1977). Quite scholarly and well documented. Essential reading for all caring people on Earth.

20. Ibid.

21. If we believe the accounts of alien molestation, it would seem that more advanced peoples have evolved in intelligence, but have devolved physically. Apparently they use human ovi and semen to upgrade themselves physically before they perish from sheer puniness and are doing this without devolving their intelligence because they use genetic engineering rather than simple fertilization.

22. Ibid.

VI. Charity and Welfare

"I celebrate Dr. King's birthday, but for only half of the day.
Half of the time he spoke about rights. I like that.
The other half of the time he spoke about entitlements.
I don't like that." ~ Jack Simons, Vermont ~

1. Good feelings are engendered within through helping others, especially if one has been carefully conditioned since childhood to feel guilt about not doing so.

2. Since it is more blessed to give than to receive, the giver will often betray himself by thus rendering his own person the "more blessed" thereby.

"It is more blessed yet, to earn what one gets and keep it in a totally free society, than either to give or to receive."
~ Dirk the Sun Warrior ~

3. There are those who have said "Live simply so that others may simply live." This well-intentioned but bogus statement is based upon the false idea that there is a limited amount of

wealth in the world. It is also based on the false assumption that quantities in mediocrity are somehow more desirable than smaller numbers in excellence. Evolutionary destiny is served through qualitation, not quantification. Maximum joyful manifestation for smaller numbers is superior to minimum meager manifestation for vast suffering multitudes. Awaken and fight back! We are not imbued with life merely to endure it.

4. The trend in evolution for three and a half billion years has not been towards simplicity and sameness, but towards complexity and diversity in the manifestation of individual organisms.

5. Those who violate natural law usually point to irrelevant, exceptional, or extraordinary examples in their vain attempts at self-justification. While it is important to look at individual instances, this should not be seen as an excuse to blindly disregard what is generally true.

"A few exceptions do not annihilate a mega-trend."
~ Dirk the Sun Warrior ~

6. The "morality" of any action must be judged as much for the effect in the long term as for any short term "intent." Working to alleviate unnecessary suffering for any living thing is a worthwhile and noble task, but only if that is what is really accomplished. Charity has no moral justification if it will increase the need for charity. In that instance, it is effectively a crime against society.

7. Indiscriminate charity usually leads to the perpetuation of traits having no survival value, because it gives artificial sustenance to weakness or degeneracy, and thereby reverses the process of evolution. Often what seems cruel in the short term is kind in the long.

8. Those who refer to the "unfortunate" or "underprivileged" seem completely detached from the idea that, in a relatively

free society, an individual's behavior could possibly have any connection whatsoever with his situation, or that his viability as a life form could possibly have any connection with his behavior.

9. If one form of weakness is allowed to feed at the expense of strength, then this must "logically" be allowed to all forms of weakness. Militant "philanthropy" seeks ultimately to destroy us all with sheer beneficence by undermining the evolutionary destiny of mankind.

10. Whoever originated the idea that it is an obligation, or even a worthwhile goal, for society to use coercion to collectively alleviate human "misery" and the resultant poverty, was one of the first dire enemies of evolving life to appear on Earth.

11. A free society is a society based upon natural order. In a free society unproductive individuals are not sustained at the expense of productive individuals or vice versa. Besides any question of liberty itself, the prosperity and full employment in a Libertarian society render social programs unnecessary in the first place. Ongoing social welfare has never worked anywhere it has been tried. The number of recipients invariably increases, it never decreases. One can help others only by teaching them to help themselves.

12. The riff-raff in any country will invariably seek to vote themselves a free handout at the expense of producing individuals. This will always be referred to as "justice" of some kind. In a country where the injustice of welfare becomes firmly established, members of a more employable group may attempt to keep members of a less employable group from voting because they do not wish to be victimized via the voting booth, through "the right to do wrong." Let us note however, that they choose this method rather than trying to get rid of the injustice of the welfare itself, because even they enjoy stealing from the most productive members of society.

13. There are those who live on welfare who sit in apartments all day watching television while others work. We are told that they are too "discouraged" to work. This discouragement however, never seems to sap their energy enough to prevent many of them from producing four or five children who inherit, are taught, and grow up to manifest this same discouragement.

14. The welfare state has been compared to a mother pig with sucklings. This is a good sentiment, but is actually an insult to baby porkers because, although adult pigs do have disgraceful manners and make the most extraordinary and wonderful sounds when they eat, as a species they are not intrinsically parasitic and eventually outgrow their dependency at a normal age.

15. Self-sustaining individuals who support a system of deficit spending for social welfare will usually do so for one of two reasons. One is that they have been taught the false idea that we can never have economic stability because nobody really knows what causes the business cycles which result in unemployment. The other reason is a simple lack of confidence in the continuity of their own viability. They want the welfare machinery in place to "protect" them in case of emergency. As we know, such "emergency" usually occurs because of the economic cycle, which ironically is caused only by the system of fiat currency used for the deficit spending in the first place.

16. Notice that those who speak overmuch about "brotherhood" in connection with society, often live or seek to live at the expense of others, or at least to earn their living as a champion of those who do.

17. It is astounding how naive is the young brainwashed collectivist who seeks endlessly to find better ways to "use the money" confiscated from those who earn it, as though he doesn't in any way associate money with work - the hours and days of people's lives. How glibly he allocates the hopes

and dreams of others to the "revolution in human consciousness" and in so doing, how foolishly he imagines himself to be "rebelling against the insensitivity of the Establishment." How arrogantly he laughs at those "ignorant reactionaries" who refer to him as a mere "dupe."

18. Whenever one speaks out against the unworkability of welfare in any situation where a noticeable percentage of the recipients happen to be of a particular racial or ethnic group, let us note the almost reflexive reaction of Socialists to make accusations of "bigotry." Character assassination from those who condone government theft at least shows moral consistency.

19. No nation, or the people in it, have ever become prosperous in a climate of moral relativity or because of guilt ridden drones sharing what they earn "in a spirit of brotherhood," but only because of inspired individuals striving for themselves and their families in a climate of individual liberty.

20. The "compassionate" have no moral right to feed the professional hungerers using stolen money, or even earned money, unless reproductive sterilization is made prerequisite to the option of receiving sustenance on a continuing basis. The sustenance option must be offered by private charity, not by government.

21. Be "greedy," but individually. Restrict this normal self-interest only at the point of dishonesty. Demand that your government respect your natural right to liberty. Not only the quality of life, but in the long term, life itself, depends on it.

VII. Society and Apathy

[Warming: chapter is boring because the subject is boring]

1. Anyone who is gainfully employed, self-sustaining, and living in accordance with Libertarian principals is a credit to his country and to the world and should be respected. Nobody should never look down upon another for doing so called "unskilled" work. Most so-called simple jobs require a good deal more knowledge than those in more prestigious positions will ever realize.

2. Why is it that certain very "educated" individuals are so frantic to "elevate the lower classes"? Why make a sad silk purse out of a happy sow's ear? If you change one thing about a person, you will change other things. Teach a simple man the ideas of a genius, and he will want to occupy himself as does a genius. There is only so much room at the top. Interference with natural hierarchy produces distortions. One distortion leads to another, and another. When you bring all of the lower classes into the middle class, who then will do the work of the lower classes? Will you train monkeys to do this? (23).

3. On the average, differences in intelligence only partially account for the great disparity in individual manifestation among human beings. The rest is primarily a function of belief. Marx called religion the "opiate of the masses." Freud said that the practitioners of popular religions need psychoanalytic "help." In the larger view however, we see that fantasy religion is perfectly normal for many people. The freedom to worship is absolutely necessary for a workable society. A proper division of labor depends upon it.

4. Unthinking individuals will make synonymous things that are not. Country, government, and "the people" are not the same thing. Country is a geographically defined area within which exists the potential for absolute individual liberty. Government is that group of subverted collectivist

functionaries in the service of international finance who prevent this liberty from occurring. The "people" are that majority of naive, brainwashed, and deluded individuals who aid and abet government in doing this.

5. Among so called "moderate" and "stable" elements in society (cowardly and apathetic) anyone advocating truly constructive social change will usually be labeled a "radical" or "extremist." Conservatives are usually just people who happen to be doing fairly well under the existing system. Usually they will perceive almost any change, for good or for evil, as a very great risk to their investment portfolios.

6. The naturally apathetic individual is easily conditioned by collectivist government. He has no sense of any inner power to change his own destiny or that of society. He will refuse to believe that anything past, present, or future, is or ever could be, better. Doing so would require him to think or to act. To such an individual, any questioning is seen as "complaining." He would rather be "thankful that things aren't worse." Indeed, there is a certain primitive wisdom in a swaggering and bellicose defense of clearly unworkable policies, if one hasn't the character, the will, or the courage to work for constructive change. Since the natural laziness of apathetic individuals will allow only a slavish rationalization of the present, motivating them quickly to action usually requires emphasizing any obvious short term threat to their precious status quo.

7. A person who is made weak and prone to non-self-blaming by cowardly religion will usually gravitate to collectivist government ideology. The irony here is that natural order depends as much as anything upon the freedom of individuals to manifest spiritually at their own level. The task then is to educate the general populace that ultimately they can have more for themselves as individuals, not by having to better themselves, but simply by supporting a system which in the longer term will make them more prosperous even though it will not allow them to victimize

others. They have to be shown that simply ridding ourselves of the wastefulness of welfare, war-based, fiat-monetary economies will result in a higher standard of living for everybody without having either to work harder or to steal.

8. The collectivist has a slave mentality and yearns to throw away his natural right to liberty with both hands. He will try to justify throwing away yours by speaking to you about your so called obligation to do your "fair share" to help.

9. Minimal human decency is simply the unwillingness to advance oneself unjustly at the expense of another. Minimal patriotic effort is simply this principle applied in the larger arena of one's country. This is absolutely all that is necessary from a small majority of individuals to have a continuing prosperity based upon natural order.

10. Most people "believe" themselves to be patriotic in some degree. We must however, distinguish between the patriotism of "intent" and the patriotism of effect. Patriotism manifests itself tangibly only through activity oriented to making the country a better place, not through blind obedience to leaders or merely singing the country's praises. The only true patriotism is the heroic defense of individual liberty, no matter how many of your countrymen this may put you against. The unpatriotic individual is one who will relentlessly support that which is detrimental to evolutionary destiny and to his country despite reasonably discernible evidence of this detriment.

11. The collectivist will think only of himself, and then only in the very short term. He will rarely think of his country, although any serious questioning of government policy will almost always be angrily regarded as "running down our country" and will often elicit a self-righteous, belligerent exhibition of flag-waving. In this way flags are used as a weapon against any intrusive insights which might inspire the flag-waver to give up unjust advantages given him by government. It also allows him the illusion of great

legitimacy, because he recognizes the "duly constituted authority" in his country as an ally with whom he can more easily intimidate the "eggheads." Don't ever let these cowards take your flag away from you. If, as a caring individual, you can assert that your country has at any time in history ever upheld the ideal of individual liberty, then in the name of that ideal, fly your country's flag proudly over all your proceedings, challenge the cowards' patriotism, and meet their onslaught with an iron fist.

12. The apathetic collectivist will gladly surrender his own liberty and that of his neighbor to anyone promising to relieve him of the need to reason, to plan his future, to assume responsibility for his actions, or in many cases even to earn his own livelihood. Rhetoric in this connection is used by unproductive individuals to justify stealing through government, but even more effectively by the very capable "champion of the underdogs" who rides to power on their backs. It is astounding how openly politicians will represent themselves as the candidate of some special interest group, speaking only about how he will further the "interests" of his supporters, and how seldom they will address simple moral principles like right and wrong.

13. The lower classes oppose Libertarian social policy in the short term because they want giveaway programs. The upper classes in turn, want to finance giveaway programs or at least not to alienate wealthy friends who do. It is mainly middle class people who want to earn what they get and to keep it in a free society. The struggle is not one of the rich exploiting the poor as is popularly believed, but of the rich exploiting sympathy for the poor and throwing them a few crumbs while using taxation to rob the middle class, thus keeping them from competing as they would in a truly free society.

14. A good balance between labor and management exists when the number in the labor force is relatively small enough so that the laws of market will allow them individually, or in

small groups, to command a decent wage. When such a balance is achieved however, there usually follows a large influx of immigrants seeking the "good life." This in turn changes the supply of labor relative to demand. Management starts paying lower wages. Labor starts organizing unions and screaming for Socialist government benefits. If we can get most countries Libertarian all at one time, then every nation will begin to prosper simultaneously. People will not want to immigrate, and a natural balance between labor and management will prevail everywhere because it will be determined smoothly by the laws of stable market instead of erratically by influx.

15. Any individual who believes that he has the right to ask government to coerce from his employer the wage which he dictates as being fair, simply does not believe in a free enterprise system. A fair wage is the highest wage which a worker can negotiate, and the lowest which an employer can get away with paying, in a totally free society.

16. Keeping in mind that there is only so much room at the top, those of us who work for natural order simply want to see upward mobility occur because of natural ability and personal effort rather than because of institutionalized plunder.

17. Immoral individuals with ambition seek crude power over or through others because they haven't the depth or character to seek and find power within themselves. Those with enough capability to act as effective crusaders for unproductive people against the producing elements in society are adept at appealing to men's lowest motives and are usually not above making use of popular prejudices as part of their strategy. This can be done in many ways, but in today's more "enlightened" atmosphere, can be done by subtly imputing "prejudice" to one's adversaries, especially among naive young "revolutionaries" advocating "justice." This type of attack is strangely one of the most widely used,

but little recognized, tricks employed by collectivist governments against individual liberty.

18. Liberty, in its true sense, subconsciously scares the collectivist because it threatens him with facing up to the long term consequences of his own decisions. Being subconsciously aware that he has no personal integrity, he is also unable to trust his own judgment. His ideas frighten him and he will seek to validate perceptions almost exclusively by consensus rather than logically with facts. Add to this the fact that mass opinion is mainly created by individuals seeking low worldly power through the flattery, manipulation, and harnessing of the collectivist tendency towards short term, dishonest, and acquisitive thinking, and we have a mass of people who will "believe" almost anything their masters tell them. These are simply the dynamics of carefully manipulated mob rule.

19. Relative to "greed," humanity is normal as it is, even though it does not conform to latter day ideas of "perfection" which are usually held as a defense against one's own weaknesses, as a way of masking one's own motives, or as a means to instilling guilt in others so that they can be more easily exploited.

20. Perfect unity and uniformity of will are not characteristics of human societies, but of beehives and ant colonies. Society is not a single organism, will prosper only if individuals prosper individually, and must be based on the way that people really are, not on the way that fools think people should be.

21. To rob a person of the quality of his life is very little different from robbing him of life itself. The only incentive for hard work that any normal individual will have is the confident expectation that he and his loved ones will be able to enjoy the full fruits of his labor. Any society which slowly kills this natural expectation of just reward in the individual by always sacrificing him for the group is inevitably doomed

to failure. Ultimately the group is nothing more than an aggregation of individuals. If you hurt either one, you hurt both.

22. It is perfectly natural for individuals to be motivated exclusively in their own interest. This is the way of things in the world of actualities. Governments not structured on this premise will never prosper. Entrepreneurs must not be seen as "criminals" for operating their businesses on the profit principle rather than the philanthropic. Capitalism is the only system which has ever worked, ever can work, or ever will work because it is the only system which is based upon going with natural laws instead of against them.

Footnote:

23. A bit more joking here ~ Will the monkeys be the new lower class? Who will replace them in the trees? What will the elevated spending power of monkeys do to the price of bananas? How will this affect the slash-and-burn rate of rain forest clear cutting? How will this affect the ozone layer and global warming? How quickly will this cause the melting of the Polar ice caps? How high will the oceans rise? Will the "tongues of perdition" come out of the Pacific to cleanse San Francisco as so many now believe?

VIII. Government and Collectivism

The False Premise of Collectivism

1. In the world at large, good seems to be more organized and more in control than evil simply because the popular notion of good is on the surface of the social structure. "Good intentions," greed, and ignorance determine the destiny of nations because they determine collective action. Human nature cannot be changed, but social action can be. Only mass education can accomplish this.

2. Evil operates on the "I only" principle. Good operates on the "I, but also you" principle. Collectivism is evil and is based upon the "I only" principle disguised as the "We" principle and the "We" is always coercive.

3. The only workable first premise in any society is that of absolute individual liberty. All else must be subordinated to this or the society will slowly degenerate or remain degenerate if it is already. The only truly free and workable system known to man is a Libertarian society with an Capitalist economy.

4. All forms of collectivism are contrary to the laws of evolution and the laws of market. All lasting prosperity and progress that has ever been achieved has been due to the extent to which the society involved has been free. All failure and stagnation have been due to collectivist control of some kind.

5. Lurking at the heart of most false ideas which find popular acceptance is the irony that, in the smaller view of things or in the very short term, they are often "true" ideas.

The Myth of Left and Right

1. "We will produce a new generation of change, and a lot of change for a new generation. We will generate change, and we will change a generation" babbles the golden-boy collectivist candidate inanely.

"All this 'gridlock' stuff is horse manure. Both left and right are serving the bankers. Neither side is advocating a return to a precious metal standard. When I was a kid, anyone with a sixth grade education knew that a metal backed currency is necessary to a stable economy. When in Hell are we going to move against these God-damned traitors?" asks Dirk the Sun Warrior as he eagerly fondles a hangman's noose.

2. The only difference between "Socialist" and "Fascist," between "left" and "right," are their respective preferences for collectivist interference in what would otherwise be a naturally ordered and workable society. The term Democracy today has become a mere euphemism for the shared, but endlessly embattled, alternating dictatorship of left and right wing thugs in business suits.

3. In a collectivist society, left and right produce the "see-saw effect." First the left pulls the country down, while the right goes up in public opinion. Then the right pulls the country down while the left goes up in public opinion. Let us observe that the only thing which goes up is public opinion in the short term. The only thing which goes down is the country over the long term. Some have called this the "Decline of Western Civilization." The rate of this decline is accelerating rapidly.

4. Among the general populace, left and right in essence want government henchmen with guns to enforce unjust advantage in their behalf. A Libertarian is simply what any reasonably intelligent left or right wing individual might aspire to be with more education and higher moral development.

5. The fundamental reason most people will support a collectivist government is that they believe it will benefit them individually more than a truly free society. This is always at the expense of others. There is however, the sometimes just idea about getting even financially for past exploitation. If we go Libertarian right now, it is reasoned, money owed from the past won't get paid back, so we have to have a little more of the opposite brand of collectivism to balance accounts. Then it has to go the other way, and then back again. This is another aspect of the "see-saw effect." If cognizant of the long term bad effect of collectivist policies upon even themselves, most people would not support such a system. Education can accomplish Libertarian goals without a complete moral remake of society. Those who have been unduly victimized thus far will ultimately be compensated much more completely, and in an ongoing way, by the advantages of a stable economy.

6. The fact that most who favor economic liberty want civil slavery, and vice versa, shows us that a person's politics are usually a product of emotion, not of logic. Economic and civil liberty are not mutually exclusive, but actually work best in conjunction with each another. When people begin to think clearly, rather than just reacting immorally to the equally immoral reactions of their adversaries, then a true ongoing liberty will be able to flourish, rather than merely a short term partisan illusion of liberty.

Who Determines Values?

1. Candidates for public office will often try to obscure the real issues by saying things which are admirable and true, but which somehow do not quite ring true coming from their lips.

"All of this 'family values' bullshit makes me sick to my stomach. These parasites don't care about families. They have caused and financed both sides of every war in the past two hundred years" observes Dirk the Sun Warrior as he inspects a big family size bag of quicklime at the local hardware store.

2. A lot of high sounding talk about the importance of family values, although perfectly true, is somehow particularly offensive, and does seem to be pushing luck a bit, coming the worst enemies that families have ever known - mere traitors who have served the interests of those responsible for the destruction of more families than anyone else in all of human history.

3. It is not the business of government to instill values in the individual citizen, except a deep and abiding knowledge relative to the natural workability of absolute individual liberty, and that preferably only by example.

Equality Under Law

1. It is not a legitimate function of government to provide a livelihood for the citizens. The equal chance to succeed guaranteed in a free society should not be confused with the equal "success" guaranteed in some measure by a collectivist society. The former works in the long term, the latter does not. Government is not supposed to "help" people, but to create and preserve an environment within which people can help themselves.

2. Government never generates new wealth, although it almost always coerces wealth away from those who do. It is never a provider of anything, its victims are. When "benefits" are gained, liberty is lost. Whatever is subsidized by government will eventually be controlled or regulated by it. Government is at best a necessary evil and the less of it we have, the better. The primary goal of Libertarian Nationalist Revolution is simply to privatize as many activities as possible which are now allocated to government.

3. There is absolutely nothing which is immoral for an individual to do, which is not equally or more immoral for

government to do. This includes theft and extortion. Government policy is supposed to reflect the calm deliberation of many minds, not dishonesty numerically multiplied behind the shield of unaccountability afforded by power.

4. In today's climate of moral decay, election to political office does not require promising the people a country in which they can have the freedom to work and keep what they earn as it once did. It requires promising to give them what someone else earns. Today if people give their vote they want something "concrete" in return. This is euphemistically called "politics." For a person to give someone a vote on the promise that he will enlist government thugs to coerce money from others is no different than if the voter were to coerce the money himself. For a person to use his vote to steal, renders him morally no better than the man who would come through a second story window at three o'clock in the morning with a crowbar and a gunny sack, except that the man with the crowbar has more courage, self-knowledge, and personal integrity.

5. Just because an individual feels that the poor "can't help" the way they are, doesn't give him the moral right to use a voting booth to allocate the resources of another to his dream of the way the world "should" be. Observe that the Socialist "loves" everyone, but advocates what seems best for himself in the short term. The Libertarian loves mainly those near and dear, but advocates what is workable for all in the long term.

6. If two men are equal, and one by his own efforts "betters" himself, then he becomes "better" than the other man who did nothing, unless there are in this instance, two meanings for the word "better." Equality under law should not be confused with equality of individual human viability. Although all men must receive equal, fair, and impartial treatment under law, it is not government's job to cheat nature or to

eliminate the deserved consequences of bad moral character.

7. The single most detrimental assumption which is commonly held by humankind today is that all men are "entitled" to be well fed, regardless of what they do or do not do individually to bring about this condition, and regardless of the detrimental effect upon those who are victimized in their behalf. Augmenting this myth is the idea that it is somehow desirable, obligatory, or moral for productive individuals to provide for ever increasing numbers of unproductive individuals. This in turn, has everywhere led to the further assumption that people have the right to collectively coerce the productive individual in order to bring about this utopian "equality." Such ideas have inevitably led to increasingly unstable war and welfare based economies everywhere.

8. If a person is not being supported financially by others, he is not being kept down. If he objects to such non-support, he is seeking to be kept up. Let there be no institutional theft, so that anyone can be kept at the expense of another, and let those who try to gain unjustly what is not theirs be kept neither down, nor up, but simply apart, from those whose behavior has survival value in a free society.

Taxation is Theft

1. Government wealth redistribution for any reason constitutes mandatory charity, and in the long term has the same devolutionary results because it sustains human weakness. Effectively it brings human excellence down to a level of mediocrity in order to elevate human rottenness up to a level of mediocrity.

2. Taxation of any kind is wealth redistribution because it allows use of government services out of proportion to payment for that use. User fees do not have this effect, nor do lotteries of designated purpose. Lotteries are simply a

more generalized form of user fee, because they are funded voluntarily by those supporting the particular policy paid for by the lottery.

3. Taxation is theft. There is no justification for it whatsoever and there never has been. It was long ago established that all legitimate government services can be paid for directly by those utilizing them, in direct proportion to that use, just as in the private sector. User fees are not theft because they are not taken at gun point the way taxes are.

4. Government has only one legitimate function: to provide redress when people unjustly assault, coerce, defraud, or encroach upon each other or the environment to the detriment of any living thing. This function is performed by military, judicial, and correctional branches at the federal, state, and local levels.

"All this Socialist hair splitting about who owns the means of production is a big steaming kettle of pig crap cooked up to keep people talking so they won't think. If government can exact at gun point any part of what you earn, then who owns the business, you or your silent partner?" inquires Dirk the Sun Warrior as he toys expertly with his consecrated war dagger, Liberator.

5. He who would tax you commands that you not only acquiesce in your own servitude but that you actively participate in the devolution of your own species.

6. To permit taxation in a free society is the exact equivalent of introducing disease into a healthy body. Well informed rational people would never do either.

7. Unlimited power to borrow and tax leads to unlimited spending and growth in the size of government. It becomes like The Blob - "The more it eats, the bigger it gets. The bigger it gets, the more it eats. It's already sniffin after ya, an one o' these days it's gonna catch up with ya !"

"It may be very difficult in a collectivist society to disseminate truth without being harassed. In most countries it is smarter for now to pay all of your taxes and keep very clear and simple records. The day will come when we will have it back a thousand fold because those who rob us now, in the end, will polish our shoes" foretells Dirk the Sun Warrior.

8. Government agencies in a collectivist society usually reach a point where they begin to exceed their authority. They develop lives of their own with agendas of their own, often in conflict with each other, usually in conflict with individual liberty. Only the unlimited flow of stolen funds an allow this.

9. The collectivist has an endless faith in the ability of government to make everything better, although he often curses "those crooked politicians" individually. It is power over others which creates all social problems. It never solves them. Other than the organized military, judicial, and correctional defense of individual liberty, there is no legitimate activity currently allocated to government anywhere that cannot be performed better and more efficiently by free and inspired individuals in the private sector than by regulated and lethargic bureaucrats.

10. It is not government's place to play the puppet master by trying to "motivate" people with tax "incentives" or incentives of any kind, except towards the preservation of liberty. It should be appreciated that any amount of taxation provides a disincentive towards work for the victim, while at the same time providing an increasing incentive for inactivity to the recipient.

11. The equivalent of a naturally balanced ecology in the sphere of human relationships is possible only in a Libertarian republic. Under such a system, all incentives, sanctions, deterrents, and rewards, either of a social or of an economic nature, are determined by the natural laws of supply and demand, rather than by pompous bureaucrats

whose only activity is the interference in the activity of others. These agents of impediment usually are what they are simply because they haven't the courage, the character, or in many cases the basic ability necessary to succeed as entrepreneurs.

Protectionism Doesn't Work

1. The protectionist wants us all to be "safe" - at any cost. He has forced manufacturers to make power lawnmowers so safe that retarded children (?) can use them without hurting themselves. The only problem is that they no longer cut grass unless the owner spends an hour or two with a hammer, chisel, and hack saw removing fifty dollars-worth of unnecessary mandatory safety equipment, invalidating his warranty in the process. All of this, multiplied by millions of lawnmowers, is only a minor consideration to be sure, now that we are all "safe."

2. In a perfectly safe society we would all be legally required to remain in bed while being fed intravenously by government, because if we got up and went outside we might "hurt" ourselves. If the world is made perfectly safe, so that the individual never experiences any of the consequences of his own actions, then natural selection is blocked and evolution stops.

3. The next time that you are awakened at two in the morning and can't get back to sleep because of the loud beeping two miles away when the snow plow backs up, just fall upon your knees and give thanks for the fact that the great legions of blind people out walking in the blizzard are "safe."

4. The collectivist wants government to compel hotel owners everywhere to change their hot and cold water faucets to mixing valves so that nobody can get scalded. Any plumber will tell you that on most hot water supply heaters there is one control that will regulate hot water temperature to all the

faucets. Is there anywhere a hotel where the water is hot enough to get even a decent shave, let alone to scald protectionists? Underlying all this "concern" for peoples' safety, of course, is the desire to increase deficit spending to fund periodic government inspections of hotels. Recent history has shown us that it's always best whenever possible to view human interactions as contracts between individuals. If we think of the right not to be scalded while showering, as an implied warrantee granted by hotel owners, then someone who is scalded can simply sue for damages. This provides the hotel owner with a natural free market incentive to make the proper temperature adjustments. No government deficit spending needed here.

5. Countries with no highway speed limits have fewer accidents because the expectation of higher impact on collision increases caution. We can think of bad accidents as contractual relationships between skilled drivers who accept the increased risk of greater speed, and inept individuals who are weeded out by their own stupidity. Those who have to clean up afterwards are paid for what they do, so who can logically object? We understand that in this example that "fast" does not mean reckless. Those who object here are the lazy people who don't want the added responsibility of extra caution which sometimes comes with increased individual liberty.

6. Statistics are worthwhile only when they serve truth, not when they allow mediocrity to fester at the expense of excellence. The less time one spends on mundane activities, like going from one place to another, the higher will be this individual's evolutionary expression. Those who attempt to justify low arbitrary speed limits always point to the number of lives saved. Some have even advocated banning automobiles altogether so that no lives will be lost. None have yet computed the total number of man-hours lost with lower speed limits because of individuals having to take longer going from one place to another. This lost time is also lost life, because time is what life is made up of. The amount

and quality of this life certainly exceeds that of the few inept sluggards who are culled naturally by an environment with higher risks.

"High performance lifestyles needn't be hampered by low performance thinking" proclaims Dirk the Sun Warrior robustly, as he masterfully wheels his 911 Porsche through the treacherous High Kancamagus on the way to Mount Cranmore for a splendid day of skiing.

7. Foreign business ownership should never be allowed in any country. Items offered in world markets should be produced solely within each country by the citizens of that country. No nation, however, should try to dictate product choice to the buyer. Some claim to be more patriotic because they advocate forced buyer choice. They feel that the worker is more important than the consumer, but the consumer is usually also a worker, and has the right to buy the best product, at the best price he can get, in a competitive free world market. Good intentions are praiseworthy, but people should read first, then advocate workable rather than destructive policies. Notice how many of these individuals never want to get rid of government handouts which necessitate fiat currency, causing the economic upheaval and trade deficits which hurt workers in the first place.

8. In business, simple dishonesty and the desire for government enforced monopoly often hides behind high sounding rhetoric about "protecting the public." A good example is the real estate business. Years ago any reasonably intelligent person could broker a real estate transaction without any special training at all. Even now attorneys often handle the legalities. Originally the requirement for a license was merely a way of collecting a user fee so that brokers as a group would justly pay the court costs for the disproportionate amount of litigation which accrues to real estate practice. Then came the rise of certain "professional" organizations comprised of well-established

prosperous brokers. First they established special codes of "ethics" in order to seem very moral and public spirited. Next we see them offering their support to politicians who then sponsor legislation enacting strict licensing requirements with ridiculously difficult exams to "protect the public from curbstone brokers" or to protect "leading citizens from unfair outside competition." These exams of course, did not apply retroactively to those already licensed. Some will argue that the increasing complexity of laws renders necessary a higher degree of training for brokers. In actuality this very complexity itself only represents other unjust interferences by government in parallel areas of human endeavor. It is simply not a legitimate function of government in a free society to regulate business in any way other than to outlaw and prosecute clearly fraudulent practices.

9. There has been a lot of phony talk recently about tobacco use. We have always known that nicotine is addictive. It is the only reason people smoke. Since tars do not enhance the pleasure given by nicotine, but are also very unhealthful, then obviously the most "safe" cigarette would be a high nicotine, low tar cigarette, any way that this can be produced. For tobacco companies to be put on the defensive about all this is just another way that government servants of international finance seek to increase deficit spending for government regulation of individual behavior. The only just ban on smoking would be indoors in all public places, at the base of occupied buildings, near gas pumps, around oil refineries, etc.

10. What smart people should not do, and what government should outlaw, are two very different things. It is not a legitimate function of government in a free society to dictate to anybody about what they can ingest into their own body. The one exception would be any substance taken in any amount expected from experience to always make the user likely to endanger others. There are very few such substances. All potentially unhealthful products of course, should proclaim themselves with proper labels.

11. A person cannot effectively love others if he does not first love himself. Using government coercion to keep adults from reaping the just consequences of their own weakness is a direct and unforgivable interference with evolutionary destiny because it interferes with natural selection. It is better to let these weak elements destroy themselves any way they can, so that those left will be the stronger, more rational people truly capable of loving both themselves and others.

Liberty Differentiated from Democracy

1. Nine bums in an alley can democratically reach a majority decision to relieve an approaching wage earner of his wallet, but that doesn't make it right or just. Somewhere along the way the terms liberty and Democracy became thought of as synonymous. They are not. Democracy is majority rule. If most people in a Democracy want slavery, then everybody will have to suffer under it. The fear of liberty is cowardice. The prevention of liberty is criminal despite "intent." A Democracy not based upon Libertarian principals is nothing more than a dictatorship of the morally inferior.

2. Implementation of natural order cannot occur unless the average individual in society has at least a rudimentary understanding of what works in the long term and what does not. Democracy can succeed in the long term only if there is a strong base of constitutional law based on Libertarian Capitalist principles. Such constitution must be the supreme law of the land and subject to none but literal interpretation. Without this there is only the immoral consensus of the mob.

3. "The only way that majority rule will be workable, is if the majority, as a rule, are willing to work." A Libertarian republic is essentially a Democracy enhanced by a Libertarian constitution, and functions with people being exactly what they are, in precisely the same way that a Democracy without such a constitution would function if most of the people were of the highest moral character.

4. In a totally free society the right to vote allows one to indicate his choice as to who can best manage things in accordance with known Libertarian principles. In a non-Libertarian Democracy the right to vote allows one to indicate his opinion as to how things might best be mismanaged in accordance with any of several competing unworkable collectivist theories. In a Libertarian society a vote is an expression of trust in a candidate's competence and honesty, rather than an expression of the voter's ideas about how to make policy, which would almost always be tainted by ignorance.

5. Representatives in a Democracy rule only by popular consent. It is important to vote Libertarian. The individual can at this stage however, do more to promote Libertarian revolution with an occasional letter to an incumbent representative than he can ever do merely by voting. Politicians know that for every dissatisfied voter who writes, there are five hundred who don't. Act now. In the USA: "All that is necessary for the triumph of evil liberals and conservatives is that good Libertarians do nothing." (24)

6. Among the profane it is proclaimed that "If you are not liberal when you are young, you have no heart. If you are not conservative when you are old, you have no brain." Among the wise it is remarked that "If you are not Libertarian when both young and old, you have neither a heart nor a brain."

7. It is power over others which results in unworkable societies. The true Libertarian candidate is not seeking power either for himself or for "the people." He is seeking to put an end to anyone having unjust or unnecessary power over anybody else.

The Atavistic Berserker, Dirk the Sun Warrior, yearns now only for the final conflict, that he may perish heroically after drenching himself in the blood of the vile enemies of our lives and liberty. "If I can't have total individual liberty by Democratic means, then I will have it any way I can get it, even if it has to be over the dead bodies of all those who serve darkness!" Let us hope that the founding of Libertarian societies by democratic means will soon relieve Dirk of these feelings.

8. The short term vested interests now opposing worldwide liberty will eventually fall because their ideologies have no internal coherency or long term workability, and as such, constitute mere technical elements to be eliminated before the inevitable triumph of truth and justice. Because of the rapidly escalating consequences accruing to past mistakes however, we do not have the luxury of patiently waiting for people to slowly awaken. Conditions necessitate their immediate awakening. The one and only thing that can accomplish this is for courageous people to develop an active and imaginative commitment to the principles of Libertarian Nationalist Revolution, right now.

Footnote:

24. This reworked quotation was communicated by the author to a certain luminary of the Libertarian Party in 1988. Apparently this chap forgot our conversation and rediscovered the idea on his own, because he later credits himself with it on the cover of a party publication. Imitation, of course, is the sincerest form of flattery. In 1994 a copy of this entire book was sent to this same individual...

IX. Opponents and Strategies

1. When making judgments about the morality of others, always first project yourself into their circumstances, whether these circumstances are more desperate or less desperate than your own. Then, ask yourself honestly how you would behave. Then, in a further empathy, appreciating the differences between yourself and the other person, again contemplate the appropriateness of their behavior. Not just you in their shoes, but them in their shoes. In this way one can avoid allowing zeal to become fanaticism fed by unnecessary self-congratulation.

2. The only true enemy an individual can have is one who would make encroachment against individual liberty. All others, regardless of how peculiar, obnoxious, or tiresome, should be perceived as friends of varying degree, or at least as allies.

3. There are those who foolishly label fighting back as "negative." If, in the process of building a house, every night enemies come and tear down three quarters of the work, it can only be construed as positive to stop them, if indeed one's goal is to someday finish the house. This must apply also to the enemies who continually tear down the building of a completely free society.

4. In daily living, before a person can help others, he must first help himself. If a person behaves rightly, he does so as well in destroying if necessary, any who would encroach upon him. One can lead a moral and happy life only if one survives in liberty.

5. Natural feelings will not produce guilt in right thinking individuals. It is perfectly natural to desire the elimination of one's true enemies. We may however, take a good deal upon ourselves in attempting this. The core goal here is only to eliminate the problems caused us by the enemy. This can

be accomplished three ways: by conversion of the enemy to an ally, through his isolation, or through his destruction.

6. Destruction should be caused or applauded only reluctantly, and then only when it will produce evolutionary progress and is the only possible alternative (25).

7. Only social masochists nurture unpleasant emotions within themselves. Feeling hatred is unpleasant and is physically unhealthful. Like any other unproductive emotion, hatred should never be nurtured to any degree whatsoever.

8. A capable human being would not hate an animal for endangering him, nor should he hate a less capable human being for doing the same. In either case, they are doing the only thing they can do.

9. One man's capability has little tangible reality except in terms of another man's incapability. The more capable man should not therefor, resent the existence of the less capable man. He should however, resent their excess and ever increasing numbers.

10. It has been said "the pen is mightier than the sword." Sometimes it is, sometimes it isn't. But why must we choose? Use your pen when you can, use your sword when you must. One can only educate the educable.

"All government policy is enforced ultimately at gun point. A person who will vote for any policy which encroaches upon individual liberty is effectively committing an act of aggression against society and is just as much an enemy of that society as any soldier in an invading army. He is however, an enemy that one would want to convert, at least to an ally, since he is also a countryman and possibly even a relative. We can't kill everybody!" reasons Dirk the Sun Warrior benignly as he examines a young olive branch.

11. Conversion of an enemy into an ally is done through education. In discussion, until another clearly demonstrates his level of development, it is usually best to adopt a posture facilitating mutual exchange, with the emphasis upon learning, not upon teaching. Even a militant jackass can teach many things if one listens.

12. It is well to remember that even in revolution, there are areas of emphasis which may be more appropriate to one personality type or another, or to one gender or the other. Discussion which leads to personal discord or unhappiness at home is counter-productive, not only to individuals but to the Quest itself. Work of this exalted nature is on a wholly different plane from interpersonal relationships. One need not discuss anything relating to any of this with a lover, or even a spouse, if it will cause personal difficulties of any kind. One must try to live the Libertarian ideal at home even as one works to actualize it on a worldwide basis.

"The key to Libertarian understanding is to put the pig on the shelf and let the human within oneself address the human within others. If, within the other person, only the pig will address you, then try talking to someone else."
~ Dirk the Sun Warrior ~

13. Talk is usually an imperfect medium for communicating truth. Often there are too many other things going on. For instance, with an urgently argumentative chap, is he perhaps striving so very hard for himself because you remind him subconsciously of a neighbor's child who used to periodically chase him around behind the garage, and mercilessly pinch him, until he screamed with a bright red face when he was only three?

14. The argumentative individual will be frantic to interrupt when another is talking. He will begin "reacting" immediately, often on the basis of massive stereotype, to what he wants you to be saying. He will jump down your throat saying "but, but, but..." before you can utter the second part of a

sentence which would mitigate the first part. Then you have to retrace and patiently explain that you were not saying any of the things which he falsely attributed to you. Conversation with such individuals, unjustly puts you on the defensive, is unnecessarily time consuming, and should be avoided.

15. Even though most people spend little or no time actively seeking new facts which might qualify their overall perspective, they will stubbornly believe that their basic view of the world is totally correct. They could not sleep at night if they didn't. While the average person will quickly defer to a specialist in matters of technology, if you seek to alter someone's basic view about society, attempt it slowly without unnecessary insult, and you may gain an ally rather than an enemy. Remember that non-Libertarians have absolutely no idea of how ignorant they are and the goal here is not personal enhancement, but the triumph of liberty over corruption.

16. When advancing truth among the ignorant, it is often best to state only facts and allow them draw their own conclusions. The inference that others will derive from given data will depend upon their goals, which in turn will depend upon their personal spiritual development. The status of a person's knowledge can be changed easily, but changes in their basic development must come slowly from within. If you state a conclusion first, the other person may react strongly against it and will be in the position of losing face to admit their error when you start citing factual instances which prove the conclusion.

17. Give others the chance to make true, perceptive, Libertarian statements, and when they do, be just as ready to agree with and elaborate upon their ideas as you are to disagree and correct them when they are speaking erroneously.

18. The un-Libertarian individual usually knows at some level that his attitudes are morally inferior. Show him this subtly,

without anger or discourtesy. Let him keep a veneer of intellectual and moral dignity and you may win his allegiance.

19. When thrown by fate into discussions with doggedly un-Libertarian elements, avoid defending justice to them, except casually, and then not for its own sake, but for its sole workability for them in the shortest term demonstrable. Subtly keep them on the defensive for perpetuating injustice. Leave them angry with themselves, but not in any way that can allow them to blame anyone but themselves. Never be personal with such individuals, but avoid any unnecessary "ivory tower" remoteness which might lead oneself to being dismissed as a mere "intellectual."

20. Respectful truth-seeking people will listen with an open mind to what others say, and will treat each individual as a new person. Such people may seek to persuade others to their viewpoint, but will use only facts and logic to do this. Those striving only for appearances will use authority, browbeating, pettiness, pedantry, glib negative summary, forced belly-laughter, and insult. They will often try to intimidate by moving closer than is normally considered polite, or by raising their voice. When their arguments are defeated logically they will often quickly proclaim their "right" to their opinion, as though to imply that you are somehow being aggressively dogmatic to disagree, and that their opinion is therefore, "right." Individuals of this sort are people of little commitment to anything of value, and should not be taken seriously either as intellectual or as moral entities, regardless of their degree of formal education or popular reputation.

21. Morally inferior individuals never seek true wisdom, only the appearance of wisdom. They usually care little about truthfulness, scholarship, merit, achievement, earning, worthiness, decency, or honor. They will invariably substitute self-serving philosophy for facts and will use every rotten little coward trick and logical fallacy they can muster to twist

the truth. It seems that to "win" is all important to such individuals.

22. When speaking, especially about serious topics, never use "obvious" exaggeration for effect. The enemies of truth will always interpret what you say literally when it suits their purpose. Be exact. If you mean "some," don't say "most."

23. Only a petty individual will react strongly against something which is not a measurable threat to individual liberty. Over-reacting to something which one deems "part and parcel of a certain mentality" will usually produce an equally hysterical counter reaction from the insultee. Much of the immorality of both left and right lies in the tendency of petty individuals to think of themselves as the embodiment of all goodness. Clarity of understanding will occur only when the individual begins to differentiate what is actually an encroachment from what is merely a matter of personal taste.

24. Should you inadvertently cast pearls before swine, let this slip quickly from your mind. Pearls are not tarnished by swine, nor can they be misused effectively, because they are simply not recognized as pearls.

25. Deep awareness about the workability of Libertarian policy will at times seem like a great intellectual burden which one must set down by educating society. Strangely though, at other times, it can lead one to feel "overly unburdened" in a more personal sense relative to others, because of what their ignorance does to their lives. The key here is not to feel that you necessarily have to assume the burden of unburdening them on a one to one basis, if they are only going to make you feel sorry that you tried. If you find that you have a low threshold of tolerance for people who insult you merely for speaking the truth, it may be better to find another way to educate them. If the hour spent talking with one person is instead spent writing a letter to the editor of a magazine with a circulation of three hundred thousand

readers, the benefit produced is multiplied accordingly. This also gives you the chance to do necessary research, and to think through and hone the clarity of your statements.

26. In or near one's own community it is better to be well liked than otherwise. Sometimes it is smarter to fight the good fight a bit further from home.

27. When confronted in conversation with true evil in it's most subtle forms, be calmly oriented to helping the individual gain insight into the disadvantages of his path. Think quickly; be subtle, impersonal, positive, just, forceful, and cool.

28. A sincere Libertarian should never allow himself to be put on the defensive unnecessarily about the morality of his values by any collectivist. For a Libertarian to condone moral criticism from any Socialist, for example, especially if the tone is vicious or disrespectful, the language nasty or slanderous is the exact equivalent of a loving husband permitting similar criticism from a serial rapist who just finished with his wife. There is simply no spiritual integrity in tolerating these elements any longer. Keep tract of them and deal with them covertly. Make a list. Take your time. Be very objective and completely just. If there is any question of any lower personal motivation on your part, do nothing until the question in clearly resolved without false rationalization.

29. It is foolish to engage an enemy that one cannot individually defeat. To do so openly is suicidal. One must after all, live to fight another day.

30. A true gentleman (one who has lived in accordance with Libertarian ideals) needn't worry about giving his enemy a "fair" fight, as "between gentlemen." If the enemy were himself either fair, or a gentleman, there would be no bone of contention in the first place. When you are the victim don't let the enemy dictate the terms of your reprisal.

"When dealing with lambs, behave as a kindly shepherd. When dealing with rats, study and master the technique of the barn owl." ~ Dirk the Sun Warrior ~

31. Those who would contemplate the destruction of an enemy should first determine with absolute certainty whether those who will replace him might prove to be an equal or even worse enemy. This should be balanced against the level of risk and the effect of the enemy's possible martyrdom upon the popularly perceived morality of either movement. Usually it is more productive and can be more satisfying to see the day when the enemy and all of his vile crew are devoid of power. This may require patience and can best be accomplished by making others aware of the enemy and the true long term effect of his actions upon their lives.

Footnote:

25. Of course, dealing with an enemy can be deeply satisfying. The author recalls an acquaintance who was badly beaten and made to watch while his girlfriend was raped by four thugs. He didn't involve the police in any way. When he finally caught up to the leader, he killed him with a baseball bat. An approximate quote: "I split his head open just like an egg. He fell forward and his brain came out onto the ground. It was unexpectedly large. I said aloud to myself, "How could such a smart man have thought that he could get away with raping my girlfriend?"

X. Solutions and Implementation

Excess Population

> "Hell is other people."
> ~ Jean Paul Sartre ~

1. Those urging us to disregard titanic natural forces claim that we can keep ourselves from long-term consequences by modifying all short-term symptomatic effects through "regulation." This is like fooling with the salt content of a tulip bed near an ocean dike as you begin to feel the spray from a five-hundred-foot tidal wave ten miles away.

2. Most people's behavior seems founded on the assumption that, because man is able to exert a certain amount of control over his environment in the short term, that he can blindly disregard the laws of nature - that science will always compensate for man's unwillingness to control his destiny. Man's plans for the long term have to be based, within the realms of reason, upon his existing technology, not upon blind faith in science to produce last minute emergency solutions.

3. Every living organism needs a certain life space within which to manifest and actualize separately from others. People are not an exception to this.

4. Carefully controlled scientific experiments with animal species have shown that merely increasing population within a given space, with all other factors remaining constant, will cause a sharp rise in all types of behavioral aberration including sexual perversion, arbitrary violence, cannibalism, and starvation death from catatonia. "People are not animals" argue the enemies of their own evolutionary destiny - and everybody else's.

5. The ideal population on Earth was passed around the year 900 A.D, if by "ideal" we mean a level consistent with concepts like individual self-actualization and opulent joy in living, rather than mere subsistence in anguished mediocrity. Common sense reveals that the ideal population for any sovereign nation is to have just enough people to easily sustain a volunteer military capable of defending the borders. The ideal total number of people for a planet the size of Earth is 320 million. All nations should immediately begin programs to reduce their populations to ideal levels.

6. No matter what else man accomplishes, if he does not immediately deal with the problem of increasing population, nothing else he does will matter.

7. The very great and rapidly increasing number of non-self-sustaining humans constitutes the primary obstacle to the triumph of liberty over collectivism on Earth. In an un-Libertarian society this indiscriminate increase impedes the progress of evolutionary expression because it makes unjust demands upon productive individuals which keep them from learning, and ultimately from teaching or passing on genetically, as much as they would in a truly free society.

8. War, famine, and pestilence are natural consequences of human collectivism. Only these conditions currently exist as ways to limit the indiscriminate increase of non-self-sustaining humans. These methods however, unless contained, present dangers to, and put limitations upon, productive humans.

9. At man's current level of spiritual development we have the problem of collectivist thinking with it's natural cowardice towards addressing human population encroachment. This has led to an ethic of indiscriminate subsidy of non-self-sustaining people. Even though getting rid of institutionalized wealth redistribution will remove the subsidy, it will still be necessary to directly address the problem of escalating reproduction among non-producing people.

10. Many are now saying that it is socially irresponsible, arrogant, and immoral for any couple to do more than merely reproduce themselves - that they should be legally limited to the clearly just number of only two children. Others have suggested that because incapable people have been unjustly subsidized in proliferating their numbers for so long that much stronger measures must be taken to undo the damage already done. This is a good example of how indefinitely putting off what is right can lead to distortions which seem to call for extremely unpleasant counter-measures. History offers many such examples.

11. We all know that ontogeny recapitulates phylogeny in human prenatal development. It also does this relative to neuronal imprinting during the postnatal growth process. At birth the child's ability to perceive and experience is at an invertebrate level, and it is quite some time before any uniquely human perceptions are experienced (26). This should be contemplated by those who would deny parents their natural right to terminate either a pregnancy, or a malformed or retarded child, at or shortly after birth. No unique human consciousness would be cut short, because none would yet have come into existence.

12. Those desperate to promote the proliferation of human quantity for some cosmically masochistic reason, have even insisted that those using contraceptives are "mass murderers" because of all the potential life which they keep from manifesting. There is of course, one area of agreement between the opposing sides in the abortion debate. This is that there should be birth control education which would prevent the occurrence of unwanted pregnancies in the first place. Since preventative medicine is always the best, this area of agreement should be stressed to the utmost.

13. The indiscriminate proliferation of non-self-sustaining humans is ultimately a direct initial encroachment against the liberty of all self-sustaining organisms. Most of these people wouldn't buy a dog knowing that they couldn't afford to feed

it, and yet would think nothing of having three or four children and would expect government to support them in this. Only education can get rid of the false idea that the highest function a woman can perform is to produce children, regardless of the consequence to others.

14. In a free society it must be the merciful option of parents to terminate at birth any child who is born retarded, deformed, crippled, or incurably sick. For example, a constitutional psychopath is someone in whom the cerebral function of moral conceptualization is dysfunctional. The day will come when hereditary psychopathy will be routinely diagnosed intrauterinely via MRI Scans. In such these cases, if parents elect to keep and raise a psychopathic child, a just society must hold them jointly liable as accomplices if and when the child hurts others.

15. If we do not condone poisoning the public water supply, then people with genetic defects which result in malformed children must be prevented legally from contributing these defects to the gene pool. This can be done with genetic engineering or if necessary through sterilization. In either case natural selection will not be reversed.

16. Opponents of population control speak of government "invading the bedroom." Proponents speak of inaction as aiding and abetting all of the new mouths-to-feed in ultimately "invading the kitchen." Both are good sentiments at gut level. The one and only thing which can prevent the ultimate necessity of population control is massive education about increasing population, human devolution, and birth control. Even this can only save us if it happens immediately. To be, or not to address the proliferation of non-self-sustaining humanity? That is the question. Many now think that the quality of living has already been ruined to such extent that numbers should be actively reduced by any means necessary, not merely prevented from increasing.

17. The continuing success of any political movement requires not only that it be consistent with natural law but that it have, at least in its externals, popular support in the long term. Although voluntary restriction of human numbers and elimination of all organized sustenance of unproductive humans are requisites in a free society, popular acceptance is currently impossible. This is essentially to ask ignorant, immoral people to live justly. If the majority of people were currently capable of grasping such exalted concepts as liberty, self-development, and justice, these problems would not exist in the first place. This, of course, simply underscores the sheer depth of education necessary to reverse destructive population trends. Remember, at the current rate, world population will double in only forty more years (27).

Population of the World 1950-2050.

World	World Population	% Growth
1950	2,556,000,053	18.9%
1960	3,039,451,023	22.0
1970	3,706,618,163	20.2
1980	4,453,831,714	18.5
1990	5,278,639,789	15.2
2000	6,082,966,429	12.6
2010[1]	6,848,932,929	10.7
2020[1]	7,584,821,144	8.7
2030[1]	8,246,619,341	7.3
2040[1]	8,850,045,889	5.6
2050[1]	9,346,399,468	—

1. Projected.
Source: U.S. Census Bureau, International Database.

Prison or Death? A Third Alternative

1. In a Libertarian society there will be full employment. The small numbers of truly non-self-sustaining people will be kept alive by private charity. Government should not have to placate people who simply refuse to work with "entitlements" in order to keep them from robbing banks and burning down the cities. A minuscule fraction of this expense can be used to solve these problems justly and in a way consistent with the principles of evolution.

2. Societies have traditionally designated certain areas within which non-self-sustaining humans are placed to protect the liberty of productive individuals. Such areas need not necessarily have cell blocks, guards, or even "rehabilitation" programs, all of which cost others a good deal of money.

3. A prison, if large enough, can be self-sustaining when it's inmates are prevailed upon to make it so. Within the walls of such a prison, any degree of liberty can exist which the inmates are capable of sustaining. There can be fields, gardens, livestock, manufacturing, and even smaller prisons. A prison of this sort can be a nine square mile, autonomous, but contained, microcosm of society. There can even be free trade with the surrounding country just as there is among sovereign nations. Such prisons can be referred to as "isolation communities." One or two per country would be adequate.

4. A Libertarian, out of deference to the loved ones of criminals, might well stand against the death penalty. There are some crimes, however, that make such huge breech with humanity that the perpetrators can never again be trusted and, for public safety, should be executed. The crimes in question are rape, child molestation, kidnapping, human trafficking, snuff or child pornography, torture, arbitrary and serial murder. If these crimes carry the death penalty even

the constitutional psychopath will avoid committing them simply as a matter of practicality.

Some cases of murder are different and demand specific scrutiny. For example, in some cases, the public might want to award a good citizenship badge to the perpetrator depending on the victim, perhaps with an admonition against private justice and a small fine to cover court costs. With murder there can be extensive mitigating circumstances. With the crimes mentioned previously there cannot.

Victimless Crimes

1. There is nothing worse than a bad cop, and nothing better than a good one. We lament the fact that unquestioning police today will enforce unjust laws. Remember though, that when just laws are finally enacted, this will be very unpopular in many quarters. In that time, unquestioning police will be every bit as helpful to liberty as they are detrimental now. There are of course, limits as to what will be tolerated in the meantime.

"No reasonable citizen with nothing to hide should ever object to having police break down his door at three in the morning to come in brandishing firearms, bellowing 'Freeze, Dirt Bag!' How could we mind having these heroic champions invade our homes to defile our family memories associated with everything they touch? It's all for our own good, after all. On the other hand, since I personally don't possess, use, or sell drugs, since it wouldn't be police business even if I did, and since I will not compromise my liberty at any cost, if any of these 'War on Drugs' morons ever enters my home, there won't even be enough left of them for their families to bury with a cocaine spoon!" explains Dirk the Sun Warrior embodying a higher lawfulness, as he polishes his deluxe engraved twelve-gauge shotgun, Pig Slayer.

2. Certain areas of individual liberty are so fundamental that those trying to make encroachment need not even be reasoned with. Such people should be dealt with in the same way that any chivalrous warrior would deal with any other unredeemable mortal enemy.

3. In a free society anyone over the age of eighteen should be able to go into any pharmacy and purchase a painless suicide kit without any medical certification at all. People who do not support the right of an individual to decide about the time and method of his own death are sadistic enemies of human dignity. Their immoral opinions and vile rationalizations don't matter. Their cowardly religious beliefs and insane scriptures don't matter. Hospital personnel who keep a person alive against their own will, are nothing more than torturers, even if they are "only obeying orders" from other more important torturers. Those who aid others in their natural right to die, legally or illegally, are courageous heroic angels of mercy and should be honored, and whenever possible, rescued from legal oppression by decent liberty loving people everywhere.

"Prostitution should not be, and never should have been, illegal. Besides the false morality of impotent slave religion, the main reason that prostitution became illegal was because married women resented the competition and made a big fuss at home. One important reason that prostitution remains illegal is because the police get payoffs, discount rates, or freebies from the whores. Many other things which make no encroachment against anyone's liberty are also unjustly illegal for these same kinds of reasons. Any cop who arrests whores is a pee-wee. Any man who thinks of an honest whore, or any other free and easy woman, as a "tramp" or a "slut" is a misogynist pantywaist. This is usually the same kind of dink who will try to make a woman dependent on him financially, or who thinks that women should get paid less than men for doing equal work. If any cop ever interferes with me for going out with a whore, his testicles will end up in a block of polyester resin in my den, that is if I can find them with my portable electron microscope" chuckles Dirk the Sun Warrior roundly, as he sharpens the stainless steel castrating tool that he always carries in his boot when he goes to town.

Law Enforcement

1. Offensive behavior becomes increasingly fashionable as human societies decline. The vile culture of excess posture is fast becoming a societal norm. On television we see insubstantive young people trying to be very "in your face" by coming right up to the camera lens. In person, someone coming into another's life space this way, would normally be pushed away or struck, as a perfectly natural reaction to what would be an act of aggression. In advertising, we see those who act threatening, yelling out their message, sometimes filling the entire field of view with a cruel, tough-talking mouth. In music videos, we see wishful individuals standing over us putting their shoes on our face or neck. Products using advertisements which show all this Hellish behavior, glamorizing unjust aggression or unnecessary violence, should be boycotted by good people.

2. There is today a terrible tendency to over psychologize. In discussing criminal behavior, people seem almost embarrassed to speak about good or evil. Psychology is so much more fashionable. We are so much more "educated-sounding" and humanitarian if we call a criminal "sick." We are insensitive and ignorant if we call him evil. All this stems from the popular misconception that evil and sickness are the same thing. Sickness can be cured. Evil cannot. If the criminal's behavior were not evil, we would find no need, nor would we have any right, to try to change it in the first place.

3. Sometimes an evil person is also sick. Curing the sick part is often easy and may get rid of a bizarre impulse, but not necessarily the evil which allowed the criminal to make the volitional choice to act upon the impulse to the detriment of another. Explaining that a criminal became what he is

because of an unhappy childhood does not suddenly transform him into other than what he was before the "explanation," nor does it place any contractual obligation upon anyone not personally involved in creating his "unhappiness."

4. It is perfectly natural for a person, even of Libertarian morality, to sometimes develop a Fascist attitude towards criminals, welfare bums, greedy jeering masses, and decadent Socialist pseudo-intellectual phonies who have continually deprived him of his own liberty. Fascism is simply a normal moral reaction among healthy, but ignorant, adults to the deeper immorality of Socialism, which itself is a cancer of the soul, stemming from a desire to live parasitically at the expense of others. The key here is never to nurture Fascist attitudes, because such methods don't work in the long term, no matter how tempting they may seem in the short term.

5. The relative "deterrent" value of various criminal penalties makes little difference to the criminal who has little or no expectation of being caught. Conversely, the criminal will almost never commit a crime no matter how small the legal penalty, if he has a high expectation of arrest. If potential victims are generally known to protect themselves, criminals planning coercive action will know that they run the very real risk of being killed, hurt, or arrested. An increase in the expectation of effective resistance will produce a proportional decrease in crime. There cannot be one policeman to protect every civilian. People must relearn the natural tendency for self-protection that they relinquished to "civilization" so long ago.

The Right to Bear Arms

"Lately I have been encountering incredible numbers of people in the streets who hurl insults and make threats of violence without any provocation at all. Usually they are in groups, not all young, some even middle-aged. Many will soon find that neither their numbers, size, strength, nor the false bravado given by drugs will render them bullet proof. This is my country too and I am not going to be intimidated by these people or by the Socialist pigs who rob us to protect and sustain them" urges Dirk the Sun Warrior enthusiastically as he loads a hundred rounds into his Thompson rotary magazine machine gun.

1. In a free society the individual has the legal right to own or carry abroad any weapon he chooses, except the intrinsically unsafe weapon. This is one that cannot possibly be used without injury to innocent bystanders. Even governments have no right to own a weapon such as that. The popular objection that an "assault" weapon is designed to kill people misses the main point. What else, other than hunting, would any liberty loving person want a weapon for? To kill flies? It is not flies who invade countries and private homes to rape, torture, and murder. It is people who do that.

2. The individual has the natural right not to be treated as a criminal before the fact of committing a crime. Owning a weapon is not evidence of intent. In a free society it is up to the individual to decide what measures he will enact to insure the safety of his own person or home. These decisions must be made based on his individual expectations about other people and the future of his country, and must not be usurped by "optimistic" pacifists who would slavishly thirst to lick the boots of an invading enemy rather than to ever resist anything. Observe that these cowardly collectivist life managers would gladly see their oppressive confiscatory laws enforced using deadly coercion if necessary, by government bully-boys with guns. Learn well the names of the true enemies of liberty who reside within your own country.

3. Any individual advocating the confiscation or undue regulation of safe weapons in the hands of responsible citizens is a clear traitor to the country in which he lives. Such a person is guilty of treason, and will by liberty loving individuals, be dealt with as such immediately, using

whatever means are available. Any government attempting to deny it's citizens the right to purchase and bear arms has been subverted and will, by courageous spirited people, be thrown down immediately, using any degree of force necessary.

Problems in the Schools

"In the 1950s, nobody ever carried guns to school. We did carry switchblades, but only after school or on weekends. 'You want the knife, Mr. Dadiae, you come and take it! Come on! Take it! Step right up and get a taste of this, Dadio!' We never had to use them because we had no enemies and were mostly decent kids to begin with" reminisces Dirk the Sun Warrior as he hefts the old bone handled stiletto that he used to carry for protection against perverts and murderers when thumbing over to the movies in Needham. During those years 1958-1963 he never encountered even one unpleasant person. Recently Dirk asked a physician friend about thumbing north from West Palm International Airport to Jupiter, Florida. After an initial admonition not to do this, Dirk mentioned that he could carry a knife. The doctor, in absolute earnest, warned him, "Forget it! They have bigger knives and faster hands!"

  1. The teenager is at heart rarely a rugged individualist, but rather a gregarious tribal moralist. Adolescence is difficult because the warmth and safety of childhood is being left behind. There are many mixed emotions and signals. The parents are trying to push the fledgling out of the nest in some ways while trying to hang on to the cute little baby of memory in other ways. It's hard for the parents too. There is sadness, frustration, and anger. The kid wants independence, but not certain responsibilities. The parents refuse the independence, but insist on the responsibility. Teenagers seek with each other the total acceptance which they don't get from parents, but when given total leeway, usually end up forming group bonds which recapitulate prehistoric barbarian warrior clans. This is consistent with

their level of neuronal imprinting at this age (28) and is perfectly normal when there is no other influence to offset it. Observe the rise in personal decoration expressing oath-like commitment to in-group value codes, especially tribal self-mutilation like tattooing and piercing. The real problem arises when teenagers are not forced by their parents into at least a superficial adherence to a decent role model. The undeveloped but individuating self becomes too strongly assertive and massive behavior problems arise reflecting peer clan values. In terms of personal swagger, many teenagers have begun to act the same way that self-important adults will act when they have too much authority, especially in primitive tribal cultures. Teachers today are on the defensive for allowing teaching to interfere with the disruptive free flow of personal style. All of this is consistent with today's emphasis on the quick false lift gained through posture or drugs, as opposed to a more permanent self-esteem based upon long term attainment. This is the culture of in-substantive posture (29).

2. Parents went wrong when they adopted the notion that self-expression is more important than education. A classroom should not be a stage upon which the youthful player acts out for an audience of his peers. It is supposed to be a place where the status quo of the unlearned self is willingly put on the shelf for a few hours, so that something new can be learned. The student should be expected to become empty of himself during school time so that he can be filled up with knowledge. Self-expression can occur during after-school hours with friends, in any arena the student might desire, from club activity to hanging out on a street corner with "attitude," just so long as something new is learned in school. The emphasis on self-expression is wonderful in itself. It began with a free dress and grooming code that made leeway for all kinds of interesting clothing and hair styles. Parents simply allowed it to go too far. Factions arose, usually based on the manner and dress of slightly older musician heroes. Identification with rock warriors in itself is fine. There is much in rock music,

especially heavy metal, which is heroic in it's ferocious intensity and excellence. At some point however, all this self-expression simply became much too serious and led ultimately to tribal warfare with gun play. Recall the degeneration of schoolboys in "Lord of the Flies". Similar primitive behavior has been observed in modern warfare when discipline breaks down, such as the collecting of scalps, ears, and penises by kill-crazy soldiers (30).

3. Private schools can provide better education more cheaply than public schools. This would eliminate institutionalizing the culture of in-substantive posture, plus all the endless debate about what should and should not be taught. We would also be rid of most of the collectivist brainwashing of students because of the influence, through government, of international finance. Even from a Libertarian standpoint, however, it is reasonable to argue that, since we have thus far allowed the schools to produce a generation of acquiescent, drug-crazed, murdering, suicidal, Socialist cowards, that it might now be a good idea to utilize a centralized public school system for just another thirty years or so in order to produce a healthy new generation of natural kids with workable Libertarian values. Since the privatization of schools is one of the most popular objections to Libertarianism it wouldn't hurt to stress that we intend to wait thirty years. If after three decades of total Libertarian leadership the voters aren't happy with freedom, they can always vote the evil parties back into power and return themselves to slavery.

The Military

1. Patriotism is not blind obedience to government, nor is it the love of war. It is the love of country. This love can be expressed in many ways. In a free society these different ways will be respected. Let us note how the term "patriotism" is almost universally equated with support for whatever war the particular society is involved in, regardless of the causes leading to the conflict. This reflexive tendency reveals far

more about the level of evolutionary development of the human psyche than any amount of well-reasoned rhetoric.

2. Attention, soldier! It is always glorious to fight against the enemies of liberty, no matter how this is accomplished. People however, should not die merely for recreational purposes. This includes oneself. Good loving parents haven't raised children to throw their lives away on battlefields for no good reason, even if the parents themselves are fooled by government propaganda. Any individual who begins marching just because some guy starts beating a drum is not using his intelligence. Most wars are effectively nothing more than publicly sponsored athletic competitions for homicidal morons. A thinking individual may or may not decide to fight for individual liberty, but will never fight merely for "our country, right or wrong." If the country is wrong and we love it, let's change it. Nobody but criminals would ever ask anyone to fight for anything other than individual liberty, preferably their own. It is simply the only thing that developed people are willing to kill or die for. The choice to die is a very individual one that should not be influenced by social pressure from boot kissing slack-jaws and war mongering bully boys trying to sound patriotic (31).

3. In most cases the worst enemies of any country live within the country itself. The enemies are the financial interests who plan and profit from most wars, not the equally brainwashed soldier-children of a foreign land. It is well, before pledging one's life to a cause, to be absolutely sure of the true goals of those who are coordinating the action. This will usually require considerable investigation and can almost never be gleaned from statements coming from any official source, including popular news media. We know of those who have a history of lending money to build up a potentially aggressive nation with the planned intent of financing a war against that same nation later. Anyone who acts in allegiance with this element is effectively a coconspirator in treason against his own country. He renders himself a traitor because he aids and abets the real enemies

who reside within the borders, even if that is not his "intent." Those who will not give any of this a second thought are not good soldiers or patriots, but just another variety of parasite seeking free martial arts training, travel, and adventure at the expense of those who work for a living. They are not warriors of light, but slaves of darkness.

4. There are many types of warrior. The warrior of light is just and knows that liberty cannot be preserved by allowing power to those who will suspend it in the short term. When this is allowed, the short term has a way of becoming the long term. There can be no military draft in a free society. Besides the encroachment on liberty it is an inefficient way of doing things. Because of individual differences, the abilities of many would be misallocated on the battlefield, just as those of an eager and skilled battlefield warrior might be mis-allocated as a journalist or film producer also in the service of truth and liberty.

5. There is no justification for the maintenance of a large standing military. When a country is attacked, it can be defended by an expertly trained militia of well-armed citizens fighting for their own liberty. These citizens would also not make very easy prey for domestic enemies of liberty in the streets. With this system, the only standing military necessary would be a skeleton crew of officers providing a chain of command to coordinate activity in the event that the country is attacked. If all the time wasted on useless team sports in schools was used for basic martial and survival training, a voluntary citizen militia could be just as effective as any occasion might demand. The place now occupied in adult society by professional team sports could then be replaced naturally by fine gladiatorial contests of various kinds. These need not be to the death as in ancient times. Get boys interested in exciting, but practical, activities and eventually men will follow suit.

6. It is perfectly natural to want to participate in history. World liberty however, will result in continuing economic

prosperity and the end of war. Ultimately, adventurous young people will be able to journey into outer space as free employees of privately owned companies seeking to develop natural resources on other planets. This will make a splendid substitute for government sponsored wars in the lives of all people.

Treatment of Non-Human Species

1. Most people will agree that to live a short happy life is better than not to live at all. Most will also agree that not to live at all is better than to live an extremely miserable or tortured life of any duration. If these two ideas are justly extrapolated and applied to the treatment of animals which people breed and slaughter for food, then there does seem to some reasonable justification for this consumption, the greater sensitivity of the vegetarian position notwithstanding. In a truly free society however, all species must be treated humanely. Animals and birds raised for food must be given free range out of doors, good food, good treatment, and painless unanticipated slaughter. Egg production or birthrates must not be stimulated with hormones and the normal sleep cycle must not be altered with drugs. In a Libertarian society ranchers and farmers will prosper far beyond what they do now even with these concessions to simple decency in place. If food animals give us their lives in the end, the least we can do is to make their lives joyful while they live. We owe them this. Anyone so cold-hearted that they don't care about how these animals feel should try to visualize himself being denied the same things he would deny to animals. These principles must be enforced by law and any society which does not do this is to that extent an unjust society.

2. Humans have no moral right to keep animals in cages. Animals are not criminals, and they do not belong in jail. Try a little empathy. You are a bird who can fly and live a normal life, but you are kept in a small cage year after year after year until you die. You never experience the joy of fulfilling

your just destiny as a bird. Every day someone comes in to feed you with the usual "Pritee Bird. Pritee Bird." The permanent caging of animals as pets or in traditional crowded zoo environments must be illegal in a free society. Free-range situations, as in the bio-park type of zoo, are the only just way that man should be able to maintain a guaranteed view of animals.

The Prevailing Religious Climate

We must apologize in advance if anyone feels insulted by what we do say on this subject. All our observations are presented in very general fashion only to make a better world. Nothing is intended personally.

We consider the history of the twentieth century to have been an absolute disgrace - ongoing economic upheaval interrupted by war. This presents us with a question. If the prevailing spirituality operational in the world during this period were adequate, why then did we have all this trouble?

We feel that any person who truly believes in and practices the Golden Rule will agree with us that it is not enough for individuals to manifest simple moral decency. Governments must do so as well. Do spiritually developed people condone ongoing immoral government activity? Evil is not rendered into goodness just because it the result of collective human action.

Please approach this material in the spirit in which it is intended. We are working to establish liberty, prosperity, and peace on Earth. If we have to rock the boat a little by asking people to think, then that is what we will do.

"God is the totality of All. Most other ideas in this connection are merely indigenous mythology. The only real morality is absolute Libertarian reciprocity. All other ideas in this connection are merely criminal rationalization."

1. The natural inspiration towards liberty for all, when acted upon, renders the individual metaphorically a warrior of light. Along with the idea of voluntary self-sacrifice, this principle is the only thing of universal positive value to be found in any moral system or religion. All other elements simply reflect peripheral things, sometimes of great archetypal value, but only to the particular cultural groups among whom they occur. The flip side of this of course, is that any individual who works against individual liberty is to that extent a slave of darkness.

2. The vast majority of people on Earth live in a fantasy world based upon false prophesy, unnatural religion, and economic misdirection by collectivist governments. Unfortunately this lower majority threatens the evolutionary destiny of all living things. The only people who stand against this rottenness and who are able to minimize the affliction from these causes in their own lives are Eclectic Freethinkers practicing Libertarian Capitalist principles.

[The rest of this chapter and all of the next are reproduced from the "Evolutionary Psychology" by the present author].

3. A person who will deny what is readily discernible through science in favor of belief is "insane." This is an insanity however, which is normal to lower types of people. There is no cure for this and none should be attempted.

4. People demand more or less of themselves intellectually and spiritually because of their individual level of development. The proportion of fantasy directed behavior of fundamentalist religioners parallels that of deeply disturbed mental patients. The sheer numbers of such people however, give them a consensus for their delusions, eliminating the sense of alienation usually present in clinical psychosis. However little, this is all that such people demand for themselves and they should not be ridiculed. It is their right in a free society.

5. One who will unnecessarily insult another because of religious differences is not a genteel person. Those who will actually prevent freedom of religion are enemies of society. Religious freedom is absolutely necessary to natural order because it allows people to find their proper level of actualization. When however, the beliefs of unnatural religioners cause them to encroach upon the liberty of others it then behooves us to at least educate them before more rigorous methods become necessary.

6. Imagine a highly advanced intelligence visiting Earth from another planet - people who have solved all their social problems and who fought their last war 25,000 years ago. Consider deeply and objectively their probable reaction to the bizarre iconography, fanciful mythologies, and ritual procedures of major world religions. Then consider also their reaction to the vast institutionalized difference everywhere between what is practiced and what is preached (32).

7. The deities of any people are merely those fantasized particularizations of the Totality of All which reflect individual origins, struggles, and goals. Historically these subjective interpretations of God have been used to justify the kind of divisiveness which finds expression in the exercise of low advantage such as vandalism, plunder, rape, and torture. Apart from the veracity of individual mythologies, the spiritual rectitude of any belief system can ultimately be measured only in terms of the amount of justice manifesting in the behavior of the practitioners. Only those who are free of unnecessary intolerance show integrity in demanding the same for themselves.

8. Religious cowards hold strong beliefs which keep them from worldly success and have been taught since youth that weaklings will be successful in the next world and that those who are successful now will be punished later. Underlying these feelings of course is the false notion that the unsuccessful are somehow always "exploited" by the successful. They fantasize that after death all this will be

sorted out by a "just" God. Those who swallow this nonsense are inevitably people of apathetic nature whose own laziness makes them perceive much of normal goal oriented behavior as somehow dishonest or immoral. This sort of thinking is common to lower class people. It is what makes them what they are, and proceeds as a characteristic thereof. The problem here from a standpoint of individual liberty is that this same apathy, besides leading to Socialism, is also evoked as an excuse for not dealing with people who really do exploit others.

9. The ambassadors of shamefulness sound just like cheap little robots as they mindlessly regurgitate their pathetic spiel about belief in some anointed person or another as their savior. They will often counter with this nonsense as a postural surrogate for moral substance politically - faith offered as an excuse for immoral allegiances. They think they can do anything they want on Earth because their savior will forgive them later. When their aggressive criticisms of others are challenged by one who points out their own total lack of tangible activity towards making the world a better place, they make alibi by accusing the constructive person of not having faith in God, who they feel should implement all right action in the world without any human participation. If you offer constructive political solutions for societal problems they accuse you of trying to supersede their savior. Mindless parroting of scriptural fantasy as an excuse for apathy and moral lassitude. People who actually live moral lives don't need saviors. Educated Libertarians can easily demonstrate the superiority of our values in just a few sentences. We don't need to hide behind a thousand pages of tricky talk and falsified history.

10. Religious fanatics who champion ancient prophesies of worldwide destruction are the sickest and most nihilistic of all. All these fools want our children to look forward to is worldwide destruction, because they really have no faith in anything, especially the power of knowledge in the service of goodness.

11. Doomsday paranoids think that the normal effects accruing to human disregard of environmental laws can only be dealt with by an angry God. They even believe that seismic activity somehow constitutes a supernatural referendum on human evil. These Slaves of Cowardice spend endless time trying to reconcile current events with ancient scriptural prophesy. They ignore the knowledge of present day affairs which would easily allow them something besides the "lesser of evils" at election time.

12. The only true test of value for a major religion is the effect that it has on society over the long term. A viable spirituality intended to exert major influence must not only attract widespread adherence but must also have a positive effect upon society. Coward religion attracts many but does this only because it promises supernatural revenge to apathetic weaklings. Slave dogma contributes to all that is devolutionary. The cowardly majority is responsible for condoning today's Socialism. Nobody should adhere to a tradition which has clearly failed. Religions based upon false values and unnatural principles are not worth following.

13. Absolute separation of church and state is impossible because what the people are spiritually determines the form of government they will create or condone. The economic system of a country will never exceed the soul wisdom of the people residing therein. Wherever we find the institutionalized cowardice of scarecrow religion, we also find Socialism or some other unworkable form of collectivist government. We can't expect an inferior prevailing spirituality to result in a superior way of running society. If the people are no good, the government will be even worse.

14. One of the main reasons that prevailing religions don't work is because they mix lies with truth. They demand literal interpretation of what is obviously mythological and teach a lot of self-effacing foolishness about sex. They then mix common sense truth about not hurting others in with all this. The nonsense part brings apparent discredit upon the true

part. Essentially it robs people of a moral basis for their behavior.

Towards a More Libertarian Spirituality

> "Philosophers and ploughmen
> Each must know his part
> To sow a new mentality
> Closer to the heart" ~ Rush ~

"One who farms out most of his spiritual activity to a clergyman can be likened to the man who would hire someone else to romance his wife. There are simply some things that one should do for himself. Spiritual activity is probably the most important of these. The man who does not perform independently in this regard is a spiritual gutter-crawler. He who strives towards a transcendental ideal will achieve things intellectually and spiritually as much beyond the average as the average is beyond the baboons" invites Dirk the Sun Warrior, one outspoken Freethinker of the New Aeon.

1. The only "creed" a truth seeker needs is a loving and just reaction to the total of his knowledge. This should be well organized, systematically increased, and periodically contemplated. It is appropriate to have an area of belief which seems to be the most plausible extrapolation beyond factual data. This area however, must never fall prey to dogmatism and must be subject to immediate revision to accommodate new factual data. It is also appropriate for this to incorporate the heroic myths of one's ancestors for the archetypal inspiration and sense of rootedness thus conferred.

2. In this context the term "spirituality" is differentiated from "religion" in that it represents something much larger. It includes all of a person's values as these are reflected by actual conduct over the course of a lifetime, rather than merely by the parroting of doctrine with only partial

adherence as we usually find in religion. A person's spirituality comprises everything in life. This may include religious activity or no religion at all.

3. A truly viable spirituality must have perfect integrity between three basic components:
~ an intellectual premise consistent with all known science
~ a moral basis reflecting absolute Libertarian reciprocity
~ a source, not of irrational belief, but of archetypal inspiration, grounded in one's own ancestral mythology."

To summarize in this context ~
~ Intellectual Premise - evolutionary dualist viewpoint (33)
~ Moral Basis - "Basic Libertarian Impulse"
~ Archetypal Inspiration - indigenous mythology

4. Those who follow "outland" religious traditions are docile spiritual bondsmen. People who find joy in the heroic myths of their own ancestors feel only pity for those who would demand so little of themselves intellectually and spiritually as to raise up a foreign philosopher and make him into a god. Most of these spiritual turncoats can't even blow their own noses without asking cultural infiltrators how to do it.

5. Those who are obsessed with trying to reconcile every aspect of modern experience with foreign scriptures written thousands of years ago are being false to their own heritage and to the present day world. Slavish dogmatism renders the individual an ineffective participant in modern society. People need not seek so far away for their spirituality nor aid and abet missionary monoculture. The vile dispiriting nihilism of wandering internationalists is a poor substitute for the spiritual integrity of being rooted in one's own ancestral tradition. There are today many fine natural spiritualities being reborn. These represent diverse ethnicity. One must seek however - they will not come to you.

6. For moral excellence to prevail in society nobody needs to be converted to anybody else's national tradition. The most

educated and spiritually developed persons of today are rediscovering the ancient spiritualities of their own ancestors. Sometimes there is justified resentment because most of the early writings were destroyed by fanatics of some other dominant religion in the past. This very fact however gives those who are resurrecting these old spiritualities much leeway for conceptualizations based upon ancient archetypal ideals while at the same time incorporating the knowledge and science of the modern world. This emerging spirituality is not encumbered by the dogmas of the past. Nor is it based upon subservience, cowardice, and hypocrisy, but upon integrity, courage, honor, truth, and liberty. The new indigenous spiritualities are superior to the original in that they do not countenance the barbaric sacrificial practices that characterized earlier systems.

7. Indigenous spiritualities have more spiritual integrity and archetypal relevance for people than any identification with outland personifications. The bland faceless beehive religion of worldwide universalism however, will only be rejected if people know there is an alternative.

8. Information about superior spiritualities and political choices must be made generally available. Usually it is better if the two things are presented separately. If this is done anonymously, the poor lost sheep who constitute most of society will not have to lose face in upgrading their allegiances. In this way all that energy they spend talking about how moral they are might actually be channeled into constructive activity.

Footnotes:

26. Robert Anton Wilson "Cosmic Trigger" (And/Or Press, Berkeley, 1977) Unusual and interesting.

27. Actually this problem might eventually be remedied by a new age of volcanism. Let us hope that somehow only Libertarians survive this.

28. Robert Anton Wilson "Cosmic Trigger" (And/Or Press, Berkeley, 1977) Unusual and interesting.

29. Adults are guilty of this too. This is the same lazy trend we see in pretentious modern art where the smaller the effort made in accurate portrayal, the more complex the explanation of what is supposedly depicted, and the more falsely superior the tone of that explanation.

30. Viet Nam War. This is simply un-chivalrous.

31. "Landmine
Has Taken My Sight
Taken My Speech
Taken My Hearing
Taken My Arms
Taken My Legs
Taken My Soul
Left Me with Life in Hell."
~ Metallica: "One" ~

32. "Khaki priests of Christendom, interpreters of love
Ride a stone Leviathan across a sea of blood and
pound their feet into the sand of shores they've never seen
Delegates from the western land to join the death machine
And we send cards and letters."
~ Country Joe MacDonald: "An Untitled Protest" ~

33. For evolutionary dualism see "Evolutionary Psychology"

XI. Revolution

"The tree of liberty must be refreshed from time to time with the blood of patriots and tyrants. It is its natural manure."
~ Thomas Jefferson 1787 ~

1. This is a very exiting historical period in which to be living. Libertarian Nationalist Revolution has begun and is being accomplished through the systematic dissemination of truth. The revolution is only in it's infancy and the stakes are higher today than they have ever been before. Liberty loving individuals must get involved. It is not enough to merely talk and "sympathize."

2. Tangible interest in anything is measurable only by activity, such as reading from "forbidden" sources. Most people demonstrate absolutely no real interest in past, present, or future. In spite of this, many are very aggressive about expressing opinions. They will speak about the value of "intellectual discussion." Even those who initiate talk however, will often meet truth with insult, usually of the jokey kind which mocks all genuine seriousness. Such people are only seeking concurrence, not truth. This element tries to sound very moral and patriotic about social issues until the lies they live by are refuted. Then they turn to silly putty.

3. The use of currency not backed by something of intrinsic value is the one and only cause of the destructive economic cycles which seem to necessitate deficit spending by government. Lending requires spending and the international bankers manipulate politicians and events. They have created and financed almost every war in our history. This is not philosophy or anecdote. It is not "conspiracy theory" but verifiable fact. There is a tremendous body of highly specific data about all of this. Not knowing about something does not render it theoretical. There is simply no excuse for ignorance in this area.

4. In America the poison has spread so far that from an economic standpoint even "conservative" candidates are Socialists. Democrats are Socialists who talk like what they are. Republicans are Socialists who talk like rugged individualists, but are not. These misguided leaders effectively serve only the New World Order international banking crowd, who do not represent the interests of America, and have not since well back into the nineteenth century. Voters who understand the Libertarian alternative to this, but who continue to support these parities are making volitional obeisance to evil. Those who don't seek knowledge of these matters are not good Americans. It isn't necessary to become a historical expert on the Council on Foreign Relations or the Trilateral Commission or to link these groups with ancient occult conspiracies, only to understand a few of the activities of international finance since 1913. What is called for is simply to bone up on a small portion of history which isn't taught in school.

5. There is nothing more pathetic than the fool who can spend hours quoting fables from his holy scriptures or reciting endless statistics on dead ball players back to the 1880s, but hasn't even a rudimentary knowledge of who runs his own country or how they do this. Ignorance about institutionalized evil doesn't make it go away. Parroting subverted media slogans about "conspiracy theory" won't make these problems disappear. Prayers and religious fantasies will not liberate mankind. The only "saved" souls are those who practice righteous behavior and work diligently for Libertarian goals right here on Earth.

6. This international financial elite who work for global monoculture must be defeated at any cost. The trend in evolution for three and a half billion years has been toward diversity, not uniformity. Human devolution and tedious cookie-cutter sameness should not be the destiny of mankind just to make a few wealthy people richer. The means to all the ends discussed here should be

contemplated dispassionately. Creative energy must be diligently applied to their implementation.

7. Most people will not be motivated to any real action until they have lost almost everything. It is only at this point that the risk involved in fighting back seems acceptably small, because the enemy has no target left except the individual himself, whose life is already ruined. Having almost nothing material, ironically, permits nearly the same freedom of action which is possible with the kind of liquidity given by great wealth. Many in power now are going to find this out to their very great detriment if Libertarian policies are not implemented in time.

"Investigators now believe there are four hundred (34) separate instances where The US government has secretly exposed large groups of innocent citizens to radioactivity so that they can study the long term effects - the number of deformed or stillborn babies, how soon the children will develop leukemia, the cancer death rate for mothers, the suicide rate for fathers. This is to ascertain the "feasibility" of having a nuclear war for profit (35). Anyone who doesn't want to see this vile criminal element overthrown is a worthless coward. Anyone who supports these vampires is a co-conspirator in treason. The pigs who murder us think they can rob us of the very meaning of our lives and that, if we object, we must feel obliged to justify ourselves in debate, as though meeting upon a field of honor. The next time we are threatened by rats with bubonic plague these 'gentlemen' will expect us, by the same logic, to engage the rats, hand to tooth, in the sewers. I would sooner do this, since the rats in this instance, are actually more the gentlemen because they are not volitional servants of evil," elaborates Dirk the Sun Warrior as he blows off steam while loading his Walther P-38 with silver bullets.

8. It is perfectly all right to become deeply angry with those who heartlessly victimize. Those who do not, lack integrity and courage. If great advantage is gained over such an

enemy, however, and there is no peril to oneself, the chivalrous individual will practice generosity.

9. Before becoming angry with any particular individual or group it is well to study the complexities of situations thoroughly. Any government not run in accordance with Libertarian principles has been subverted to the purposes of evil, but this does not necessarily mean that it operates against the will of the people. Exploiting masters can never do what they do without eager slaves in the form of obedient functionaries, ideological cowards, and greedy shortsighted masses. All are equally to blame because of immoralities of their own.

10. Liberty loving people have the right to overthrow the tyranny of evil people wherever this occurs by any means necessary. Libertarian Nationalist Revolution today mainly involves teaching people everywhere what liberty actually is, that it not only can work, but is the only thing that can work in the long term, and that the apparent "obstacles" imposed by governments are only temporary points needing resolution. People must learn not to deny in their hearts the essential rightness of individual liberty simply because in some countries it seems temporarily unattainable. The true Libertarian must not despair the seemingly endless length of the Quest.

11. Always attempt first to educate, and do this with gentility. People, however, who go along too easily with the treasonous men who run societies today, especially the glib insulting ones, should be remembered. Make and maintain a list, but justly take account of personal growth as time passes.

12. When an enemy and it's aims are clearly defined, a war against such enemy can be fought and won by individuals and small groups unknown to each other and without any central coordination of activity. Individual clandestine activity actually confers advantage since it makes mass retaliation

impossible and completely eliminates any capacity for infiltration. There must however, be a strong spiritual unity based on clearly defined goals and principles.

13. Let the warrior of light become proficient in the use of weapons and in some area of unaided martial attainment. These skills may well be needed in the years to come, but let us hope they will not.

14. The history of mankind is perfect because the highest capability of mankind as a whole, is always happening at any given moment. Evil currently predominates on Earth because injustice is to some degree institutionalized by every nation on this planet. Once Libertarian Nationalist Revolution is complete, good and evil will then be in perfect balance on Earth. The difference will be that the wielders of light and of darkness respectively, will more frequently and perfectly derive the normal just consequences of their actions (36).

15. The day that good will have the upper hand on Earth will come only when noticeably more than half of the people are simply unwilling to advance themselves by encroaching upon the liberty of any living thing. This includes the indiscriminate increase of their numbers through mindless reproduction.

16. The young often have a fierce and idealistic love of liberty. Today this is skillfully misdirected by collectivist governments into subverted cooperation with entrenched financial interests in all countries. When the passion of the young can everywhere be fused with knowledge and wisdom before life has a chance to first confuse and then beat them down into low apathetic obedience, then "Liberty Triumphant and Eternal" will prevail.

Footnotes:

34. The 400 figure is from CNN, Autumn 1994

35. "Darkness at the break of noon
Shadows even the silver spoon
The handmade blade, the child's balloon
Eclipses both the sun and moon
To understand you know too soon
There is no sense in trying."
~ Bob Dylan: "It's All Right, Ma" ~

36. "Now in darkness world stops turning,
ashes where the bodies burning.
No more War Pigs have the power,
Hand of God has struck the hour.
Day of judgement, God is calling,
on their knees the war pigs crawling.
Begging mercies for their sins,
Satan, laughing, spreads his wings."
~ Black Sabbath: "War Pigs" ~

Part II: Liberation of the World

> "Aye, the king hath set us a grim table!
> Tis a bitter draught, I tell ye!
> A scabaceous broth and a turdsome loaf
> which hath been served up to us.
> And worse yet, the people still have no idea
> of what finer thing liberty can make in its place."
>
> ~ Elof II ~

1. New Look at Western Civilization

Spiritual monism is the popular belief that either good, or evil, is the predominant moral force on Earth. This involves imaginative wishfullness about the supposed destiny of one to eventually triumph over the other. In this mode of error, evil is thought of as being a mere pathological deviation which can somehow be "cured." Ironically, the ongoing "cures" institutionalized by collective human action have been responsible for most of the real evil faced by human societies throughout the ages.

The majority of exploiting masters in history have made use of monistic spirituality to misdirect populations into serving their purposes. To what extent this has been done with contrived awareness is of no real importance. It is actions which effect other people, not intentions. Usually such leaders have accomplished their goals by identifying one group in society as being somehow responsible for the plight of another group, and then exploiting both the feelings of guilt on one side, and a desire for "justice" on the other. The leaders explain that when the "evil" individuals are finally defeated, that "good" will prevail.

Out of the rise of monistic Judaism came Christianity and it's popularization in the third century AD. The most sophisticated exploiters of monistic Christianity were the clergy, and in their desire for worldly power, they succeeded in throwing away most of the vast accumulated knowledge of ancient civilization through the destruction of many of the great libraries (1). At the same time, they renamed, reapplied, or revised whatever Pagan wisdom they deemed useful to the achievement of their own objectives.

The following centuries saw a continuation of all the usual war, plunder, rape, and torture but also a tremendous decline in the arts and sciences accompanied by a tremendous rise in the kind of murderous bigotry which always accompanies insane religiosity. This became institutionalized and provided the rationale for the murder of over nine million "heretics," often people of dualist spirituality: Zoroastrians, Manichaens, Albigensians, Cathars, Templars, and "Witches." (2)

Christianity further consolidated it's power by teaching the flocks that man, through his natural desires had fallen from grace, and that since God had sacrificed for him, that he had incurred a debt thereby. The way that all these "sinners" could absolve their guilt, avoid eternal damnation, and pay their debt to God was through His emissaries, the clergy. The believers were very conscientious in this, dressing their holy men in silk, adorning them with jewels, and ensconcing them in vaulted marble palaces, surrounded by priceless treasure, great libraries, and works of art.

Accompanying the stubborn rise of an entrepreneurial middle class came the Age of Enlightenment with a tremendous decline in the worldly power of Christianity. Interestingly today, even most Christians refer to the period of their own domination on Earth as "The Dark Ages." The modern Christian is however, usually very different from those of the Medieval Period (3).

With the rise of the international banking families came a new specter to haunt mankind (4). These families who live in great luxury at the expense of brainwashed populations continued the use of monistic ideologies appealing to apathetic masses. Exploitation of the dishonest idea that wealth earned honorably can somehow be "excess" and that not sharing is first under Judeo-Christianity, sinful, and later under collectivist government, criminal, has been increasingly used to rationalize escalating government theft. The effect has been to negate a great deal of what humanity might have otherwise accomplished, because of constant interference with the natural progress of the producing elements in society (5).

The insidious behind-the-scenes manipulation of virtually all western nations by international finance, and the establishment of institutionalized wealth redistribution began the process of what is now rapidly accelerating into the destruction in humanity of everything that is strong, solid, and viable, while at the same time giving temporary artificial nurture to, and thereby increasing, everything that is weak, rotten, and non-viable. Non-producing elements can only be relieved of the consequences of their unworkable life strategies for so long.

The deliberate creation by international bankers, through the Treaty of Versailles, of conditions which would inevitably lead to a Second World War and their subsequent financing of both sides in that conflict, has understandably lead to the massive falsification of history since that time. For those who seek the truth however, there is a considerable body of highly specific, factual, and well documented literature dealing with this period. The truth has not been lost, it has simply been propagandized into obscurity by those very powerful people who gain immensely from doing so (6).

One may well reach the point of feeling that there is no real way to know what is true and what is not. What it finally comes to, is simply who one prefers to believe. Is it those, who by war and economic upheaval, profit through manipulative and coercive power over others? Or is it those who would profit only by being allowed to justly keep what they earn, honorably and peacefully, in a free society? Choose!

The student is sternly advised to pursue unflinchingly a specific knowledge of these matters. Those who will not seek further in this are just apathetic boot-lickers with no effective patriotism, moral courage, or genuine love of liberty.

Footnotes:

1. In all fairness we must credit Roman Pagans with doing this as well.

2. Students of comparative religion need not be told that many of these victims were advanced intellectually and spiritually beyond the loftiest of Christians.

3. We can all of course, think of a few exceptions to this.

4. Allen, op. cit.

5. Apathetic slaves trying to sound very Darwinistic will rationalize that government interference weeds out weakness. Actually it is fierce unhampered competition which does this most naturally.

6. The reader is urged to be open minded, seeking out those "forbidden" sources which might on the surface seem to be the least likely avenues of truth in any area.

2. World Power Through Misdirection

> "The very Deep did rot: Oh Christ!
> That ever this should be!
> Yea, slimy things did crawl with legs
> Upon the slimy sea."
>
> ~ Samuel Taylor Coleridge ~

Central banks controlling the currencies of so-called free nations are usually owned privately as corporations. Investor participation is primarily among various international banking families. The financiers discovered long ago that having a currency not backed by something of intrinsic value like gold can cause massive financial upheaval in society. It became government's job to deal with the consequences of such upheavals. This requires vast amounts of money. Most of this money has to be borrowed from international banks and paid back at high interest rates. It is to the advantage of the lenders to see that there are plenty of upheavals. Since government officials receive large salaries connected with new spending programs, their interests are aligned with those of the bankers, but unfortunately not with those of society, even though on the surface it may seem otherwise.

There are two main types of upheavals caused by the fiat monetary policy used to finance deficit spending by government. The first is the inflation-unemployment cycle, seeming to necessitate government borrowing for social programs. The second is trade deficit problems caused by the fluctuating values of fiat currencies in world markets. This leads to itchy trigger fingers between nations and seems to necessitate government borrowing for defense build-up.

What the government cronies of these banking overlords fail to mention in their campaign speeches is that, with a currency backed by a one hundred percent reserve of something of intrinsic value like a mixed store of precious metals, there is no cycle of inflation and deflation in the first place, no boom and bust - just a continuing slow prosperity with full employment and peace. The inevitable one percent of chronically unemployable people can easily be taken care of by private charity.

The politicians also neglect to mention that society can actually be run most efficiently without any taxes at all. The majority of government services can be paid for by individuals, in direct proportion to what is received, with specific user fees. Remaining collective areas, like law enforcement and defense, can be funded with lotteries of specific purpose and are merely generalized user fees (7). For example, with volunteer military service, there would exist virtually no important divisiveness within a country if those favoring a military venture to aid freedom fighters in a foreign land are the only individuals participating in and funding the venture. There is absolutely no potential for vast public demonstrations or big government scandals with this type of arrangement.

The bankers prefer a balance of power between left and right elements in government so that there will be plenty of spending by both. They know that if either faction gains ascendancy that they will lose greatly thereby (8). If Libertarians gain control, the bankers will be able to finance honest private enterprises. The stimulus of a continuing Libertarian Capitalist prosperity, with all the finance needed for business expansion, especially the push into outer space, coupled with the vastly decreased risk of business failure, will actually leave the bankers far better off than they are now, with the special bonus that they would no longer be enemies of society. Even the ones who insist on being crooked would not become impoverished while looking for new ways to live dishonorably.

The way the international bankers keep the balance of power between left and right is by insuring that the churches, schools, and media teach Socialist ideas because they know that the continued injustice and unworkability of Socialist policies will produce a natural Fascist counter reaction in much of society. In the United States the cowardice of Socialism is taught to children at an early age through the National Council of Churches and the National Education Association. Both were sponsored by financial interests long ago so that American business would be heavily taxed to pay for all kinds of unnecessary government programs. This weakens American business and insures a competition free environment and with it continuing monopolistic control for the big tax exempt foundations (9).

Endowments to specific schools are also utilized. Those who write or publish that which pleases are subsidized. Those who write the truth are slandered and glibly dismissed as "reactionary" or "paranoid." This particular label usually finds a quick audience, especially among ignorant young fledgling "intellectuals" trying to seem very recondite and profound in their understanding of the human psyche. In complex matters the readiness with which truth tellers are judged to be paranoid is directly proportional to the intellectual cowardice and moral lassitude of those rushing to judgment.

World Power Through Misdirection – Chart

Goodness (10)

permitting

Unimpeded Evolution

augmented by

Truth

leading to

Natural Order

via

Prosperity	Liberty
preserved by	preserved by
Capitalists	Libertarians

---- opposing ---- ---- opposing ----

Socialists	Fascists
perpetrating	perpetrating
False "Justice"	False "Morality"

used in

"Social Planning"

rationalized with

Disinformation

exploited for

World Domination

motivated by

Evil

Footnote:

7. Remember that a true tax redistributes wealth at gunpoint, a user fee does not.

8. A good example is with a nation's arsenal. As the parties alternate they build it up, tear id down, build it up ... This costs much more than just sticking to one policy.

9. Allen, op. cit.

10. Today when we speak of Good and Evil, we are often accused of "using flamboyant language." Approach further elaborated in "Evolutionary Psychology" by Eric F. Magnuson.

3. The New World Order

Social Planning by and for Bankers

The long term goal of a certain powerful segment of the international financial community is absolute economic domination of the world through monopoly. Fiat monetary policy produces the trade deficits which lead to international hostilities. One of the primary methods used to exploit this has been to make the world so unsafe with military proliferation that it will seem that the only way to save humanity is to eliminate trade deficits by establishing a one world government and monetary system. This would involve central computer debit cards with purchasing units replacing currencies. Even with this system it would still be possible to increase the "money" supply, and using the card would completely destroy privacy as to one's whereabouts.

The next step is the relinquishing of sovereignty of all nations to a one world government. This is what is called the "New World Order." This would give the internationalists total monopoly with nowhere for liberty loving individuals to run. There can be no off-shore accounts when there is no off-shore. If all this is allowed to happen then individual liberty on Earth will effectively be a thing of the past.

To have one world government not based upon Libertarian principles would be the worse fate, short of total nuclear war, that man could ever inflict upon himself. Complete control by international finance would accelerate the trend of the Twenty First Century in making the quality of existence on earth progressively worse (11). It would mean the endless artificial sustenance of primitive peoples through the continued victimization of advanced peoples. This kind of globally institutionalized bloodsucking would effectively put an end to the evolutionary destiny of mankind on this planet.

Third-world people usually favor globalization because it will allow them to prosper via social programs paid for by productive host populations. NWO bankers know that countries with legions of immigrant third-worlders, if globalization comes to a ballot referendum, will be far more likely to relinquish sovereignty. This is the reason for all the new indigent faces we must endure in productive countries.

Propaganda for these policies has already begun to appear in everyday television shows. Here we find fashionable young college types falsely, but very matter-of-factly referring to the "New World Order" as though it were an impending utopia of great opportunity for all. Dissenting individuals are portrayed as racial bigots and violent rednecks.

A suggested exercise for college students would be to determine, from employment and entitlement statistics, the ratio between the total numbers of producing and non-producing people on the entire Earth. The next step is to compare this to the current ratios in existing separate nations and to assess from this what would be the average effect of a one world economy upon the standard of living of producing people on earth as a whole.

Even the Great Plague of medieval times ultimately benefited humanity by reducing excess numbers. It increased the quality of consumption by diminishing the quantity of consumers. A collectivist world government would have the opposite effect. Ultimately the numbers might be reduced by a new plague, but not until most of the beauty of this planet, the general quality of human manifestation, and the simple morality which accompanies joy in living had been utterly destroyed. This is already happening almost everywhere on Earth now. The rate is increasing.

Can the reader think of a single movie or television series which portrays a peaceful and productive Libertarian future on Earth? Entertainment now usually involves only themes of destruction and control rather than building and personal growth. Most of the human advances postulated are based only upon technology or individual prowess such as empathy or telepathy. The future is portrayed as Post-Apocalyptic with the same old crew running things and the people racing around devastated landscapes in souped-up jalopies killing each other over life's basic necessities like fuel (12).

The efforts of the international bankers are aided and abetted by the short sighted reactionism of brainwashed masses whose limp-wristed spirituality and collectivist values lead them to support banker approved politicians. These candidates promise the immediate triumph of "good" if certain sacrifices, namely individual liberties, are lovingly made. Everything will turn out fine "if we all just work together." Actually all we have to do to have a glowing prosperity all over the world is simply to strive selfishly, but honorably, on an individual basis in a climate of absolute individual liberty.

Again, there is an interesting, well documented, fact-filled literature dealing very specifically with all of this. The aspirant is now grimly admonished to pursue understanding in this area. This is not philosophy or "bias," and the truth cannot be glibly psychologized or slandered away. These facts must be learned and taught to younger people at a grassroots level. All it takes to make the average mesmerized boob-tuber quickly dismiss verifiable truth out of hand is to have some subverted, but respected "news" person refer casually to the truth teller as being an "extremist" or a member of some ideological group, which has been popularly "discredited" by the slandering puppets of international finance.

Footnotes:

11. The author freely acknowledges the improvements in life which have accrued to advances in technology - especially communication, transportation, and medicine.

12. And if an Earthling is not turned on enough to date or marry an alien with horns, scales, a nose like a summer squash, ears like cabbages, and all manner of protuberances, he is, of course, considered to be extremely bigoted and provincial.

4. Superior Options for the Future

Difficult Choices

Democracy without evolutionary Libertarian principles is itself only mob rule and will usually degenerate into some form of collectivism with a little behind-the-scenes help from international finance.

Consider all the terms denoting so called "free" societies which are special pairings of the words Democracy, Christianity, and Socialism. None of these societies are truly free, nor are they workable in the long term. Separation of church and state has to be not only in name, but also in practice. Institutionalized mandatory religious charity (taxes) must be eliminated. This can be done without hurting anyone and will produce a virtual rebirth of any society where it occurs. There can be no moral or logical objection to this from anyone, especially since humanity will devolve at an increasing rate if we do nothing.

Archaeology and history show us that there have been cycles throughout the ages, first of human evolution, then of devolution. Man has made slow progress culturally, but has declined markedly in intelligence since the Cro-Magnon (13). What we face today however, with the technologically efficient methods used by collectivist leaders for engineering of popular consent, is a massive trend towards the reversal of human evolution. The decline in human intelligence has been going on for a very long time, but in the Twentieth Century the rate accelerated (14). Many may dispute specific studies and data, but common-sense should suggest that the basic laws of nature cannot be ignored indefinitely.

None of these bad things have to happen because economic history shows us with absolute clarity that the total economic mobility present in an Evolutionary Libertarian society will result in spontaneous natural order. We are the first generation of humans to have any real understanding of these principles, but young people must be educated about how things work before the triumph of natural order can occur. Libertarian Nationalist Revolution will not occur because of virtual reality games at the local video arcade.

Without the establishment of Libertarian societies the only chance that evolving humanity can possibly have in the long term is through the escape to other planets of self-sustaining humans (15) or through the mass sterilization of non-self-sustaining humans. Both of these "alternatives" are tall orders at best, and even if possible in the short term, have no long term integrity. Without finding a way to end the false ethic which leads to collectivist sustenance of human degeneracy, no society can long endure. The same problems would only recur and must be faced eventually. Technology cannot substitute indefinitely for moral courage.

Although all men must receive fair, equal, and impartial treatment under law, all men are most certainly not born with an equal potential for complex manifestation and nothing that government can do will ever change this. An equal chance to succeed normally results in wide individual differences in the degree of success, not in perfect beehive uniformity, nor should it.

If the relative number of non-self-sustaining humans becomes too great, then one of the short term solutions already mentioned may become necessary. We must insure not losing even more of what man has attained through evolution, and with it, the chance of ever establishing truly free societies so that evolution can resume it's normal upward progress. This ideal is only attainable with Evolutionary Libertarian principles.

In a totally free society people manifest only up to a level consistent with their natural abilities. There have to be differences in manifestation for a proper division of labor. Capitalist economic systems will yield the kind of earned prosperity that naturally results in lower birth rates. We must, to survive, move towards an adult, realistic, and informed understanding of the problems facing humanity as a whole. If we begin this in time, it will eventually result in separate sovereign Libertarian Republics everywhere. This is what is referred to as a World Libertarian Order.

In the time when all countries are basically Libertarian, the idea of a one world government won't seem necessary for peace and harmony, and it won't be, because it isn't now. Separate sovereign nations will always be preferable to one world government, because it's easier to subvert one government back to collectivism than a lot of individual ones. A world court to arbitrate land disputes arising among nations colonizing space will, of course, become necessary just as courts are necessary within individual countries now.

Young people are eager to participate in historical change for a few years before settling down. Look at the NASA photographs below. Imagine if their eyes could see views like these from space probe windows instead of the war-torn bodies of their fellow humans.

Footnotes:

13. Pendell, op. cit.

14. Ibid.

15. "All in a dream, all in a dream
The loading had begun.
They were flying Mother Nature's
Silver seed to a new home in the sun."
~ Neil Young: "After the Gold Rush" ~

10. Declaration of World Independence

> "All men recognize the right of revolution;
> that is, the right to refuse allegiance to
> and to resist the government,
> when it's tyranny or it's inefficiency
> are great and unendurable."
>
> ~ Henry David Thoreau ~

Introduction

What follows is a spontaneous inspired writing which preceded most of the other material in this volume. It is offered only as an emotional posture for constructive action within individual countries. There is no suggestion here, as certain weisenheimers have chided, that it should be sanctified historically or appended toany official document.

Declaration of World Independence

Let it generally be known that there exists a sovereign nation of indigenous population now lying primarily dormant everywhere, and yet morally above all others; a nation which will be rendered actual by any means necessary through the uncompromising courage and perseverance of just men and women everywhere; a nation mighty and prosperous wherein all and sundry may live and strive unhampered either by exploitation or unnecessary aid; wherein there will be no foreign ownership of business or lending of any kind to those residing outside of the national borders, wherein all may live in complete and absolute liberty with success dependent only and totally upon those circumstances pertaining to the individual; wherein liberty is defined as one's right to pursue life and happiness in any way which does not unjustly impact anyone else; wherein government is limited to its legitimate functions of creating and regulating the national currency, defending the national borders, and of redressing any unnecessary assault, coercion, fraud, or other unjust encroachment against any person, or the environment, to the detriment of any living thing; wherein it is recognized generally among the populace that indiscriminate charity inevitably leads to the perpetuation of traits having no survival value, and thereby reverses the process of evolution; wherein taxation is called by it's true name, theft, and government services are paid for only by those utilizing them and only in direct proportion to value received; wherein the freedom to worship or not worship according to one's understanding in the privacy of one's home or church, is jealously guarded everywhere; wherein the right to secure, keep, and bear arms is defended even unto death; wherein individual liberty is held to be the first and highest ideal of all, is creatively implemented as the one uncompromisable premise, and is imaginatively and aggressively preserved at any cost; and wherein all matters of government will be clearly outlined in a constitution based upon these principles, and which document will, without favor to any vested interest, be subject to none but literal interpretation, and will, by just men and women, be regarded and enforced as the supreme law of the land.

5. Liberty Works Best Everywhere

Speed Traps

As we all know, some municipalities use unreasonable speed and seat-belt laws with large fines for revenue enhancement. This is done under the guise of public safety and is simple extortion. The people involved are nothing but common criminals and will by good people be treated accordingly.

We urge all liberty loving people to boycott towns where this injustice occurs. In this way business people will bring pressure on city government to make necessary changes. When you are victimized by criminals masquerading as police or magistrates, be sure to get their names and addresses so we can punish them later.

We have very few listings here, but are large speed trap sites on the Internet. Towns listed will be removed from this list only when the town government changes it's policies, makes public apology for past extortion, and makes restitution, plus interest, to the victims.

Speed Traps:
Grass Valley CA
Framingham MA
Franklin NH
Meredith NH
Virginia City NV
Dewitt NY
Moscow PA

Seat Belt Traps:
Port Townsend WA

March 22, 2003

The War on Drugs

One striking example of the destructive effect upon society of entrenched banker-government interaction is the world crisis in "pleasure" drugs. It is normal in any society for a small percentage of the population to use drugs of addiction. Originally the numbers were small, but un-Libertarian elements, wanting to impose their values on others, lobbied government to make these drugs illegal. This interfered with supply, but demand remained the same. Increased risk in supplying the drugs made prices rise drastically.

This increase created a huge profit incentive for black marketeers. They began to recruit new users, especially of addictive drugs. Because of the higher price, most of the existing users could no longer work at normal jobs to supply their own habits. They in turn, began to recruit new users. As the competition and risk of selling drugs increased, the users began to sell to children, then turned to burglary, robbery, and mugging. At this writing, eighty five percent of violent crime is drug related. This is what collectivists call the "War on Drugs."

Government interference in the normal laws of supply and demand is the one and only thing that caused the escalation of drug use as it now exists. To perceive all this as simply one consequence of a "War on Liberty" would be more accurate. The financiers love all this because they lend the money to government for the massive enforcement expenditures, phony "rehabilitation" programs, and the bulging prison systems. That's why they lobby government against the legalization of these drugs. "It's the politics of contraband..."

Of course, all this seems to give government an excuse to deprive the populace of an ever increasing number of other liberties, such as reporting requirements in the private transfer of funds. What difference could it make that this is never done in a truly free society? After all, anyone transferring money "might" be a drug dealer. And of course, how could any good citizen demure at giving his employer an occasional squirt of urine for analysis?

In fact, no good liberty loving person would ever require drug testing of employees. Pay can be increased or decreased based upon job performance. The personal life of employees should remain their own. Besides this, the tests are not accurate. Poppy seed rolls and several common prescription medicines will give a positive reading on drug tests. Those who are denied employment because of false readings are urged to sue prospective employers. Take these no-good swine to the highest courts in the land and let the pubic see their cowardice (16).

It took three generations of un-Libertarian policy to produce the current epidemic in drug use and ironically, legalization would produce a dramatic short term increase in use. This however, would be followed by three generations of slow decline until a normal level of use is once again reached. The longer we put off doing what works, the longer it will take to work when we finally do it.

The slave mentality will glibly parrot the collectivist slogan that legalization is "giving in to the problem." It is not giving in to anything. It is the one and only solution to the problem and can be likened to simply putting the problem into reverse gear and slowly backing up out of an expressway tunnel which leads only and irrevocably to more of the same.

How many more decades will the opponents of legalization keep making the same mistakes while always expecting a different result? Prohibition itself is the one and only problem. Dealers should be seen merely as ruthless businessmen, because usually that's all they are. They kill each other because the profit incentive is increasingly great and because they cannot arbitrate disputes in the courts like everyone else. Try making lawsuits in other areas of business illegal and watch the murder rate go sky high.

The three generation time frame could only be shortened by drug education in the schools and the adoption of Libertarian policy in all other areas. As life and hope for the future improves people won't want to escape with drugs. Even with the triumph of liberty however, there will always be at least a small percentage of people who seek to destroy themselves in one way or another, with or without drugs. This is normal even in a free society and is a manifestation of natural selection in the arena of human affairs.

Footnote:

16. Here's another tactic. When they ask you to sign the urine test form, insist they sign a counter form reading thusly:

"Employee will agree to urine testing if employer will reciprocate with the following assurances:

Employer will have authorized agency submit results of projective psychological test showing that employer is not a practitioner of urolagnia or any other perversion related to urine.

Employer will submit notarized affidavit promising that urine sample will be used only for drug testing, will be discarded immediately after test, and specifically will not be-
 - delivered into the hands of any third party
 - drunk, sniffed, or savored in any way
 - used in any practice of sex or masturbation
 - used in any ritual or ceremony of religion or magick"

Later, when you have found a new job, just before you quit, fill the cup to the brim, accidentally trip, and spill the contents onto employer's bikini area.

Soaring Medical Costs

In a Libertarian society, government needn't get involved in health care. The only reason for the ridiculous cost of medicine today is because the loss of financial assets caused by collectivist societies has led to such desperation that medical malpractice suits have become an almost routine way of trying to make ends meet.

This has led to increased costs for everything medical. For example, a small switch used in a medical application will cost seven times what it would cost at the hardware store. This covers lawsuits if the switch fails (17).

It's not at all unusual today for a general practitioner of medicine to have an annual insurance premium of a hundred and twenty thousand dollars. The amount for surgeons must often be two or three times greater. Doctor rates must cover them for this (18).

Certain kinds of damaging effects which have come about very slowly in a collectivist society can only be expected to go away very slowly, even under a Libertarian system. People learn values in response to conditions, over time. Changing to a workable system of economics doesn't automatically change human values.

Doctors won't suddenly drop their fees just because of a change in economic policy which they may be too busy to read about, nor will people suddenly stop filing lawsuits. The only thing that can speed the return to normalcy will be a massive education program accompanying the triumph of Libertarian candidates everywhere.

Lately doctors like to ask if the patient is still taking specific medications prescribed by his other doctors. Then they write it up to make it look like a consultation with them, and bill the government insurance two or three hundred dollars. We leave it to the patient to devise their own method for defeating these scoundrels.

Footnotes:

17. Private communication with hospital purchasing agent, White River Junction, VT, 1986.

18. Private communication with general practitioner of medicine, North Conway, NH, 1993.

Sanctioning of Marriage

This is not even a real issue, but a phony one. People have forged their own chains in this regard. All people need is to deal separately with the personal and property aspects of interpersonal relationships.

It is not a legitimate function of government in a free society to sanction either spiritual unions or promissory sexual arrangements between individuals. It's doubtful whether these agreements even possess all the elements of a legally enforceable contract (19).

Personal unions can be meaningfully sanctioned only by the parties involved. Government has no business in the approval process. Those seeking a sense of validation by ceremony may, of course, wish to involve friends or spiritual organizations.

For the protection of adults and children the state has traditionally made provision for tenancy and the distribution of property upon the sundering of personal unions, whether by death or other means. These provisions apply to all people equally and can be utilized by them without any reference to the nature of the union itself.

Any of the the following legal arrangements can be put into place by any number of individuals living either together or apart. Details relating to these options can be easily researched elsewhere:

1. Sole Ownership
2. Joint Tenancy with Right of Survivorship
3. Tenancy by the Entireties
4. Tenancy in Common
5. Various Forms of Business Ownership

This entire business has become an issue only because collectivist types are seeking majority approval for sexual conduct which is not in keeping with evolutionary principals. The laws of nature and the laws of man are not one. If a person's behavior makes no unjust encroachment against anyone else then there is no legitimate political issue. In the case of marriage all people need to do is simply unchain themselves and "Just say no!" to big government.

January 2, 2004

Footnote:

19. Essential Elements of a Valid Contract -
LO = Legal Objective
CP = Capacity of Parties
LC = Legal Consideration
RC = Reality of Consent - "Voluntary Agreement"
OA = Offer and Acceptance - "Mutual Assent
"If agreement falls under "Statute of Frauds" contract must be in writing.

Hackers, Spam, Censorship

Web Hackers:

Under certain circumstances large numbers of people could die because of ruined Internet access. Hackers who tamper with the lives of others for their sick amusement should be tried and convicted for attempted mass murder. Let's see how amused they are by life in prison.

Email Spam:

We cannot ban unsolicited Email without banning capitalism itself. If we analyze the situation it becomes clear that the real problem is not spam, but the amount. This occurs because Email is free. We need only insist that reason prevail.

Our suggestion for legislation is that the amount of spam sent to any one address should be limited to one ad per week for two months followed by one ad per month thereafter.

It should be illegal for the sender to use an address

that the recipient cannot reply to. The addressee should be able to request removal from any and all lists and that his address not be sold. These requests must be honored.

Unexpected pop-over windows should be illegal. Expected pop-over and normal pop-under windows are not a problem. There should be severe penalties, however, for using windows which cannot be closed without rebooting the computer. This should also apply to windows which automatically minimize or maximize other windows.

Huge avalanches of spam and un-closable windows are not acceptable behavior among decent business people. Such practices are clear encroachments and should be illegal.

These simple measures will get rid of all the real problems associated with spam in a way which is consistent with individual liberty and free enterprise. Until we have proper legislation, people can only boycott those who reach the point of immorality in their business aggressiveness (20).

May 28, 2003

Internet Censorship

Everywhere there are libraries, community centers, and senior centers which provide Internet access to the general public. Everywhere also there is arbitrary censorship.

Community institutions will, of course, ultimately be paid for by user fees, but even when they are, the same problems of access could arise and must be addressed as a separate issue.

Unfortunately, many of the present institutions are controlled by people who have no respect for individuality or liberty. Their computer labs are funded publicly, but the viewing polices are not public, but based upon personal or parochial values being touted as the "community standard".

All decent people want an end to both child and snuff pornography. These involve the worst possible type of encroachment against the victims. But these are exceptions.

The general rule in a free society must be to allow no unnecessary censorship. The narrow and particular must not be allowed to interfere with liberty on the Internet or anywhere else (21).

August 17, 2005

Footnotes:

20. The author once received 650 spam letters every day. Usually there are several different persons who send from 3 to 8 each. In one case, until it was discovered and stopped, there were 40 every day from one person, but disguised to look like it was from many different people.

21. A friend of ours tells us about public access Las Vegas. "The public libraries are great. Their access policy is American and based on the Bill of Rights. Unfortunately, many of our city and county community centers are controlled by people who are not well psychologically and have jealous contempt for those who are. The censorship reflects their personal problems. We have nutcase religious fanatics and domineering butch lesbians acting as malicious webmasters. At one center the system is configured so that if there is any word the webmistress objects to in an Email you won't be able to open the inbox even to delete the letter. One man had searched for information about breast cancer for his wife and was awaiting response. He couldn't open the Email inbox because the word 'breast' had been flagged to shut down access. When he mentioned this to the morbidly obese bull sow running the place she said with a dismissive air of cruel exultant triumph 'Sir, I don't know that I want you viewing that word.' "

Mega Business Frauds

Massive losses to stockholders because of dishonest business practices have lately caused some to question the workability of Laissez Faire Capitalism. They claim that we need government regulatation of business to protect us from crooks. It's really much simpler than that.

All we need is better disclosure laws with heavy penalties for violation. Government doesn't need to tell executives how to run the business, simply that they cannot maintain long term secrecy from their stockholders. Investors are initially told what information to expect. They are then notified about business procedure as it occurs.

If there is non-compliance by management, or if investors don't like executive policy, all they have to do is put their money elsewhere. This provides a natural free market incentive to management rather than a meddlesome or coercive one.

November 5, 2002

Noise Pollution

If a person looks unpleasant we have the option of looking away. High volume sound doesn't give us this alternative. All people have the right to the quiet enjoyment of their lives and homes. Those who rob them of this in a defiant ongoing manner are volitional enemies of society (22).

Today we are unjustly besieged by noise of all kinds, from the unnecessary bleeping of automobile security systems to the highly amplified dirty-mouth chanting of emotionally disturbed individuals masquerading as "artists" (23). We can't even get away from this in our libraries where moral dopes blast us with it using tinny sounding head-sets. And then there is the cell phone...

The laws for some reason will not protect us from this ongoing encroachment, so we must be vigilant. We are at war with those who care nothing about individual liberty, and these noises are the sounds of war. When you hear these sounds, go looking for the source and do whatever you have to do to stop them. Always make legal remedy the first choice, but never close out your options.

June 27, 2004

Footnotes:

22. Case History
Struggling writer, with no options for moving, every night for three months is robbed of his sleep by a bellowing amphetamine psychopath. His immune system breaks down, he becomes deathly ill with pneumonia, is hospitalized, and nearly dies. Attorney advises that greedy negligent landlord cannot be held liable only because pneumonia is not an "easily foreseeable consequence" of being robbed of sleep. Writer has no insurance and the huge debt incurred ruins a lifetime of good credit and this in turn in many ways effectively ruins the rest of his life.

23. Case History
Sole purpose of sub-woofer is to blast pavement with sound which user knows will disturb everybody within a half mile radius. For example if anyone objects...
2004 in Reno NV at 3:00 AM two young savages with caps on backwards are parked outside a big hotel with woofers thundering, blasting the entire south face of windows with dirty mouth monkey music. At least two hundred sleeping people have been awakened by this. When night manager comes out and politely asks them to please turn down the volume he is told - "Fuck off bitch! Stick it up yo ass, motherfucker!"

Part III In the United States

Proposed Additions to the Constitution of the United States of America

Introduction

The American Revolution began primarily because of a tax without representation on tea, which if we adjust for inflation, amounts to about one dollar per individual per year.
There should be no question in the mind of any liberty loving American that the people of the United States today have infinitely more just grievance against the subverted collectivists and servants of international finance who run our country than the Founding Fathers ever had against the British.

America is today little more than a Socialist slave state, with consent occurring primarily because of apathetic reaction to false information. Members of the two evil parties like to quote the Founding Fathers, especially if the party name is the same. The problem is that the party platforms are not the same. Libertarians are getting a bit tired of hearing Socialists quote, as ideological allies, individuals who by today's standards, are Libertarians.

There are many now who would scrap the Constitution of the United States and write a completely new document. This particular patriot would never agree to such a thing, being much too sentimental about the history of America. Besides, a new Constitution isn't necessary. The original is almost completely a Libertarian document, even though the principles were not at the time, equally applied to all people.

The existing Constitution remains a living testimony to the growth of a great nation, reflecting the hopes and aspirations of its people. In it we can see many of our mistakes, and in some cases, our recognition and admission of these mistakes. It should be preserved for the children and be continually amended as we grow in understanding as a people.

What follows are proposed additions to the Constitution in order to help bring this venerable document to its highest potential as an instrument of Libertarian action. These ideas are offered to help establish a direction for enlightened discussion among those genuinely concerned about the future of America. The timing for any particular change, of course, must be such as to minimize any potential short term bad effect upon individuals or the economy.

The suggestions are formatted as additions to existing paragraphs in the Constitution. They correspond numerically to the original. In reading these proposals, most would want to have a copy of the Constitution at hand for purposes of comparison. See link below.

Additions to the Constitution

Article I Section 8

1. To establish user fees to pay for government services in direct proportion to specific value received by the payer, and to establish lotteries of specific purpose, relative to the common defense and general welfare of the United States.

2. To borrow money through the sale of internal treasury securities to be held only by citizens of the United States of America and only in that total amount equivalent to the usual expenditures incurred by government during a period of one year. Such reserve would also serve in case of national emergency.

5. To establish currency as a body of warehouse receipts representing a fixed amount of scarce and durable commodity, and backed by a one hundred percent reserve thereof, the value of which to be determined in a free world market.

14. (pertaining to the military) ... service in which will, at all times, be on a voluntary basis.

Additions to the Bill of Rights

Amendment 2. Nor shall the right of the people to keep and bear arms for the protection of life and property, hunting, or recreational purposes ever be infringed for any reason.
Amendment 16 is hereby repealed and the Federal Reserve Bank nationalized, with just disbursements.

Footnote:
Article I, Section 8, 1 and 2:
Foreign military ventures would be paid for only by those supporting them, in direct proportion to that support, using lotteries of specifically designated purpose.

Invasion of the United States

"We often give our enemies the
means of our own destruction."
~ Aesop ~

"It is passive genocide for a
nation to admit into its territory a
different, more rapidly breeding
population. The genes of one
group replace the genes of the
other. This is genocide."
~ Garrett Hardin ~

US National Debt $21,872,391,074,242   Update 12/15/18

America is being invaded by third world parasites who come here to profit unjustly via social programs paid for by more productive people who are taxed at gunpoint by government. Fools and cowards call this "social justice". See Wikipedia Untied States Demographics.

The New World Order bankers profit from this in the usual way through lending, but are especially motivated here because the immigrant hordes will favor globalization should the issue come to a referendum or plebiscite. If the reader has not read Worldwide Racial Displacement, now would be a good time. It explains the problem clearly, first at a global level, then with a specific section on the United States.

It is most important to read Ten Steps to Libertarian Nationalist Revolution because it explains the long term solution. In the short term, we need to quickly stop the infiltration, independently and in groups, using imagination and whatever means at our disposal.

November 20, 2014
9:00 A.M.

Part IV. The Future

United Nations
General Assembly Chamber
New York, USA

Address to the
United Nations General Assembly by
President of the United States
Roswell R. Benedict
October 8, 2034

State of the World
in the wake of
Libertarian Nationalist Revolution

"The state of the world has never been better, never in all of human history! Everywhere on Earth there is now absolute individual liberty, free enterprise, full employment, active trade, and growing prosperity.

Achieving this has been a big job. What helped us most has been the faith that people everywhere have shown in the possibility of making a better world through persistent rational effort. The particular best approach had to be varied from one region to another because of what had occurred in the past. The variations, however, involved only short term emphasis and sequence, not basic policy or principle. The time frame for phasing in any particular policy was always of sufficient duration to insure smooth transition without any disruptive effect on economies or individuals.

People everywhere now understand and accept the premise that government is at best a necessary evil, and that the less of it we have, the better. There is a new level of personal independence. Individuals are even beginning to deal with gross encroachments upon their personal liberty, justly, on an individual basis.

Permanent worldwide economic stability has been achieved. In all countries, privately owned central banks, like the US Federal Reserve, have been nationalized, the national debt repudiated, and demand for reparations for the amount already swindled made to the creditors as a civil alternative to being put on trial for engineering every war and ruined economy over the past two hundred years, or being the beneficiary heirs thereto, all of which is easily provable from existing historical records. There has been a return to currencies backed by durable commodity of intrinsic value, either gold or a mixed store of precious metals, the value of which is determined in the world marketplace.

Consumers worldwide now have total product choice. Goods offered in the world market are produced solely within each country by the citizens of that country, with no foreign ownership of business anywhere. Now that all nations are prospering under free enterprise, few think it good practice to invest away from home, and the imbalances have begun to subside. All subsidies and unnecessary regulation of banks, business, trade, and financial transfers have been eliminated. Balance-of-trade deficits are a thing of the past.

For any bank, including a nation's central bank, to maintain less than a one hundred percent reserve at all times is dishonest and has been made illegal everywhere. There is mandatory disclosure to depositors about amounts in reserve, with information about how it all works.

Taxes everywhere have been replaced with user fees and lotteries of designated purpose. This insures that unnecessary foreign adventures by governments will have to be paid for only by those who support them.

In this new climate, war is fast becoming just an unhappy memory. The energies previously squandered in these conflicts is now being channeled into undersea farming, renewable energy technology, space exploration, and interplanetary mining operations. The career opportunities in all of this are practically unlimited.

Defense spending everywhere is being cut to a safe minimum, substituting standing military with a skeleton crew of officers for the coordination of voluntary citizen militias as needed. Frivolous athletics in the schools have been replaced with basic martial and survival training. The students enjoy this every bit as much, and it has far greater utility for them long term.

Unnecessary social programs have been phased out as the improving economy and rising employment has made this possible in each locality. How quickly this was able to happen has been a happy surprise to a great many people. For people with a prior history of productivity, there are ample funds available to eliminate hardship caused by unpredictable local catastrophe or incurred disability. These are maintained with designated lotteries at the federal and regional level.

Prisons have been replaced by large self-sustaining isolation communities with agriculture, livestock, and small manufacturing. The really bad guys: rapists, human traffickers, kidnappers, child molesters, child and snuff porn filmmakers, arbitrary murderers, and serial killers are now recognized as irredeemable constitutional psychopaths who have made an unforgivable breech with humanity. For the safety and simple moral integrity of societies. they are now being put painlessly to death. We point out to opponents of this method, that one needn't be a rocket scientist to figure out that all it takes to avoid being executed for these terrible things, is simply not to do them.

Victimless crimes are those involving consensual areas of human contract, and now are off the books. Those previously confined for these things have been released with public apology, modest funds to tide them over, and a list of realistic job offers. The inevitable one percent of humanity who simply cannot support themselves by normal means are offered permanent sustenance by private charity as per specified terms, usually reproductive sterilization. Those refusing this option must provide for themselves. If this causes them to make unjust encroachment against anyone, they are sent to isolation communities.

As the distortions produced by hundreds of years of unnatural coercive government are gradually subsiding, all unjust protectionist measures, such as unnecessary safety regulations, are being cautiously phased out.

Along with traditional subject matter, programs have been instituted in schools to teach children about what was wrong with human societies in the past and how Libertarian policies are improving everything. This includes explanation about the manipulative relationship that existed previously between international finance and politicians. This is supplemented with rigorous teaching about control of excess birth rates, disease, and all classes of drugs. Understanding these things is requisite for promotion. We are in hopes that teaching the whole truth for forty years will make it possible to eliminate public education altogether.

All unnecessary environmental pollution has been ended. Requirements have been enacted in livestock production, zoo administration, and pet ownership based upon humane, free-range, and hormone/drug free models. The cruel, decadent down breeding of pets into evolutionary non-viability has been stopped. The existing animals have been sterilized.

There has been a complete overhaul of medicine, stressing nutritional solutions, both preventative and therapeutic, as opposed to the former mostly pharmacological and surgical options. The duplicitous role of physicians as both personal doctor and commission salesman for drug companies has been eliminated, Doctors are now allowed to prescribe only within generic categories. The specific choice of drugs is left to the patients who select for themselves on the basis of price and manufacturer reputation.

Respect is finally given to the right of individuals to decide when their life is no longer viable. Regional centers have been established where people can be put into cryonic suspension, or receive a lethal injection and be cremated.

National park and forest lands have been given back to the native populations from whom they were originally stolen. This has been done with the provision that the recipients continue to run the lands at a high standard for the enjoyment of all within their country. Previous non-native employees are offered life tenure or new jobs.

History has shown that the smallest number of people in any given place always works best, just as long as there are enough to defend the borders. The ideal population of 320 million for the land mass of Earth was passed c 900 A.D. By the word *ideal* we mean a level consistent with vital self-actualization and opulent joy in living, rather than mere subsistence in anguished mediocrity. Maximum varied manifestation for small numbers is superior to minimum meager manifestation for vast suffering multitudes. We are not imbued with life merely to endure it. To this end, we rigidly enforce a limit of two children per couple. More than two is an unjust encroachment against others, like house burglary. World population is slowly beginning to decline back to workable levels everywhere. The projected ideal numbers are as follows:

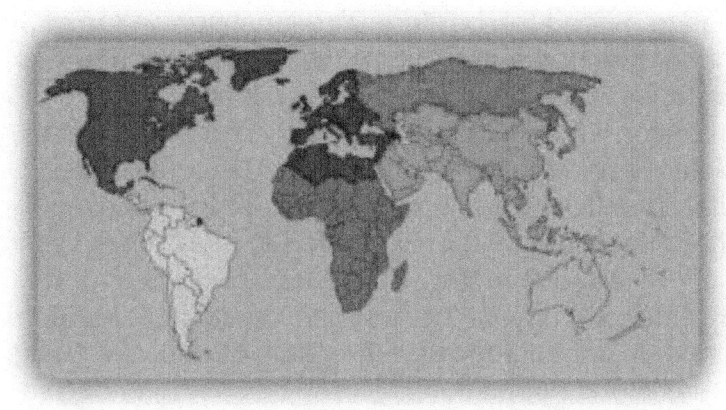

Canada, United States, Mexico
50,000,000

Central, South America
50,000,000

Greenland, Europe, Northern Africa
50,000,000

Southern Africa
50,000,000

Russia
50,000,000

Near, Middle East, Asia
50,000,000

Australia, New Zealand
20,000,000

Workable societies must be based on natural principals. It is normal for people to feel most comfortable among those of their own race and ethnicity. Globalist bankers, who worked for totalitarian Socialism and world monoculture, wanted everyone to mix together, so they could lend money to national governments who must deal with all the resulting social problems. In all of human history there has never been a multiracial or multicultural society which did not self-destruct because of the unnatural mixing.

All people have the natural right to grow up among their own racial kinsmen. Resident racial outlanders are simply an unjust encroachment upon personal liberty. The conniving internationalists wanted to destroy national cultures because they knew that one world government, giving global finance monopoly, would have been more acceptable to people with no racial or ethnic identity. To survive, we now emphasize race preservation and the prevention of global monoculture. Interracial marriage advocates were attempting to murder all existing races. They tried to sound interested in human variety, but their breed-up quick programs, long term, would have completely obliterate human variety by making what are now separate races into one race. Variety is the spice of life. Imagine a world where everybody is the same. "We are Borg. We are one. You must join us!"

One falsehood perpetrated by politicians serving big business who want cheap immigrant labor is that ongoing immigration is necessary to keep industry alive. In actuality, business simply expands to accommodate any available work force. With worldwide liberty and prosperity, people will not want to flee their ancestral homelands.

Third-world people have always favored globalization because it would have allowed them to prosper via social programs paid for by more productive host populations. The predatory bankers knew that countries with hordes of immigrant third-worlders, if globalization came to a ballot referendum, would have been far more likely to relinquish sovereignty. That's why we've had to endure so many indigents invading productive countries in recent decades.

Borders everywhere are being closed to immigrants of non-indigenous race. Anybody can leave, and a great many are returning home. Voluntary sterilization is being requested of all who choose to remain in host countries, with special retirement programs for those who cooperate. There are also adoption priorities for qualified couples within this category. There are no restrictions on tourism. Those who travel from now on will be able to enjoy the full undiluted potency of indigenous cultures everywhere.

The new technology for determining constitutional psychopathy, even in the prenatal state, along with intrauterine diagnosis of fetal deformity, mental retardation, and genetic predisposition to sexual perversion are leading to the elimination of human non-viability everywhere.

And... last but not least, we have finally hit upon an equitable solution for the problems caused by a century of Socialism in unnaturally increasing the quantity, while undermining the quality, of people everywhere. The new foolproof brain-scan method for determining intelligence is being used to assess IQ in populations worldwide, with voluntary sterilization requested of all those having an IQ of 94 or less. Special retirement programs and adoption priorities are also being granted here. Because higher moral conceptualization is a function of the cerebral cortex, these IQ adjustments, along with the elimination of constitutional psychopathy, will effectively spell an end to commonplace moral stupidity on this planet.

All of these splendid changes have been accomplished far more easily than anyone could have imagined, because they were not prolonged for the benefit of lenders, but done efficiently to insure prosperity, peace, and joy of living on this planet. Evil will no doubt continue to flourish at interpersonal levels, but it will no longer rule the day, nor will it ever again be institutionalized by governments anywhere on Earth. The legions of darkness at last have been vanquished!

I see nothing but smiling faces in this room, and it's getting on that time, so I'm going to lunch! It should be sufficient to say that what we have left to do is mere fine tuning compared to what has been accomplished already. Natural order is now prevailing on our planet. Thank you all for your help and support."

* * *

The response to this address is overwhelmingly positive. Within weeks there are special guidance programs being set up worldwide to help young people make early career choices from the bewildering selection of new possibilities.

The Beginning

Part V Quotations for World Liberty

"The destiny of humanity depends upon the attainment of it's highest type." ~ Friedrich Nietzsche ~

"It is far better to grasp the universe as it really is than to persist in delusion, however satisfying and reassuring... For small creatures such as we the vastness is bearable only through love." ~ Carl Sagan ~

"Most people are little more than sleepwalkers living is a fantasy world of mythology, intoxicants, spectator sports, and delusionary games. The true journalistic impulse proceeds from a desire to change this tepid, limp-wristed approach to living with truth." ~ Garrett Valdison ~

"To see a thing uncolored by one's own personal preferences and desires is to see it in its own pristine simplicity." ~ Bruce Lee ~

"Life is harsh. It leaves only one choice, that between victory and defeat, not between war and peace."
~ Oswald Spengler ~

"In an age of lies, such as our own, the greatest threat to it's existence is the truth, which like the blade of an invincible sword, is effective only when fully exposed and wielded by a man with death in his eyes." ~ Michael Miller ~

"If the individual is born into an un-free society, he will have no legal rights corresponding to his natural ones, since these depend upon other people. He is endowed, however, in many cases, with the potential to be something more than merely a slave, and always with the choice of turning his will towards this end." ~ Dirk Aubrey Lokison ~

"He who wills the ends must will the means."
~ Plato ~

"We often give our enemies the means of our own destruction." ~ Aesop ~

"When ghettos become the mainstream of society, islands of individuality cannot help but harbor an elite."
~ Anton Szandor LaVey ~

"It is more blessed yet to earn what one gets and keep it in a totally free society, than either to give or to receive."
~ Dirk Aubrey Lokison ~

"They that can give up essential liberty to obtain a little temporary safety deserve neither safety nor liberty. A people or individual without purpose will end up being used to achieve the goals of other races or individuals."
~ Benjamin Franklin ~

"It is passive genocide for a nation to admit into it's territory a different, more rapidly breeding population. The genes of one group replace the genes of the other. This is genocide."
~ Garrett Hardin ~

"Those who would rob you of your liberty, or threaten the survival or evolutionary destiny of your race, are your mortal enemies. There are two ways to deal with them. You can either have them at a distance or eliminate them completely, at very least by stopping their further reproduction. Which you choose should be determined only by your perception of possibility and cost." ~ John Hobart Farris ~

"...excepting in the case of man himself, hardly any one is so ignorant as to allow his worst animals to breed."
~ Charles Darwin ~

"It is better for all the world, if instead of waiting to execute degenerate offspring for crime, or to let them starve for their imbecility, society can prevent those who are manifestly unfit for continuing their kind." ~ Oliver Wendell Holmes ~

"There is a putrid cauldron aboil and the stench of it hath befouled the entire earth." ~ Elof II ~

"Single acts of tyranny may be ascribed to the accidental opinion of a day; but a series of oppressions, begun at a distinguished period and pursued unalterably through every change of ministers, too plainly prove a deliberate, systematic plan of reducing us to slavery."
~ Thomas Jefferson 1774 ~

"Lasting happiness is not possible in this world. What we should strive for is a heroic passage through life. A more enduring sense of commitment, a higher form of joy results when we champion a noble idea greater than ourselves."
~ Aurthur Shopenhauer ~

"Cattle die, kinsmen die, we ourselves also die. But the fair fame never dies of that man who has earned it."
~ The Havamal ~

"Achieve much. Stand out less. Be more than you appear."
~ Alfred Von Schieffen ~

"The most difficult thing is the decision to act, the rest is merely tenacity. The fears are paper tigers. You can do anything you decide to do. You can act to change and control your life; and the procedure, the process is its own reward." ~ Amelia Earhart ~

"Every single person should act as if the fate of the nation depended soley on his or her actions."
~ Karl Fichte ~

"Risk-taking is a recipe for success, all within the idealized framework of high purpose and self-abnegation."
~ Alfred Borth ~

"Nothing is ever done in this world until men are prepared to kill one another if it is not done."
~ George Bernard Shaw ~

"The point is doing them, rather than the accomplishments. There is no actor but the action. There is no experiencer but the experience. ~ Bruce Lee ~

"A Man who is doing his True Will has the inertia of the Universe to assist him."
~ Aleister Crowley ~

"We are not to expect to be translated from despotism to Liberty in a featherbed."
~ Jefferson to Lafayette, April 2, 1790 ~

"All men recognize the right of revolution; that is, the right to refuse allegiance to and to resist the government, when it's tyranny or it's inefficiency are great and unendurable."
~ Henry David Thoreau ~

"Rebellion against tyrants is obedience to God."
~ Benjamin Franklin ~

"The tree of liberty must be refreshed from time to time with the blood of patriots and tyrants."
~ Thomas Jefferson ~

"If I can't have total individual liberty by democratic means, then I will have it any way I can get it, even if it has to be over the dead bodies of all those who serve darkness!"
~ Dirk Aubrey Lokison ~

"True heroism is proclaimed through deeds alone."
~ Elof II ~

"A wise man and his weapon are never separated."
~ Viking Proverb ~

"The beast within is a valiant steed whereupon the man doth ride." ~ Elof II ~

"For the strength of the Pack is the Wolf, and the strength of the Wolf is the Pack."
~ Rudyard Kipling ~

"Under the thunder of liberating vengeance!
Woe to the people that are still dreaming today!"
~ Dietrich Eckart ~

"Our swords are not bent, nor are they broken, and will be sheathed in the bowels of thee and all thy minions."
~ E. R. Eddison ~

"Speed is everything."
~ Bernard Goetz ~

Song Lyrics:

"Philosophers and Ploughmen
Each must know his part
To sow a new mentality
Closer to the Heart."
~ Rush ~

"It's not how you play the game.
It's if you win or lose, you can choose.
Don't confuse, win or lose. It's up to you."
~ Ozzy Osbourne ~

"Between the velvet lies
There's a truth that's hard as steel.
The vision never dies.
Life's a never ending wheel"
~ Ronnie Dio ~

"And so we're told this is the golden age
And gold is the reason for the wars we wage."
~ U2 ~

"Call out the border guard.
The castle is crumbling.
The king is in the counting house.
Laughing and stumbling."
~ The Electric Prunes ~

"The core principle of freedom
Is the only notion to obey
The formula of evolution and sin
Leading the way"
~ Dimmu Borgir ~

"Let the dark do what the dark does best"
~ Deathstars ~

"I am born to live, fight for glory.
I am born to die, memento mori."
~ Hammerfall ~

" With dreams to be a King, first one should be a man.
I call them out and charge them all with a life that is a lie,
And in their final hour, they will confess before they die."
~ Manowar ~

"Rise those who despise the weak
Spare none and ride proudly on the winds of death"
~ Immortal ~

"They choose the path where no one goes.
They hold no quarter. They ask no quarter."
~ Led Zeppelin ~

Quotations for Good Living

"All truth passes through three stages. First, it is ridiculed. Second, it is violently opposed. Third, it is accepted as being self-evident." ~ Arthur Schopenhauer ~
"Intelligence without ambition is a bird without wings."
~ Salvador Dali ~

"The key to Libertarian understanding is to put the pig on the shelf and let the human within oneself address the human within others. If, within the other person, only the pig will address you, then try talking to someone else."
~ Dirk Aubrey Lokison ~

"Have no intimacy with worthless men."
~ George Washington ~

"God helps those who help themselves."
~ Benjamin Franklin ~

"Let your tongue speak what your heart thinks."
~ Davy Crockett ~

"And while the sun and moon endure
Luck's a chance, but trouble's sure,
I'd face it as a wise man would,
And train for ill and not for good."
~ Alfred Edward Houseman ~

"When dealing with lambs, behave as a kindly shepherd. When dealing with rats, study and master the technique of the barn owl." ~ Dirk Aubrey Lokison ~

"The admiration of a quality or of an art may be so strong as to deter us from aspiring to possess it."
~ Friedrich Nietzsche ~

"Affairs are easier of entrance than of exit; and it is but common prudence to see our way out before we venture in."
~ Aesop ~

"All government policy is enforced ultimately at gun point. A person who will vote for any policy which encroaches upon individual Liberty is effectively committing an act of aggression against society and is just as much an enemy of that society as any soldier in an invading army. He is however, an enemy that one would want to convert, at least to an ally, since he is also a countryman and possibly even a relative. We can't kill everybody!"
~ Dirk Aubrey Lokison ~

"Be sparing with advice. Wise men don't need it. Fools won't heed it." ~ Unknown ~

Song Lyrics:

"We're off to the witch.
We may never, never, never come home,
But the magic that we'll feel
Is worth a lifetime"
~ Ronnie Dio ~

"Be the broken or the breaker
Be the giver or the undertaker...
The keys are in your hands
Realize you are your own sole creator
Of your own master plan"
~ Dimmu Borgir ~

"Besiege the thrones of reverence
Gods of all fiery fate
Besiege the thrones of reverence
Warriors crowned on this day"
~ Immortal ~

Part VI World Libertarian Order

About the WLO

Every problem in every society on Earth can be traced back to a point where someone in government decides to sacrifice individual liberty for some other goal. Like any breech of natural law this produces a distortion. One compromise seems to justify another and soon the cause and effect relationships become obscured by time and complexity. The achievement of harmony on Earth simply involves eliminating the complex of false dependencies that have arisen because of these past mistakes.

Description:

The World Libertarian Order was founded February 12, 1983 on a hilltop in Plymouth Massachusetts by Eric F. Magnuson in a company of eighty seven revolutionary Libertarians. We are a worldwide non-profit fraternal order welcoming people everywhere and now have 418 members in 50 countries.

Our guiding premise is that the highest evolutionary destiny for all living things can only be served by permanent prosperity, full employment, and peace in the human sector, and that all moral people want this. Libertarianism is the only system which can bring this about without injustice for anyone. Our job is worldwide education about the superior workability of Anarcho-Capitalist principles in order to save this planet from the destructive effects of collectivist governments (4).

The entrenched economic interests which now oppose worldwide liberty are dealt with explicitly herein. We work for a "World Libertarian Order" of separate nations interacting in a free world market. A multitude of sovereign free nations can less easily be subverted back to collectivism than a one-world government. This is the cutting edge of political

thought in the world today and is not for dilettantes or milquetoast pseudo-Libertarians.
WLO Goals:

Our goal is that, through education, government involvement in the lives of citizens everywhere on Earth be reduced to it's absolute minimum. It is only when people have legal, but unjust, coercive power over others that evil becomes institutionalized. Unjust power becomes legal in society when the majority of people simply don't realize that there is a better, more effective, way of running things.

The one thing that threatens this planet more than ignorance is the illusion of knowledge. Those uninformed about economics often label people who work for absolute liberty as hating the weak. If you refuse to be arbitrarily sacrificed for others, you must hate them. There are, however, proven better ways to help those less fortunate than by government theft and destructive economic policy. We must, however, occasionally read something besides the daily newspaper to learn about such things.

Much of our task simply involves sweeping away popular misconceptions. For instance, the withdrawal of social programs in a Libertarian society would not lead to starving children as Socialists believe. Once the destructive effects of fiat monetary policy are behind us, entitlement programs can be phased out over a suitable period without hurting anyone. There will be ongoing prosperity with one percent unemployment. There can be an emergency fund to help those in desperation because of local catastrophe or disability.

Any true goal must be based on an overriding first premise embodying an important ideal which will not be compromised at any cost. Mere technical problems will then be seen simply as points to be resolved rather than as stumbling blocks which can be used as an excuse to alter the basic nature of the goal itself. When a system is internally coherent and has long term workability, then all opposing elements will, by persistence, be eliminated.

We aspire to teach everyone everywhere the value of structuring societies and economies on the "uncompromisable premise" of absolute individual liberty as opposed to any form of collectivism in any degree whatever. Having this steadfast principle underlie all Libertarian action doesn't mean that there is one identical method for fixing everything, but it does mean that we care enough about long term workability so that we will not breech natural law. There are as many different Libertarian solutions as there are collectivist problems.

Specifically, we feel that only education can deal effectively with all of the following otherwise insurmountable problems facing evolving life on this planet:

1. The destructive rapid increase of human population everywhere, especially the practice of governments in subsidizing non-self-sustaining people in reproducing themselves unnaturally.

2. Unnecessary ongoing economic instability and the manipulative control of this by international finance. The worldwide existence of welfare-warfare slave states is perpetuated solely by fiat monetary policy, which itself causes the destructive economic cycles and the apparent need for otherwise unnecessary deficit spending (5).

3. The impending creation of one world government involving surrender of sovereignty for all nations to a collectivist "New World Order" with the ever increasing unnecessary government programs, absolute monopolies, and loss of individual liberty that will accrue to this.

4. The reactionary support of unworkable protectionist counter measures by brainwashed majorities.

5. The effect of well-meaning, but misguided, popular religion in promoting ideas which aid and abet collectivist government.

Widespread consent for all this institutionalized rottenness occurs only because of public ignorance about the superior viability of unimpeded interaction among completely free sovereign nations. Anywhere Libertarian candidates are on the ballot at this time, the machinery for right action is potentially already in place. Having Libertarians in all major government positions on an ongoing basis will solve all of the above problems each within it's own particular time frame.

To be adequately understood, this material should be read very carefully in the sequence presented. This includes footnotes. Many common terms are meticulously clarified, and a lot of unfamiliar new information is presented. The reader should not be distracted here by what is a somewhat lofty style of writing. The writer makes only small apology for this, having been influenced by the inspired high moral tone of many of those whose works he has been privileged to read.

Before getting started, here is a small exercise which may help to clarify the writer's intent. The reader should answer for himself the following questions:

1. What do I want life to be one hundred years from today?
2. What needs to be done to bring this about?
3. What have I done in the past towards this end?
4. What will I do in the future towards this end?

Footnotes:

4. We have decreased our use of the term "Anarcho-Capitalism" because the average person thinks this refers to pandemonium in the streets. "Anarcho" is actually a parasitic intensifier that we have had to add to the word "Capitalism" simply because so many Socialists call themselves Capitalists. In the past it was implicit that Capitalism works best when unimpeded by government.

5. "You fasten the triggers
For the others to fire
Then you set back and watch
When the death count gets higher
You hide in your mansion
As young people's blood
Flows out of their bodies
And is buried in the mud."
Bob Dylan - "Masters of War"

August 5, 2003. Have always felt "Maters of War" to be one of the greatest protest songs ever written, but since the early 1980s have also felt that one of the best examples of the terrible irony in all the phony left vs. right nonsense is the fact that the people Dylan describes in this song are precisely the same people regularly criticized by the John Birch Society. So much for left and right. This entry was prompted by just now reading the lyrics to "Talkin' John Birch Paranoid Blues." Long ago I stood in line at the Club 47 for two hours to see Bob Dylan. He's one of the great original hepcats and nobody likes him better than I do, but he owes the Birchers an apology for the Nazi stereotype. When a person has influence over young people he also has a responsibility to speak the truth. Being against Socialism doesn't make one a fascist any more than parroting lies about Fascism makes one a Capitalist. Only in a free market can a person become rich peddling reactionary slander to uneducated young people. Years ago I knew a pharmacist living in Athol Massachusetts.

His name was George Lindsay. He was a good friend of mine and I called him "Horheevus the Linz". He was very active in the John Birch Society and was a hard working Capitalist businessman, and a patriotic, well- educated American Jew, not a Nazi or one who shouts "Yee-hoo" or anything else remotely resembling either of these monstrous caricatures. ~ EFM ~

Brief History of the World Libertarian Order

Eric F. Magnuson
January 9, 2000
The Low Hell Motel
Grass Valley, California (2)

Selected entries from the author's journal:

1980
May 29 Boston. Visit Radical Libertarian meeting on the Common. Meet Dirk and Heidi Lokison. They join me for rib at Jake's. We speak of many things and agree to meet again in future...

1981
May 29 [Only by coincidence, but exactly one year later]... Dirk Lokison and I discuss Libertarian Revolution over rib at Jake's...

1982
Sep 24 ... Meet Dirk at Jake's. Prime rib. He supports my plans for the WLO. His parents, Lars and Greta, join us on their way to the theater. It turns out that Lars is an advanced initiate in many secret societies and when I mention some of my own affiliations he comments that this is very unusual for one my age [I proudly recall]. I tell him about my Libertarian writings. He is impressed and I am so delighted by his response that I ask him to write a description of me for the book. While the ladies talk, I return to Naked Eye Cabaret with Dirk and Lars for a brief interlude... See Venus who avoids me. See Venus dance. With ultra-long hair she resembles an Elfin Witch princess. Lars really enjoys all this immensely and seems very taken with Venus. He says that he hasn't had an evening like this since he lived in Berlin during the 1930's... Retire early [Even though I don't end up having a date, this is one of the finest and truly well rounded evenings I have ever had].

1983

Jan 24 Tell Lars more about the World Libertarian Order. He knows many radical Libertarians who he says will join, even a few in other countries, and will get information to them. To this end I send him photocopies of "A Brief Introduction to the WLO" and the "Vis in Terra" Chart for distribution to all prospective members.

[Membership drive with many phone calls by Dirk, Lars, and others during this period].

Feb 12 c 6:30 AM Leave for Plymouth MA. Scrambled and bacon at Olsen's in Templeton. Drive fast. Reach top of Burial Hill before others arrive [Location chosen because of the superior weather on the coast at this time of year and because of the connection with liberty and beginnings. The view is beautiful. I feel at home because there are a great number of my ancestors buried here]. Britt shows up a few minutes later. 12:30 PM Amongst a splendid company of revolutionary Libertarians [88], finish performance of "Ritual AYW" founding the Order of Yggdrasil in the North and the World Libertarian Order. I encourage the others to remain in Plymouth to see the sights. We then pay respects briefly at Plymouth Rock and Mayflower II. Lars and Greta are beaming with delight. Dirk and Heidi introduce me to many of the people. Talk especially with Bert Valdison about Norse stuff...

July 3 Write outline in letter explaining to Dirk about introductory material for my books. 8:00 AM Finish letter asking Lars about his contribution to the writings in the form of a description of me - "A word about the Author." ...

July 16 Lars calls me from Great Slave and reads rough description of me [as author]. Aft. Write this up. [Later decide not to use this material because I have grown to think that a personal description of me is unimportant, plus it speaks overmuch about my personal life with women in Boston].
1984

Dec 16 ... Meet Dirk at Jake's. Shrimp at China Pearl. He agrees that I can use good paraphrases of his words as quotations...

1985
Sep 22 Autumn Sabbat. At daybreak, walk Stonebridge Farm. At Solar Noon on west shore of Surry Lake with eighty six (all but two) OY Knights and Ladies, perform ritual founding the Special Orders for Valor and the WLO Werewolves [Same text as used for founding OY, but with appropriate adaptations]. Follow with nice picnic on blankets. Delicious egg salad sandwiches. c 6 PM Seventeen of us have celebration banquet at Windingbrook Lodge...

1986
Sep 8 Bert calls to tell me that Dirk and Heidi went in search of his parents to Great Slave Lake last October. Lars and Greta were on strange business connected with some arcane fraternity during the founding of the Special Orders for Valor last September. None of the four have ever been heard of since. This bewilders me. They are the finest people I have ever known. [This also convinces me to never visit Great Slave Lake as I had once planned].

[Bert Valdison calls a few times during this period about minor matters connected with the WLO].

1994
Aug 22 ... Bert calls. He informs me that we now have 273 WLO members. He is going to mimeograph his copies of the books and send these to all.

Nov 27 ... Aft. Bert calls to tell me he is returning to Stockholm, but not for a while...

1996

Jan 5 First listing of WLO with Gale Research Encyclopedia of Associations.

Jun 1 Write entry about WLO for Yearbook of International Organizations who write to us from Brussels Belgium in March requesting a listing.

1998

Jan 12 Aft. Bert calls to say good-bye before leaving for Sweden. When I begin to reminisce about Dirk and Heidi, he tells me that Dirk and his family didn't just disappear - they were murdered by an underground group of radical Socialists. He refuses to give me details and says that he has been aware of this for a long time, but didn't tell me sooner because he was afraid of what I would do. On the bright side, he also informs me that we now have a total of 392 WLO members in forty seven countries... He says that once he gets to Sweden he will not be able to recruit at all in the USA because of the distance and because he will be working long hours managing an estate. I don't know what I'm going to do without his efforts.

Jan 13 Decide that unless I can somehow increase the WLO membership markedly on the Internet that I will declare and keep the official number at 418 - Crowley's number for the New Aeon...

Footnote:

2. Where many check in, but few check out.

Membership in the WLO

For this you must visit our website.

The easiest way is to do an exact phrase search "World Libertarian Order".

The second easiest way is to type in the web address - http://wlo418.tripod.com/worldlibertarianorder/id13.html

The United Nations

The WLO wants to see Peace on Earth. There is, however, a necessary natural sequence. Worldwide peace will not happen until there is worldwide prosperity, which in turn will not happen until there is worldwide liberty and free enterprise.

There is no need for any country to surrender national sovereignty to any international body. We don't need the banker-manipulated collectivist monopoly that would be inevitable with one world government. What we need is a world of separate free nations competing like individuals in a free world market.

We can make peace happen if we all insist that international organizations who aid nations in feeding their people also insist that these nations free their people so they can feed themselves. This means that they have to take a hard line against collectivist government - Fascist and Socialist. These systems are sometimes remedial in the short term because of what has happened in the recent past, but they do not work long term, and there is no reason to pretend otherwise. It is a feeble diplomacy which will not stand fast in these matters.

In July 2002 the World Civil Society Forum invited WLO participation at the International Conference Center in Geneva. We feel very honored by this, but could not attend because travel expense was prohibitive.

Consider the purpose of the WCSF quoted below. Then consider what could come from bringing a strong Libertarian influence upon United Nations policy: permanent liberty, prosperity, and peace worldwide.

"If the UN's global agenda is to be properly addressed, a partnership with civil society at large is not an option; it is a necessity."

Kofi Annan,
Secretary General of the United Nations
1999, Montreal (WOCSOC)

* * *

Aims and Objectives

"Strengthen International Cooperation by:

Promoting cooperation among civil society organizations across the world and working in different fields of activity, especially with developing countries and indigenous peoples;

Facilitating cooperation between organizations of civil society and the United Nations system, including its specialized agencies and other international organizations;

Creating space for dialogue on the relation between the different stakeholders of the international scene, such as civil society organizations, international organizations, governments, and the private sector."

The United Nations can be a tremendous force for future good, but only if there is a strong ongoing effort towards the establishment of worldwide free enterprise and trade among autonomous sovereign nations.

When there is liberty and Capitalism everywhere, there will be prosperity everywhere. There will be no economic upheavals, trade deficits, or war. Then we can put all that energy into exploring space and colonizing distant planets.

Unfortunately. at this time the United Nations fully supports the plans of the New World Order for global oppression. If the UN is ever again to be taken seriously as a force for good on this planet, they must break with this criminal element once and for all.

To Free Market Economists

In June 2002 we began to wonder if anyone had ever compiled statistics showing the different kinds of loss to American society in dollar terms over specified periods from the unnecessary business cycle caused by fiat monetary policy.

We wrote to several economic think tanks and came up with nothing. Some told us that if we found any such data to let them know so they could publicize it. In the course of doing this we also conceived an idea about method:

An economist could extrapolate forward figures from the 19th Century and then compare those to what actually happened as a result of fiat currency.

For example, in the U.S. during the 19th Century there was almost ninety years without any rise in prices. There were no taxes except local ones on property and federal ones on tobacco and alcohol. Deficit spending was not needed even during the greatest period of expansion in all of human history. This period constitutes a model of proof and a basis for comparison regarding the superior workability of Libertarian Anarcho-Capitalist principles.

Internet Forums

Occasionally today there are unsolicited forum postings about the WLO, but usually these degenerate into discussions about things unrelated. It's a pity the administrators don't run a tighter ship.

The reader may prefer to skip ahead since we have not initiated or participated in any online forums since 2003. It's funny for us now to read what our policy had to be in those days:

"We have been delighted by intelligent commentary that has arisen from material in the WLO site. Much of our content is controversial, however, and certain problems have arisen. Debate is like a gunfight, speed is usually at the expense of accuracy. Serious matters should be weighed calmly. One should never reply the same day. Problems exemplifying this kind of frantic rush-to-judgment are as follows:

1. Laziness. We are more than happy to answer intelligent logical questions which might arise from a careful reading of this volume. We will not, however, respond to questions which clearly reflect that the individual gave the work only a cursory glance. Our time is too valuable to waste on private copy-and-paste tutorials.

2. The trigger-happy practice of skipping ahead and reacting out-of-context. Often an idea is greatly qualified by the ideas which precede and follow it. Sometimes the entire essence of what ties a book together will be found only in the preface or introduction. A good example here is the reader so anxious to express himself that he will quickly skim the text for emotionally charged keywords that he can object to. This way he can quickly express his philosophy without having to read or think. If the person doesn't have sufficient time or energy to digest this material in it's entirety, then it shouldn't be read at all.

3. The mistake of acting as though one statement is a microcosm of an entire work, defining every term and elucidating every principle in one or two sentences. If this were possible, one book would summarize an entire library. This error leads to superfluous comment resulting from the wrong assumption that specific points have not been covered elsewhere in the work.

4. The tendency to ignore the actual words a person uses and react to some complex of ideas which the reader brings to the situation rather than what the writer is actually saying. This will often involve the reader's simply ignoring words not understood. A collegiate dictionary close at hand would be a good remedy here.

5. The problem of not separating the important from the trivial. This results in petty and pedantic chit-chat. This, especially is helped by first sleeping on the idea.

6. The cheap shortcut of glib negative summary. There is unfortunately a certain element who feel justified in quickly reviewing books they haven't read. This is easier of course, than creating something oneself. Our ideas are not intended for narrow individuals who try to falsely enhance themselves by quickly dismissing that which challenges them. Those who have taken the time to write something are seeking only specific substantive comment, because only this can lead to constructive upgrade of the material.

7. The use of insult or slander. Sadly, the same anonymity which makes message boards such a wonderful arena for free expression also provides a safe haven for unhappy people who like to be abusive. We always try to be genteel and will not read the posts of anyone who is nasty. Insult is not equivalent to viable argument and always comes from people with untenable viewpoints which they simply can't support (1).

Generally speaking the kind of tedium that comes from all this intellectual slovenliness isn't worthy of reply. Serious people won't squander their time on dilettantes."

Footnotes:

1. Heavy insult is mostly from aggressive dirty-mouth boys of all ages, and usually involves remarks against a person's intelligence or family. Often there are elaborate anal or excretory references. Three unpleasant examples:

~ Fundamentalist Christian responding to a discussion of evolution with reference to imagined necessity of his opponent receiving "deep-muscle enema."

~ Liberal Democrat responding to a discussion of Libertarianism with reference to sphincters and the unlikely scenario of political philosophy emerging from the upper colon. This poor soul uses an online pseudonym which mentions a prominent birth defect. It would be too great a coincidence, but a friend of ours from Florida told us about a disfigured man who is known to spend a great deal of time insulting people online. We won't go into detail about this poor man's deformity. It should suffice to say that his neighbors refer to him as "Old Turkey Neck."

~ The author was lucky enough to learn the identity of one of these message board thugs and paid him a visit. An apology was politely requested, but the slander and vile language was loudly escalated in the presence of a lady. When the tough talker tried to claw the author's face, self-defense and simple chivalry dictated corrective action. The author introduced the attacker to a little known love-tap called the "East Boston Fluffernutter" upon which the insulting individual became very mild and apologetic. The lady wanted to instruct our dirty talker in "the art of passionate shoe kissing" but the author insistd that his apology was enough. The pen is mightier than the sword, but sometimes...

Subverted Media Alternative

Stop the Parasites

It is important to view these books and videos, because globalists control the mass media. They slant the news to destroy ethnic and cultural identity, so that host populations will accept one world government, giving their banker associates absolute financial monopoly. They do not use logical persuasion, but In a matter-of-fact way, suggest that the majority of people already believe in their goals. This is to make us feel that we will be out of step with current trends, and be disliked for not embracing the same viewpoints.

The subconscious mind is pre-lingual and cannot be influenced by words. Whenever possible, the media masters program us with pictures designed to elicit primal emotions. Even if we find out the truth from statistics later, the subconscious will still believe in the pictures.

We must rid ourselves of these hell-rotters once and for all. We cannot learn about superior alternatives to globalization until there are laws to protect societies against media monopoly. The fairest way is to require that the percentage of media ownership by any special interest group not exceed the percentage of that group in the national population. Who, but monopolists, would object to this? Read how things stand now, then ask yourself why any of this is tolerated:

Non-Fiction

New World Order: Seek and Destroy
from Viking Media Favorites
This compilation from many sources explains all you will ever need to know to maximize your resistance to predatory globalization.

None Dare Call It Conspiracy by Gary Allen
Riveting inside history of globalist bankers right from the beginning. More compelling than the best of novels. Only chumps, jokers, and sleepwalkers have not read this one yet.

The Occult Technology of Power by Robert Eringer
Explanation of how the Shadow Government rules, written as though by one of the globalist bankers to be read posthumously by his son as instruction on how to wield his newly inherited power.

Our Nordic Race by Richard Kelly Hoskins
Explains who the Nordic peoples are, how their civilizations have been destroyed in the past, and urges future preservation of the Nordic race and culture.

Why Civilizations Self Destruct by Elmer Pendell
Scholarly history of the way in which earlier societies fell into decay as the entire world is doing now.

The Fulfillment of Evolutionary Destiny by Eric F. Magnuson
Explains how we can defeat globalist totalitarian socialism with a far more workable worldwide Libertarian Free Enterprise system.

Revolution: And How to Do It in a Modern Society
by Professor Kai Murros
Things are happening in Europe that should be happening elsewhere.

Holocaust: 120 Questions and Answers
by Charles E. Weber
From the Institute for Historical Review. One of many interesting contra-orthodox volumes refuting standard wartime disinformation.

Fiction

Hunter by Andrew MacDonald
This engrossing novel explains the truth about many world problems, including how to kill the everyday public enemies of your country covertly as a heroic citizen.

The Nationalist Revolution Series by Roy C. Peterson
Exciting novels explain how to exterminate the growing legions of subhumanity in massive numbers privately, but also how to legally establish world liberty, prosperity, and peace without killing anybody.

Eric F. Magnuson Short Biography

Eric Fenris Magnuson was born in Massachusetts. His parents were corporate business people. At Northeastern University, he studied science and English. Supporting himself as an antique dealer, he amassed a library of over four thousand books and began a diverse program of private study. Moved by the need to create something that would outlive him, on February 12, 1983 he founded an activist organization, the World Libertarian Order. After a six year tour du ski. he moved to Lake Wildwood California, and at present continues his writings in Montreal, Quebec.

Fimbul Winter Books

Writings of Eric F Magnuson

Balanced Healthy Living / Absolute Individual Liberty / Viable Evolutionary Spirituality

As director of the World Libertarian Order, I have worked for peace and prosperity since the early 1980s. Most people prefer fantasy to reality. Since my books deal only with uncompromised truth, they are for the few, not the many. I offer these writings for whatever good they may ultimately accomplish in the world. They are all good quality glossy paperbacks at a low price. To see them, visit your favorite book vendor (e.g. Amazon, Barnes + Noble) and search "Eric F. Magnuson" under Books. You fill find independent reviews and author descriptions.

~ Eric Fenris Magnuson ~

Printed in Dunstable, United Kingdom